Gender, Youth and Culture

Gender, Youth and Culture

Young Masculinities and Femininities

Anoop Nayak and Mary Jane Kehily
University of Newcastle and The Open University

First published 2008 by
PALGRAVE MACMILLAN
Houndmills, Basingstoke, Hampshire RG21 6XS and
175 Fifth Avenue, New York, N.Y. 10010
Companies and representatives throughout the world

PALGRAVE MACMILLAN is the global academic imprint of the Palgrave
Macmillan division of St. Martin's Press, LLC and of Palgrave Macmillan Ltd.
Macmillan® is a registered trademark in the United States, United Kingdom
and other countries. Palgrave is a registered trademark in the European
Union and other countries.

ISBN-13: 978–1–4039–4976–9 hardback
ISBN-10: 1–4039–4976–X hardback
ISBN-13: 978–1–4039–4977–6 paperback
ISBN-10: 1–4039–4977–8 paperback

This book is printed on paper suitable for recycling and made from fully
managed and sustained forest sources. Logging, pulping and manufacturing
processes are expected to conform to the environmental regulations of the
country of origin.

A catalogue record for this book is available from the British Library.

A catalog record for this book is available from the Library of Congress.

10   9   8   7   6   5   4   3   2   1
17   16   15   14   13   12   11   10   09   08

Printed in China

This book is dedicated to our fathers, Baidyanath Nayak and John Patrick Kehily, with love

Contents

Acknowledgements

This book would not have been possible without the support of a number of people. We would like to thank Catherine Gray at Palgrave for believing in this project right from the start and providing her full support. We are especially grateful to Rachel Thomson for reading a first draft of the whole manuscript and providing detailed and encouraging remarks throughout. We would also like to thank Peter Redman for his intelligent comments on Chapter 8. We are highly appreciative of the support given to us by Australian friends and colleagues across Melbourne, especially Julie McLeod, David Goodman, Deana Leahy and Mary Lou Rasmussen. We are grateful to Kirsty Liddiard and Stephanie Withers at The Open University for their help in preparing the manuscript. Our thanks also extend to Cait Weston for providing the index.

Anoop would like to thank the numerous friends, students and colleagues at Newcastle University who continue to enrich his ideas and thinking. He is particularly grateful to Alastair Bonnett and Richard Collier for their unstinting friendship and support. Mary Jane would like to thank many friends and colleagues at The Open University for their support and encouragement throughout. She is especially grateful to Peter Barnes and the Making of Modern Motherhoods research team – Rachel Thomson, Lucy Hadfield and Sue Sharpe.

Portions of Chapter 6 pertaining to informal student cultures are published as Kehily and Nayak, 'Lads and laughter': humour and the production of heterosexual hierarchies', *Gender and Education*, 9, 1, 69–88, 1997.

Portions of Chapter 8 are published as Nayak and Kehily, Gender undone: subversion, regulation and embodiment in the work of Judith Butler, *British Journal of Sociology of Education*, 27, 4, 459–472, 2006.

Part One

Understanding Gender and Youth: Concepts, Theory and Action

1
Introducing Gender

The question of how boys become men or how girls become women may seem absurdly simple. But if the question is simple, the answers are certainly more difficult. This book is about the making and unmaking of gender. It asks how do boys become men and how do girls become women in late-modernity? What does it now mean to be a 'proper' girl or boy? What are the costs of failing to inhabit this identity? And what are the possibilities for doing gender differently in the contemporary global economy?

Throughout this book we argue for a global perspective on gender that recognizes difference and diversity across time and place. We are interested in how gender relations are produced and reproduced on a world stage and the impact this is having upon new generations. Of particular interest here is the way in which gender is embedded in national and local cultures, institutional sites and settings, as well as everyday social relationships. Furthermore we are concerned with how gender interacts with age, class, ethnicity, sexuality and a host of other complex dynamics. In large part we are motivated by a curiosity to understand how gender is experienced, enacted and embodied in daily life, frequently in ways that are competing and contradictory. In this chapter we explore the different features of the title, *Gender, Youth* and *Culture*, through the following sections: gender practices; constructions of childhood and youth; playing with gender; and youth and youth studies. This is followed by an introduction to the structure and content of the book. As an introductory chapter we outline and discuss many of the contemporary debates and issues in these fields. Our focus is upon the salient features of gender, youth and culture that inform this book. Beginning with a consideration of gender practices, we document our interest and approach to gender as a lived process. This is followed by a discussion of constructions of childhood and youth in which we recognize the shifting boundaries between these social categories and the implications of this for understanding young lives. The third section of the chapter considers some of the ways in which gender and play come together in cultural analyses of children and young people's lives before moving on to a discussion of youth and youth studies. Here we focus upon the ways in which young people have been made visible through different research traditions and approaches. The final section of the chapter provides an introductory mapping of the subsequent chapters of the book, outlining the content and main themes of each chapter.

Gender Practices

Recent developments in arts, humanities and social sciences have seen a growing interest in issues of gender, particularly in relation to young people, globalization and popular culture. Current scholarship on gender and youth is exemplified in works on class and gender formations (Skeggs, 1997; 2004), young masculinities and schooling (Mac an Ghaill, 1994; Frosh *et al.*, 2002), young femininities and girlhood (Hey, 1997; Harris, 2004; Aapola *et al.*, 2005) and young people's gendered and racialized relationships to post-industrialism (Delamont, 2001; Nayak, 2003a). This burgeoning literature points to the abiding importance of gender as a conceptual category for understanding the organization and interpretation of human relationships. While much work in the field of gender research has focused exclusively upon young women and more recently young men, surprisingly few studies have taken a holistic approach to the subject, integrating work on masculinities and femininities. An abiding focus upon the gendered subjectivities of either boys or girls has tended to privilege one or other of these identities by holding them apart. However, our own ethnographic observations would suggest that one of the primary means through which young men and women define themselves is through and against one another and alongside imaginary notions of masculinity and femininity. The impact of separate sex studies is particularly revealing where there is a tendency in at least some research to conflate sex with gender, thus identifying boys with masculinities and girls with femininities. In this way 'sissy boys' remain tied to some peripheral, if failing, notion of masculinity, just as 'tom boys', despite their name, continue to be positioned as the temporary occupants of an aberrant femininity. As even these more extreme subject positions show, sex continues to remain the ultimate arbiter of gender relations, that irrevocable grain of truth. Categorically sex relates to specific anatomical differences, chromosomes, hormones and developmental markers such as facial hair or breasts, while gender refers to the cultural elaboration of these bodily signs through clothing, hairstyle or, as we shall see, even one's taste in film or music (Chapters 7 and 8). However, as Cream (1995) illustrates through the example of intersex subjects who are born with genitalia that is explicitly neither male nor female, sex itself can be socially constituted through the surgical scalpel and parental choice at birth. When discussing sex and gender a danger haunts categories that unwittingly collapse to presume that masculinity is something all boys inhabit while girls are the sole occupants of femininity. In this way gender – we believe mistakenly – can appear as a product or outcome of the sexed body.

Looking at the working and reworking of gender between and amongst boys and girls offers a rather different way of approaching the topic. Our concern then is not to compare and contrast the behaviour of boys with those of girls and so reach conclusions – a routine means of preserving the sex/gender binary – but instead to focus upon what we might call the 'practice of gender'. In talking about *gender practices* we are moving away from notions of gender as either a biological essence or a knowable category that is fixed upon the bodies of men, women, girls or boys in the ways we previously described. Gender practices involve an understanding of gender as a lived process rather than a proper object that we are each magically endowed with as an unwritten consequence of our sex. Through this approach we aim to show how gender is a set of relations configured through technologies, bodies, spatial, discursive and material processes. Thinking about gender in this way enables us to see how it is 'summoned into life' under the weight of particular historical conditions, how it is discursively struggled over, repudiated or enacted. Exploring gender practices places attention upon the production, regulation, consumption and performance of gender in late-modernity – the structuring schematic of this book. By adopting this approach we aim to illuminate first, how gender relations are embedded in different societies; second, how they are discursively enacted and encrypted with specific indices of power; and third, how they can occasionally be reconfigured in different times and spaces. Throughout we argue that the making and unmaking of gender is no random occurrence, or *fait au accompli*, but the shaky happenstance of identification, embodiment and the rigidly routine rituals of gender demarcation that are a feature of everyday life.

By examining gender practices and in particular how they are produced, regulated, consumed and performed, we can gain a fuller insight into broader gender patterns and arrangements. This enables us to interpret the relationship between gender and power and to see how gender is institutionally organized, discursively constituted, embodied and transfigured in social life. It can begin to explain how gender relations are embedded within the social fabric of human societies and come to shape the choices and possibilities open to us as gendered subjects. This suggests that gender is not simply a matter of choice, but a negotiation that occurs within a matrix of social and historical forces enshrined in the ideological arenas of law, religion, family, schooling, media, work and so forth. And while gender structures may appear enduring, they too are continually subject to change and vary over time and place. In this respect, gender structures, rather than being determining, only come into being in and through social action, what we have been calling *gender practices*.

The production of a seemingly coherent gender identity is then the result of a series of successive, though never fully accomplished, 'gender achievements'. These 'achievements' conceal an extraordinary amount of mental and physical labour that go into making these identities appear normal, 'just so'. Yet if there is no determining link between sex and gender, the question of how boys become men and how girls become women is itself theoretically constrained by a slew of political presumptions. By raising these questions we recognize that we too are in danger of replicating sex/gender categories, and in Chapter 8 we make a concerted effort to rethink gender 'otherwise'. The theory and illustrations we draw upon indicate that gender is not an identity that prefigures action, but is an activity that gives rise to how we come to understand and experience ourselves as gender subjects. Gender is not, then, the precursor of action, rather, it is its immediacy and after effect.

This book is concerned with the *coming-into-being* of gender. For young people the phrase 'coming-into-being' is especially apt as they undergo a great deal of physical, cultural and emotional change. In beginning to unravel some of the theoretical knots that bind gender to sex we do not seek to absent the role and agency of the body. Indeed some feminist poststructuralist accounts of gender have paid an enormous amount of attention to the multiple and complex configurations of gender power, but have occasionally rendered the human body obsolete. As part of a politically informed anti-essentialist project, this tendency to elide sex difference and the 'overdetermined' presence of the body as the atomized essence of 'who we are' is understandably compelling. However, as sociologists of the body and the new queer theorists we discuss in Chapter 8 amply illustrate, bodies are not docile, passive conduits for action. Bodies are both the objects and subjects of gender process: they are socially constituted but remain wilful agents that participate in their own making and that of others. Gender practices are embodied activities that carry with them a scattering of feelings, affect and emotion. These assemblages are also affected by the corporeal mechanics of the body regarding health, dexterity, dis/ability, body mass or skin pigmentation. Gender is sculpted through such mundane bodily processes as aging, giving birth, hair loss or weight gain. It is also culturally signed and manipulated through such corporeal activities as the use of cosmetics, tanning or plastic surgery. We should, then, be wary not to 'write out' the body from existence or set sex and gender apart from corporeal activity. For young people the coming-into-being of gender is always an embodied act. The proliferation of social terms already bestowed upon them throughout their short lives – as babies, toddlers, infants, children, offspring, adolescents, teenagers, youth and so on – iterates the discursive making of young people that come to mark their bodies in altogether different ways, as we shall now explore.

Constructions of Childhood and Youth

Over the last decade or so Childhood Studies has become a recognized area of research and analysis reflected in a growing body of literature that points to the importance of childhood as a conceptual category and a social status for the study of a previously overlooked or marginalized group – children (Stainton Rogers and Stainton Rogers, 1992; James and Prout, 1997; Gittins, 1998; Montgomery and Woodhead, 2003; Kehily, 2004). How does this development relate to the concept of youth and youth studies? Is a young person still a child or does youth signal a move out of childhood and the onset of adulthood? These are key questions to ask, as they reveal how children, youth and adults are terms that gloss over a great deal of complexity and carry with them a substantial amount of discursive power. In this respect we can consider childhood and youth as contingent constructions, forever in the making.

Cultural investments in the idea of childhood as a state of innocence can be contrasted with notions of youth as difficult, 'out of control' and potentially dangerous – a symbol of what is wrong with the neighbourhood or the country more generally. The concept of childhood in the West is underpinned by twin images of children as either innocent angels or evil devils (Warner, 1994; Kehily and Montgomery, 2003; Valentine, 2004). The Romantic inspired child of innocence also calls into being its opposite – the demonic child. This duality is often used in the media and can be seen in contemporary views and images of childhood generally. Childhood figures in the contemporary British and North American imagination exist in an idealized state but children who break out of this state, especially through crime, are increasingly penalized and demonized. The potential wickedness of children seems to be reserved for some young people and aberrant children. Childhood innocence is celebrated and protected while individual children who transgress may be vilified – their behaviour placing them beyond the realm of 'proper' children and normal childhood. Central to contemporary approaches is the understanding that childhood and youth are not universal states. Rather they are culturally produced and as such will vary across time and place. An example of this can be seen in a British cultural geography study of 'fear of crime' with 449 school students aged 12–15 years (Nayak, 2003b). Those living in certain suburban neighbourhoods were repeatedly described as 'children' (i.e., those in need of protection), while those of a similar age in the inner city and nearby working-class estate were regularly depicted as 'youth' (by implication those that are likely to exacerbate fear of crime simply by 'hanging out'). Moreover these relations were gendered with boys (61 per cent) significantly more likely to be stopped by the police than girls (41 per cent). This reveals, first, how childhood and youth are contingent social constructions and, second, how notions of good/evil are tied to relations of gender, place and class. Economic and socio-cultural factors continue to shape childhood and youth on the international stage. A recent UNICEF report (2007) on the well-being of children and young people in 21 industrialized countries ranked the UK at the bottom of the table in their assessment of child well-being and the US as second from bottom. The report focused on six areas: material well-being; health and safety; educational well-being; family and peer relationships; behaviours and risks; and young people's own perceptions of well-being. The report placed The Netherlands at the top of the table, followed by Sweden, Denmark and Finland. The report offers an economic account of the findings, powerfully suggesting that despite national wealth, children who grow up in poverty are more vulnerable, their experiences of childhood more difficult, leading the UK Children's Commissioner to comment, 'There is a crisis at the heart of our society'.

Developmental psychology has documented the stages and transitions of Western childhood. Within this framework childhood is seen as an apprenticeship for adulthood that can be charted through stages relating to age, physical development and cognitive ability. The progression from child to adult involves children in a developmental process wherein they embark upon a path to rational subjectivity.

Sociological approaches by contrast have been concerned with issues of socialization: ways of exploring how children learn to become members of the society in which they live. The differences between the two approaches are outlined and discussed in an academic intervention that sets out the parameters for a 'new sociology of childhood' (James and Prout, 1997). James and Prout propose that 'the immaturity of children is a biological fact of life but the ways this is understood and made meaningful is a fact of culture' (1997:7). They suggest that there is a growing body of research that signals an emergent paradigm for the study of childhood. Key features of the paradigm as outlined by James and Prout include the following:

- Childhood is understood as a social construction.

- Childhood is a variable of social analysis.

- Children's relationships and cultures are worthy of study in their own right.

- Children should be seen as active social agents.

- Studying childhood involves an engagement with the process of reconstructing childhood in society.

Most researchers working within this paradigm take their lead from the United Nations Convention on the Rights of the Child by defining childhood as the life stage from 0 to 18 years, subsuming youth into the childhood years. Studies of young people and particularly those defined through the social category 'youth' have a history largely outside of Childhood Studies and continue to be studied as young adults rather than late childhood subjects (see below for a further discussion of youth and youth studies). We now elaborate our discussion of childhood by considering its relationship to gender.

Playing with Gender

Some of the differences between childhood and youth can be discerned by focusing upon the notion of play. Many studies of children and young people use the term *play* to refer to children's activities, while young people are viewed as engaging in leisure and youth subcultures rather than play. Children's play is commonly viewed as benign – imaginative, exploratory and a 'safe' way of dealing with difficult emotions. Play is often regarded as one of the most distinctive features of childhood. Indeed for many people, children's capacity to play, their enthusiasm for playing and the importance attached to being allowed to play define childhood. The Romantic movement in eighteenth-century Europe fostered the idea of play as essential for children, most famously in Rousseau's words, 'Is it nothing to jump, play and run all day? He will never be so busy in his life' (Rousseau, 1979[1762]:107). Building upon the Romantic idea that play encourages self-expression, educationalists in the West suggested that play was a natural way for children to learn. Child developmentalists in particular attach significance to play as a central way in which children learn the complex skills required to reach adult maturity. It can also be seen as a form of body-learning, through the development of such qualities as balance, hand–eye coordination, physicality and motor skills. From the twentieth century onwards, the consensus among professionals working with children suggests that play is significant and necessary – *the work of childhood*.

Studies of children's cultural worlds have drawn attention to childhood as a gendered experience. Thorne's (1993) US-based study of children, gender and play is especially insightful as her focus is on boys and girls (aged 9–10), using ethnographic methods to study their social worlds in a public elementary school. Her account captures the energetic and highly charged nature of children's cultural worlds where friendship involves engagement in imaginative forms of physicality, talk and action. To the adult researcher the rapid movements of children at play appear haphazard and chaotic. However, after several months of observation Thorne begins to make sense of children's play from the perspective of children themselves. Thorne's analysis suggests that children's friendships have a structure and an internal logic that makes sense to the children involved. Through patterns of friendship and rituals of play children create meanings for themselves and others. An example of this cited by Thorne is the way in which children use everyday objects such as pencils, crayons, erasers, toy cars, magnets and lip gloss. Thorne suggests that these objects acquire symbolic significance among friends. In the school context where children have little power these objects become significant as tokens of friendship that can be bartered and exchanged. Thorne observed that the objects constituted a flourishing 'underground economy' and indicated that among the children she studied, they acquired use-value in contexts where patterns of trade marked circles of friend-ship in the following ways – 'as a focus of provocation and dispute, as a medium through which alliances could be launched and disrupted, as sacraments of social inclusion and painful symbols of exclusion, and as markers of hierarchy' (Thorne, 1993:21).

Thorne identifies a further example of children creating meanings through friendship in playground chasing games. Here Thorne describes and comments upon the widespread invocation of 'cooties' or rituals of pollution in which individuals or groups are treated as carriers of contagious 'germs'. She docu-ments the experiences of some unfortunate children whose undesirability is captured and pronounced by the tag 'cootie queen' or 'cootie king'. Thorne suggests that, in general, girls are seen as a source of contamination, referred to by boys in one school as 'girl stain'. 'Girl stain' involves boys treating girls and objects associated with femininity as a polluting presence; the reverse did not readily occur. This indicates that gender power may further be used to privilege masculinity whilst denigrating femininities as subordinate.

Thorne's analysis of these games points to the relationship between children's cultural worlds and the broader context of power relations in which they exist:

When pollution rituals appear, even in play, they enact larger patterns of inequality, by gender, by social class and race, and by bodily characteristics like weight and motor coordination. . . .

In contemporary US culture even young girls are treated as symbolically contamin-ating in a way that boys are not. This may be because in our culture even at a young age girls are sexualized more than boys, and female sexuality, especially when 'out of place' or actively associated with children, connotes danger and endangerment. (Thorne, 1993:75–76)

Thorne points to the further significance of gender in children's cultural worlds through her conceptualization of 'borderwork', a term used to characterize the ways in which children tend to form single-sex friendship groups that serve to create and strengthen gender boundaries. Thorne suggests that children's friend-ship patterns create a spatial separation between boys and girls that they work to maintain through play and social interactions more generally. Drawing up boundaries, however, also creates opportunities for transgression, crossing the line to disrupt gender-appropriate behaviour or 'border crossing' as Thorne terms it. While most children adhered to gender-defined boundaries, Thorne did notice that border crossing appeared to be acceptable among girls or boys who had achieved a position of high status within their peer group. We return to Thorne's powerful elaboration of 'gender staining' in Chapter 8 where we discuss how gay subjects may especially be interpreted as defiled, polluting bodies in youth friendship circles.

Studies focusing upon children's friendships point to the fragility of gender 'borders' and the fragmentation of borderwork. Hey's (1997) study of friendship among teenage girls in the UK points to some under-acknowledged features of same-sex friendship groups. Hey's ethnographic study of girls (aged 11–18) in two secondary schools challenges many assumptions relating to girls' friend-ship with each other. Hey suggests that feminist researchers have a tendency to romanticize girls' friendship, to view them through the celebratory lens of girls' capacity for sharing, caring and mutual support. By way of contrast, Hey documents and discusses the frequent interactions between girls that centre upon the less than supportive practices of bitching, falling-out and rituals of exclu-sion. In Hey's account girls can be seen to be engaged in patterns and practices of friendship that are fuelled by tensions and conflict as much as support and care. Frosh *et al.*'s (2002) study of boys and masculinity illustrates some striking features of boys' friendship. Their interview-based study of boys (aged 11–14) in the UK suggests that boys' relationships with each other are structured around the contradictions of masculine identities. Many of the boys they spoke with saw masculinity and toughness as inextricably linked, thus making it difficult for them to discuss feelings of emotional closeness and intimacy within male friendship groups. In individual interviews with Rob Pattman, however, many boys did discuss feelings of intimacy and vulnerability at school and within the family. Frosh *et al.* comment upon the ways in which conforming to masculine norms may constrain boys and leave them with few opportunities to express their feelings. Connolly's (1995) account of children's games and friendships in multi-ethnic English primary schools imparts that the practice of gender power may be given a further twist when racist insults are deployed. As Troyna and Hatcher (1992) have demonstrated *mainly white* primary schools are also sites within which race categories are used as an exacting form of 'borderwork'. The above studies contribute to an understanding of childhood by problematizing the notion of 'innocence' and 'friendship' as a natural self-evident feature of children's lives in Western societies and pointing to the ways in which gender and ethnic alliances are continually worked at and shored up.

Youth and Youth Studies

In contrast to the creative and constructive ways in which children's play is cast, young people's play and leisure activities are commonly seen as poten-tially threatening and disturbing. It may be for these reasons that play has historically been disciplined through the rule-bound formation of team sports and physical education. The notion that young people *need* to play and that this may serve useful functions is rarely indulged. Rather young people 'at play' can become a source of evidence to indicate that they are unfit for adulthood. Studies of subcultures demonstrate how the idea of youth can be associated with 'moral panic', threat and danger (Cohen, 1972; Hall and

Jefferson, 1976; Hebdige, 1979). It is possible to suggest that young people's play can be seen as imaginative expressions of late childhood/early adulthood that have many points of continuity with children's play. In a discussion of rave culture in Chapter 7, McRobbie draws a direct comparison between the rave party and childhood. Both states share a love of carefree abandonment and enjoy the comforting paraphernalia of childhood: dummies, primary colours, lollies and songs from children's television programmes can be found among the accessories of ravers. Graham Dawson's (1994) psychoanalytic account of masculinity in *Soldier Heroes* broadens these ideas further, demonstrating how the activity of play can extend, at least in sublimated form, into manhood.

The focus on young people's leisure activities remains one of the ways in which youth have been researched and theorized. In the UK the study of young people has been marked by two contrasting approaches: youth cultural studies and youth transitions. These approaches have been distinguished by a different set of concerns emerging from different disciplinary traditions, methodologies and theoretical perspectives. The youth cultural studies approach has been characterized by the study of spectacular youth subcultures of the post-war era such as skinheads, punks, mods and rockers. Associated with the work of Birmingham University's Centre for Contemporary Cultural Studies, these studies focused on the ways in which young people's collective sense of style, attitude and self-expression could be understood as forms of *resistance through rituals*. Using ethnographic methods and semiological analysis, this influential body of literature drew upon Gramscian inspired theory to suggest that young people's subcultures opened up an intergenerational dialogue in which young people commented upon their parents, their locality and the socio-political context of their lives (Hall and Jefferson, 1976; Hebdige, 1979). Hall and Jefferson suggest that working-class youth subcultures involve young people in a 'double articulation', first with their parents' culture and second with the broader culture of post-war social change. Critical and occasionally angry, expressed through clothes, music and style, youth subcultural formations came to be understood as creative commentaries on the dominant culture in which young people imaginatively reframe their own lives. To view youth subcultures as adolescent rebellion is to underestimate the extent to which young people seek to address issues of generational change and social structures. From a cultural studies perspective, youth subcultures are purposeful interventions, imbued with meaning.

More recent studies of youth cultures have been influenced by postmodern theory rather than post-Marxian perspectives and have developed a strong critique of the Birmingham Cultural Studies approach (Thornton, 1995; Redhead, 1997). Premised upon the argument that 'we're all mainstream now', contemporary approaches to youth cultures document the significance of global media cultures and patterns of consumption as key changes in young people's lives, producing fragmented and ephemeral youth groupings rather than full-blown subcultures. Redhead (1997) characterizes these changes as a shift from subcultures to 'clubcultures' – indicating the salient presence of corporate leisure facilities and global media forms in young people's everyday lives. Redhead defines clubcultures as global and fluid youth formations that are based on media fashions and the niche marketing of dance music as a youth culture-for-all. He refers to clubbing as 'hedonism in hard times' (1997:4) suggesting that it is both an escape and a riposte to political realities. In this respect clubcultures have interesting points of resonance with the 'double articulation' of earlier subcultural formations. The fragility of youth cultures in a globalized media world has led many researchers to suggest that the term 'subculture' should be replaced as it is no longer useful for describing the connections young people make with each other and their social context. Current contenders for the newly reconfigured subcultural crown include 'scenes', 'tribes', 'lifestyles' and 'neo-tribes' amongst numerous other post-modern terminology. While 'scenes' explores musical collectivities, 'tribes' and 'neo-tribes' draw upon the work of Maffesoli (1995) to describe loose groups of young people whose stylized tastes and lifestyles come together during moments of shared interest (see Bennett, 1999; Blackman, 2005; Hesmondhalgh, 2005 for a further discussion of these themes). Maffesoli suggests that consumption patterns and practices enable individuals to create moments of sociality. 'Tribe' describes an ambient state of mind and point of connection that is not necessarily class bound or subcultural. A feature of post-modern approaches to youth culture is a tendency to produce rich and aesthetically pleasing accounts of young people at play at the expense of some earlier subcultural themes. Youth subcultures as interpreted in the CCCS moment, while focusing upon the cultural, were also a comment upon social class, economic context and social change. Significantly, recent studies of youth cultures appear to elide matters of social class and offer little commentary upon the new social divisions that emerge in global economies (Hollands, 2002). Chatterton and Hollands (2003) in their discussion of young people in the night-time economy draw upon Appadurai's global sense of place when writing of 'urban playscapes' as an attempt to recognize the place-specific role of youth identities within late-modern economic and cultural exchanges. The movement from subcultures to 'scenes', 'tribes', 'neo-tribes' and 'scapes' reflects a shift from locally bound to globally connected youth cultures.

In contrast to culturally oriented approaches to youth cultures, the youth transitions approach in the UK has focused largely on structural arrangements that shape young people's lives and experiences. Emerging in the 1980s at a time of dramatic social change for young people, the notion of transitions sought to explore the ways in which young people manage the transitional life phase from school to work and, in doing so, navigate a course from adolescence to adulthood, dependent to independent citizen and member of the workforce.

The concern in this approach has been to document the impact of structural inequalities on young people and the differences these make to experiences of work, family, community and social mobility. At a time of high unemployment, the implosion of the youth labour market and the introduction of youth policies designed to keep young people in forms of education and training that effect-ively restricted their life-choices, 'factual' accounts of the school to work journey appeared timely and necessary. Using empirical methods such as questionnaire and survey, with some follow-up interviews, the youth transitions approach can be viewed as a top-down research initiative that positions young people as the unwitting subjects of class structures and economic forces. However, this view underestimates the capacity of the approach to document the social experiences of young lives and communicate these experiences to policy audi-ences in sensitive and thoughtful ways. Studies of youth transitions have been critiqued for their mechanical, positivistic and somewhat linear approach to young lives. An aspect of the critique is the recognition that the sequential progression from school to work has become so diverse and fragmented that the idea of transitional and incremental movement from one state of being to another is unhelpful, even redundant. MacDonald *et al.* (2001) reassert the value of the transitions approach as a way of making sense of young lives. Arguing that youth transitions are inherently complex and unpredictable, MacDonald *et al.* suggest that the strength of the approach lies in its potential to understand the complex relationship between personal agency and structural constraints as played out in young people's lives. Moreover there is a need to appreciate that many studies defined by this approach have moved beyond the positivistic methods employed by early studies. MacDonald and Marsh (2001; 2006) use features of biographical life-history method to develop an analysis of socially excluded youth in the north-east of England. Their analysis generatively draws upon biographical cameos to illustrate how accounts of personal experience offer a glimpse into wider social processes of division and hierarchy that impact upon young people's lives and the ways these processes can be reproduced and inhabited. Finally MacDonald *et al.* suggest that a youth transitions approach can incorporate the cultural by taking a holistic approach to young people's experiences. The concept of 'alternative careers' referring to the drug dealing and criminal activities that replace legitimate forms of employment for many young people in their study necessarily involves a consideration of the cultural context of young lives where style, leisure and friendship groups interact in particular ways.

Recent work on UK student cultures indicates that many young people are extending 'studenthood' beyond the period of study associated with Further and Higher Education. Insecure labour markets and the financial barriers first-time buyers face when it comes to home ownership is leading a greater number of former students to take up temporary work in the service sector as a means to extend studenthood and maintain at least some independence away from the parental home. In the context of the wider culture in which youth transitions to adulthood are becoming extended, non-sequential and uncertain, youthful play may be a way of immersing oneself in the perpetual present of an in-between state. However, the contemporary construction of student night-life and the commercial links between university campuses and corporate merchandizing has led some writers towards a critique of what they term 'studentland' (Chatterton and Hollands, 2003). Within this particular market segment, 'The "corporate campus" and the surrounding corporate city are increasingly inter-twined. The future of work and place in studentland is not just up for grabs: it is also up for sale' (p. 147). In Chapter 7 we also allude to the ways in which the concept of girlhood is packaged as a desirable commodity by media cultures and sold to adult women through dreams, fantasies and images of desire. These examples further indicate the fuzzy borders that exist between childhood, youth, studentdom and adulthood.

Our own approach to the study of youth and culture recognizes the contri-bution of the different perspectives discussed above. In keeping with other researchers (MacDonald *et al.*, 2001; Hollands, 2002) we would also suggest that the youth cultures tradition and the youth transitions paradigm exist as roughly sketched categories rather than mutually exclusive approaches to the study of young people. In a discussion of these two approaches, Cohen and Ainley (2000) propose a 'third way' for the future of youth studies while Wyn and Woodman (2006) suggest that the concept of 'generation' offers a more effective way of conceptualizing youth. Cohen and Ainley suggest merging cultural and structural approaches in ways that address gaps in our under-standing of young lives. Cohen and Ainley indicate that the question of how people learn culture remains underdeveloped in both approaches and suggest that a combination of actor network theory and interdisciplinary collabor-ations between educationalists, youth researchers and social policy analysts may provide a way forward in generating new studies of young people in changing times. They also call upon teachers and youth workers to play a part in defining and implementing the research process. While the approach developed in this book would not fit into the 'third way', we attempt to hold in play the cultural and the structural in ways that make sense of young people's lives in changing times. We are also interested in exploring different 'geographies of youth' (Skelton and Valentine, 1997) in order to under-stand how young people's experiences vary over time and place. In doing so, we hope to promote a better understanding of place and its relationship to youth, as well as gaining insight into the role of youth cultures and global change in late-modernity. A discussion of our approach is documented in the following chapter, while below we outline the overarching structure of the book.

Structure

The volume is organized in two sections – Section I documents contemporary concepts, theories and ideas on gender and youth formations, and Section II crystallizes these ideas by locating them through ethnographic research into the life-worlds of young people. In the second part of the book the focus is upon the production, consumption, regulation and performance of gender in everyday life.

In this brief introduction we have described theoretical and conceptual approaches to gender, youth and childhood. In the following chapter we explore our methodological approach along with two prominent themes that have arisen in late-modernity with regard to constructions of youth and gender relations. The first theme considers the role of 'risk' and individualization in the construction of contemporary youth identities. Here the doing of youth is no longer seen as a class-bound, collective, subcultural practice – if indeed it ever was – but is increasingly regarded as a highly individual 'project of self', a perspective we critically discuss and sensitively open out for critique. A second theme concerns globalization and the postcolonial. The focus here is upon the diverse flows of subjects and objects in late-modernity and the way in which these relations cohere within a postcolonial frame. Our accounts of South Asian young graduates in Bombay call-centres, Lebanese youth fighting racism on Sydney Beaches, British Muslim young women deploying fashion to form new femininities and Korean folk singers participating in Japanese musical cultures offer illustrations of these new power-infused transcultural relations. The chapter concludes with an explanation of our research methods to investigate gender and youth – primarily ethnographic and cultural studies analyses. Here we focus on the value of biographic, ethnographic and representational methods in order to understand the 'economies of signs of space' (Lash and Urry, 1999) and the processes of globalization. A concern is to begin to grapple with the bewildering but provocative potential of global ethnographies.

In Chapters 3 and 4 we investigate gender relations in late-modernity by identifying the role of recent labour market transitions and their impact upon young lives. Using cultural studies and media analysis we argue that the defining signature of gender relations in late-modernity is etched into an understanding that young men and masculinities are 'in crisis', while young women are portrayed as the ideal neo-liberal subjects and beneficiaries of flexible labour and mass consumption. We view these cultural representations as powerful tropes that conceal as much as they reveal. The resonance of these themes and the affective qualities they carry echo back to us, we suggest, through global media images that in turn may become embodied in everyday life. The crisis of masculinity is seen and felt in such films as *Fight Club*, the *Rocky* series and *Falling Down*. The project of neo-liberal femininity with its silent promise of individualism, consumption and sexual satisfaction, explored in Chapter 4, is also virulently prevalent in such popular television series as *Sex in the City*, *Ally McBeal*, *What Not to Wear*, *Ten Years Younger*, *Would Like to Meet* and *You Are What You Eat*.

In Chapter 5 we draw upon a series of selected readings to examine gender relations in a global context. Our aim in this book is not to achieve international coherence, itself an impossible task, but to show how the practice of gender varies across time and space and is particular to specific cultures. The 'critical readings', as we have chosen to style them, further indicate that there are thematic connections to be made when we look at gender and youth in world societies. Here we reveal how gender is connected to power, how it operates as an 'organizing principle' in many Western and non-Western societies, and how it is continually being made and remade under differing conditions of social and economic transformation. The chapter draws upon ethnographic and anthropological insights to illustrate these points.

In Section II we turn to an ethnographic and cultural studies exploration of the production, regulation, consumption and performance of gender and how these processes connect with youth identities. Chapter 6 focuses upon the production and regulation of young masculinities and femininities. The chapter investigates the role that institutions, work-based cultures and regional histories play in manufacturing ideas about gender. Using ethnographic observations, we consider schools as sites for the production of gender and the making of young masculinities and femininities. This approach is designed to look at the role of national and local cultures, the significance of state regulation and the extraordinary capacity that young people have to 'shore up', subvert and indeed produce their own gender identifications. In Chapter 7 we turn to the issue of youth consumption by exploring the role of popular culture through various genres of music, film, soap opera, pulp fiction and magazines. The focus is in part upon the way merchandizing operates to produce gendered subjects through the creation of segmented and niche youth markets. However, we are also concerned with how young people negotiate global culture in friendship circles in local circuits. Here we explore not only how young people from the West position themselves through global culture but also how non-Western youth may adopt and adapt processes of globalization and Americanization. The focus in this chapter is upon the different gender subject positions made available through consumption, which remains one of the most sophisticated ways through which young people embody and transform gender identity.

In Chapter 8 we engage in a detailed discussion and application of 'queer theory'. Our argument is that queer theory offers a new moment for rethinking the subject. But although queer thinking has been a key topic of discussion rooted in North American feminist philosophy and cultural studies these ideas have too often been cut adrift and marooned from the actual experience of young lives. The absence of empirical research illustrating how queer theory can be transposed into queer practices is especially apparent. There is also a paucity of academic enquiry utilizing these perspectives within youth and childhood studies. For example the 'new sociology of childhood' proclaimed by James and Prout (1997) fails to register with these new ways of thinking about identity, action and the construction of sex categories. In using queer theory to interpret the actions of young people we focus upon the regulation and performance of gender to examine how gender can be done and undone. Here we address the interplay of gender and sexuality, the role of identification and dis-identification, acts of gender 'passing' and transgression, as well as the plethora of ways in which gender is performed, embodied and psychically envisioned.

We view queer methodologies (see Halberstam, 1998; Rasmussen, 2006 for discussion) as an invaluable and highly specialized technique for understanding the humdrum and habitual investments we each make in gender and sex categories. In particular the notion of gender as performance is especially compelling when it comes to understanding masculinity and femininity as arbitrary signs, fictions that are made to appear real through corporeal forms of embodied activity. In this way we reveal how young people can regulate the unruliness of their bodies by adopting seemingly fixed gender positions although these are not without contradiction or personal cost. Throughout this book we maintain a keen interest in locating theory through practice. In connecting queer theory to everyday practice we argue that gender performances are always sited, that they occur within particular places and that this has a bearing upon the bodies and activities made possible within these spaces. Our intention is to bring together the material, discursive and imaginative aspects of gender to move towards an embodied interpretation of young lives. We conclude by arguing for new dialogues between these repertoires and the recognition that the somewhat abstract work on gender, performativity and the body can benefit from the fleshy corporeality of 'real life' experiences. Overall we welcome the creative tension that may arise between different theoretical and political approaches and hope that these contradictions can be utilized in the search for a more complex, but ultimately more meaningful understanding of young lives.

Conclusion

This chapter has focused upon the social construction of childhood and youth. It suggests that gender and youth relations need to be looked at a global scale to understand variations across time and place. And it argues that gender is better understood as a process that is given meaning through gender practices. To illustrate this we drew upon examples of 'borderwork' in which the interplay of power led to highly exacting gender-dividing practices. These practices were seen to valorize particular versions of masculinity at the expense of femininities and subordinate masculinities. We then outlined two different approaches to youth, focusing upon youth cultural studies and youth transitions to investigate the ways in which structure and culture can be more effectively brought together. We concluded the section by outlining the two-part structure of the book and gesturing towards our theoretical approaches in the subsequent chapters.

2
Researching Gender: Towards Global Ethnographies

This chapter explores two key sociological themes through which the question of identity, gender and youth can be understood. The first concerns itself with risk and individualization. The second investigates the relationship between globalization and postcolonialism. These signatory themes are said to be significant features of young people's coming-of-age in late-modernity. In this chapter we outline our methodological approach, the genesis of this project and our personal perspectives. We consider some of the influences on our approach to gender, youth and culture as shaped by our biographies, our commitment to ethnography and our background in cultural studies.

Risk, individualization and globalization can be viewed as major themes reworking constructions of gender and youth in late-modernity. While the term 'new times' has been used to identify social, cultural, economic and political change (Hall and Jacques, 1989), it is widely thought to embody a move from an industrial to a post-industrial society in which there has been a growth in services and information technologies. We consider the impact that globalization is having upon youth and gender in various parts of the world. In particular, we offer a critical perspective on global change by placing it within a postcolonial frame in order to disturb, or at least unsettle, the accepted rubric of Western modernity to show how these ideals can be displaced, transfigured and replayed in imaginative form. The themes of risk, individualization, globalization and postcolonialism feature throughout the book as they have been influential thinking tools for scholars in youth and gender studies. Our interest is primarily with how these theories may be put into practice by young people themselves.

The chapter concludes with a discussion of our research methods and approach. Here we discuss the potential for developing 'global ethnographies' that are open to the 'flows' of global processes but capable of maintaining an ethnographic interest in the values of the local, the particular or the individual. So can there be such a thing as a global ethnography? This question poses an interesting challenge, and while it is of course impossible to represent the world in anything approximating its entirety there are other ways in which local ethnographies can be made meaningful in global times. We suggest there is much potential in working within and between different scales (e.g. local–global, national–international) to shed light upon the interconnected and disconnected worlds in which we live. We further argue that an ethnographic focus on people and process is capable of opening up researchers to a 'global sense of place'. The other research method we draw upon to develop this approach involves various forms of cultural studies analysis. This includes, but is not restricted to, textual analysis, representational methods, visual methodologies and the use of cultural theory (including postcolonial, feminist and queer methodologies). Bringing these methods together is a means of describing, analysing and interrogating the question of gender and youth.

Risk and Individualization

A characteristic of 'new times' is that they are said to be governed by greater levels of 'risk' and insecurity (Giddens, 1991; Beck, 1992). This is in part due to the dismantling of much heavy industry and the promise it was perceived to afford to lifelong labour, secure and embedded relations. Sociologists of 'risk' focus upon the 'self' in late-modernity and argue that identities are increasingly being formed in relation to a broader culture of risk. A feature of inhabiting a risk society (Beck, 1992) is that it demands individuals to become more 'reflexive' and develop 'individualized' biographies comprised of enterprising skills, technical expertise and entrepreneurial behaviour, adapted to the changing world that surrounds them. This has enormous implications for how young people must advance their lives in what is deemed to be an increasingly less secure, fragmented and postmodern world, that at least to some extent is witnessing the end of empire and industry. The break-up of the Soviet Union and the rise of New Social Movements are also thought to give rise to new forms of identity and other ways of being.

However, we dissuade, at least in part, from some of the stronger emphases Beck and Giddens give to individualization as a distinct 'project of self' where writers proclaim, 'This accelerating individualization process is a process in which agency is set free from structure' (Lash and Urry, 1999:5). We are also more cautious about the extent to which we can write about a 'new modernity' when it is evident that alternative modernities feature across the globe and continue to haunt the postcolonial present. Furthermore while sympathetic to the need to rethink the changing world through new vocabularies we feel there has been a tendency to underplay the salience of locality, tradition, class, community and family as key features in young people's social landscapes (see Chapter 6).

As such we concur with youth writers such as MacDonald and Marsh (2006) who argue that while the concept of 'individualization' allows for the creative delineation of diverse youth biographies this should not be set apart from a grid of structural processes through which common experiences can cohere. A thoroughly class-bound way in which individualization is being developed in young lives is through the Student Gap Year, now an institutionalized aspect of the transition from school to Higher Education. The 'Gap Year', once frowned upon for its associations with hippy culture and 'dropping out', in recent times has become a vital experiential prop for the scripting of individual biographies for universities and future employers (Simpson, 2004). However, as the Gap Year is rapidly becoming the norm rather than exception, it is evident that ever-more specialized forms of entrepreneurial kudos and cultural capital are likely to be sought by middle-class parents and their enterprising offspring. Inevitably for Beck, and not without paradox, 'Individualization thus means precisely *institutionalisation*, institutional shaping and, hence *the ability to structure* biographies and life situations politically' (1992:132). The project of self and the work of late-modern social theorists are further discussed in the following two chapters where we consider emotional relationships and new practices of intimacy.

Beck's remarks regarding institutionalization are in keeping with the insights generated by Halford and Savage (1997), in a compelling account of the roles of embodiment and performance evident in the restructuring of British banking. Halford and Savage reveal how particular organizations have their own institutional cultures that construct particular personal qualities as 'desirable' or 'undesirable', so that when restructuring is underway these characteristics are bound up with a redefinition of the types of personal qualities an employee must inhabit. On the surface this appears to fit neatly with theories of individualization and the way in which subjects are transformed into self-monitoring and self-reflexive beings. However, using life-history method these writers illuminate a further dynamic within the nexus of restructuring – individuals are not passive recipients of change but resist, contest and reinterpret these strategies. For these writers gender cannot be held apart from economic restructuring, rather 'gender is central to the restructuring process itself' (1997:109). This is seen in the transformation of an older, oak-panelled paternalistic banking culture once headed up by an elder male manager. In 'new times' this culture is being substituted for a chic entrepreneurial world of glass and chrome where the promotion of masculine 'young guns' to managers is available to those who meet sales targets and achieve high rates of performance-related pay. What each of these banking cultures share, new and old, is the institutional production of a powerful *gender regime*. Where the older culture is staunchly masculine, priding itself on a familial culture and longstanding relationships with staff, the newer ethos, though in principle more open to women and minorities, is experienced as more aggressive, divisive and anonymous. It

produces a higher managerial turnover as 'head-hunting' and corporate individualism come to subsume the previous culture of company loyalty. In a
world of presentation, appearance and 'signs' Halford and Savage discovered
women may regularly be deployed on the front desk as they are thought of
as smiling faces who can easily pacify customer complaints. The making of
what we might see as 'financial femininities' in this way is a power-laden and
contradictory process, seen for example when ethnic minorities claim they are
rarely permitted front-desk work and are instead allocated to the background
shadows.

The ways these identities are negotiated and embodied within business
cultures is strikingly in evidence in the competing cast of such television hit-
shows as *The Apprentice*, fronted by multi-millionaire moguls such as Donald
Trump in the US and Sir Alan Sugar in the UK. Becoming an apprentice
in adulthood is a highly stylized act of cultural reproduction: it involves an
acute investment in modes of gender performance and practices of individualization. In contrast in localities with strong regional working-class cultures
that have historically valued loyalty to an industry or firm through collective
practices and the rhythmic regularity of labour, individualization and enterprise may be difficult to realize. Labour market risk and the cost of living
not only shape work relations but are also impacting upon household transitions. For example, increasing job insecurity coupled with a rise in house
prices has meant many young adults are unable to set up home alone, so
are extending their stay within the confines of the parental home. Thus, in
a study of young people in north-east England, Hollands (1995; 1997) has
shown how 'Delayed transitions into marriage and autonomous households
is the main coping mechanism young adults on Tyneside have for dealing
with a less than satisfactory financial position' (1997:50–51). This is seeing
the production of what Pilkington and Johnson (2003) term 'obstinate identities', bound to peripheral cultures of class and locality (see MacDonald and
Marsh, 2006). In particular this may give rise to 'stubborn' forms of masculinity
through emotional investments and affective understandings of manual labour,
a theme picked up in Chapter 6. The status of peripheral youth living in
outer-city estates and remote areas wherein the intensity of metropolitan
cultural globalization is more muted has been the subject of British investigations of displaced youth (Back and Nayak, 1999; MacDonald and Marsh,
2006) and recent work on masculinities set amidst the Australian outback
(Kenway *et al.*, 2006). Indeed the idea of 'at risk youth' is longstanding and
as a discursive mode has been applied to violent, black, homeless, gay and
drug-using youth. As a discursive trope, risk has been central to the recurrent 'moral panic' surrounding young people (Cohen, 1972; Pearson, 1983). In
the following chapter we consider how 'risk' categories are currently being
applied to young women in late-modernity and the impact of the 'girls at risk'
discourse.

Globalization and the Postcolonial

Globalization is frequently associated with the 'shrinking' of time and space and the compression of world relations into a single market. Places such as London, New York and Tokyo are primary examples of global cities that exemplify the making of an interconnected world in which all kinds of global 'flows' from migrants to musical cultures can be found. Many of these transnational flows and connections are enhanced through new technologies and are linked to the production, expansion and circulation of capital in late-modernity. For young subjects who are geographically displaced and living peripheral lives, their relationship to global cultures may seem distant and remote. Similarly, for those who are economically marginalized, globalization remains a highly 'uneven' event, 'that fragments as it co-ordinates' (Giddens, 1991:75).

Of particular interest to our research is the ways in which global culture can produce new spaces and incite 'different youthful subjectivities' (McRobbie, 1994) giving rise to new femininities and masculinities. The consumption of new forms of gender identity is in evidence in rapidly developing nations. In India the role of popular media and global change is seen in the growth and popularity of a new genre of soaps, Bollywood musicals, film and novels that have all been set in telephone call-centres – the liminal space of 'glocal' interaction *par excellence*. Television soaps such as *India Calling* portray how call-centres form a new contact zone between East and West. They draw attention to the new gender relations evident in work-based cultures where young male and female graduates are thrust together in the confined space and nocturnal world of the call-centre, an arena that breaks down the traditional distance between the sexes. These examples inform us, on the one hand, how global outsourcing and changing labour markets are restructuring gender relations. On the other, they also disclose how the circulation of media images through soaps, music and fiction operate as technologies that can incite a proliferation of new gender styles and identities. In the tangled interaction between East and West there are also attempts to rewrite 'Asian' ethnicities and bring them into line with Western values and understandings. For example, many Western businesses that relocate to India encourage workers to anglicize their forenames – from Sanjay to Sam or Prabha to Pauline for example – as part of a process of whitening that attempts to modernize these identities while bleaching ethnicities.

In this respect engagements with globalization are at least in part a falling into line with Westernization. This is seen through the imposition of a Western time-space frame upon Indian employees who work through the night and are trained to avoid making calls during the scheduling of popular Western soaps – they too are encouraged to gain familiarity with. The racialized spatial divisions of labour achieved through corporate mobility and outsourcing are a cursory reminder that 'the colonial is not dead, since it lives on its "after-effects"' (Hall, 1996:248). And while the postcolonial colonies of India, China or Brazil are said to be booming there remains an enormous gulf between the wealthy and the impoverished. For example India is now tailing China at the peak of the global economy with Indian companies becoming leading global players in steel, information technology, automotive components and cement. Mobile phone connections are growing by around 5 million per month and the prosperity of India's middle class has surged dramatically. However, closer inspection of the 'India shining' narrative cannot dispel the lengthy shadow of poverty, caste and sex disparities. It is still a country where 2.8 million children die annually of malnutrition or easily preventable illnesses, and 300 million Indians live on less than 50 pence a day.

In Western nation-states there has been much discussion about the footloose nature of multinational corporations who relocate to developing countries where cheap labour is in abundance and union rights may be non-existent. If call-centre work in India is undertaken predominantly by middle-class skilled young graduates, in the UK the story is different. In many northern English towns where a tradition of heavy industry once existed, call-centre work has been aimed particularly at women. Working in call-centres has been regarded as an example of the 'feminization' of the labour market not only because women are welcomed into this sector, but also as it harks back to secret-arial keyboard office work where being friendly, polite and 'smiling down the phone' are given a new, modern technological twist in high-wire capitalism. This 'emotional labour' is discussed by Hochschild (2002) in her analysis of the management of feeling by women air-crew flight attendants whereupon the 'emotional style of offering the service is part of the service itself' (2002:194). In this respect gender practices are written through the service economy and cannot be separated out from economic exchanges. The 'reworking of work' and the role of affect and emotions are discussed in Chapter 6.

Tracing the scattered lines and fractured configurations of the global economy may then highlight some contradictory aspects of contemporary relations with regard to gender, sexuality, ethnicity and social class. On Sydney beaches in Australia, battles were recently fought between Anglo-Australian youth and Middle Eastern, predominantly Lebanese youth, accused of intimidating women bathers and assaulting two volunteer lifeguards. Some 5000 people were involved in the attempt to 'reclaim the beach'. Although race hatred against immigrants is far from new the role of global media and communications as new technologies facilitating fear and anger came to the fore. Sydney reporter Roger Maynard cites a police report stating the attacks 'were fuelled by racial prejudice, alcohol, text messages and the inflammatory remarks of radio shock jocks'. The story informs how 'In the lead-up to the riot 270,000 text messages calling for a showdown on the beach were sent, urging young Australians to go "wog bashing". Other Lebanese youth urged their fellow countrymen to 'bring your guns and knives and let's show them how we do it' (*The Guardian*, October 21, 2006:21). In the postcolonial moment the construction of white femininity as under threat from foreign predatory males continues to exert an emotive appeal that may result in a violent effort to reclaim imaginary bodies and spaces.

A postcolonial reworking of gender is found in Dwyer's (1999) interviews with 49 young British Muslim women in two Hertfordshire schools in the UK who are implicated in the making of 'new femininities'. In exploring attitudes to Western and Islamic dress (for example the loose-fitting *shalwar kameez* trouser suit and the head-covering scarf the *hijab*), Dwyer reveals the relationship between the body, fashion and gender. By examining discourses of 'appropriate' femininities and how this concept is reworked in different spatial contexts she reveals the power of consumption to shape gender ascription. For example her respondents reveal how seemingly conservative young Muslim women can be judged negatively for wearing 'Western' clothing, and how those wearing the *hijab* can use this powerful, if ultimately superficial sign to mask the fact that they may date boys and/or go out on the town. Interestingly some respondents are seen constructing alternative Muslim femininities by asserting their rights to wear skirts and other Western fashions secure in the knowledge that this does not contravene Islamic codes if the body remains covered. Furthermore, some of these young women were mixing and matching Asian and Western fashions as observed through the organization of a school fashion show. According to Dwyer the event was designed to emphasize the ways fashion crosses boundaries. It 'can be read as the opening up of an alternative imagined space – outside the bounded dichotomies that over determine the identities of young Muslim women – through which new forms of identification and femininity could be imagined' (1999:149). The culturally hybrid 'pick-and-mix' approach to clothing parallels the way musical spaces can perform as zones of interruption when it comes to racial fixing. In the postcolonial context young women are fashioning a new, ethnically assertive British Muslim identity that is as traditional as it is modern.

Another postcolonial example of the cosmopolitan dialogue between cultures and place can be traced in Yano's (2004) detailed reading of the Korean *enka* singer Kim Yonja and the star's unique place in Japanese culture. *Enka* is a traditional genre of Japanese ballad, especially popular with older Japanese men and women who form the target audience. In many ways it is a type of folk music out of tune with modern Japan, harking back to melancholic poetic expressions of longing and pre-industrial customs. However, Japan's colonial relationship with parts of Far East Asia and nation-states such as Korea and Taiwan has seen *enka* adopted and adapted by new generations of once-colonized peoples. Kim Yonja's linguistic understanding of Japanese is occasionally faltering and enshrouded in self-deprecating humour, yet part of her charm lies in the way she locates herself as someone in need of assistance from those around her. Kim is open about her Korean identity and her position as a cultural interloper. It is with much irony, humour and unflinching respect that she occasionally dons a Japanese kimono – a marker of a constrained and traditional femininity – during select performances. This is not an act of cultural and gendered submission to a former colonizer, but a carefully cultivated spectacle that rewrites the power of the kimono. As Yano explains:

> The kimono became a centrepiece of Kim's performance, as well as emblematic of her position in Japan. The kimono is a vessel into which one gets poured, yet Kim never becomes the container; instead she is always made to hold the container at a distance from herself. She at once adopts and extends the gaze of her audience in Japan. Kim and kimono do not blend, but hold one another in suspension like oil and water. (2004:164)

The fact that Kim's performance never leads to the obliteration of her Korean identity makes for a strategically powerful illustration of cultural hybridity as a complex postcolonial mode of resistance (Bhabha, 1994). The theme of mimicry, passing and the possibilities they hold for the subversion of race, class and gender are discussed in Chapter 8. What is interesting here is that Kim Yonja has a special place in the hearts of many of the middle-aged Japanese public who adore her (including a younger gay male fan club), precisely because she appears to show a reverence for the 'authentic' as she simultaneously dissimulates from it. She is, according to Yano, in some senses 'more Japanese than Japanese' (2004:170). Despite this appearance, and as her name unashamedly testifies, Kim is proudly Korean: fans wave Korean flags at her concerts, she speaks about the beauty of Korea as a place to visit and her performances are emblematic of a 'bejewelled and bedecked version of Korea' (p. 170). As such Yano's analysis goes beyond generalized approaches to global change by drawing our attention to alternative modernities, cosmopolitan flows between nation-states and the different histories and geographies of postcolonial negotiation. In many ways Kim's performances bridge the postcolonial divide, crossing national boundaries but never losing a pride of place in her Korean heritage. The interplay between globalization, postcolonialism and identity are taken up in Chapter 5 where we discuss the performance of gender and sexuality in Brazilian carnival and also within select East African tribal cultures. Each of these examples vividly illustrates how sex and gender is being resituated in global times through postcolonial frames. Having discussed our critical approaches to notions of risk, individualization, globalization and postcolonialism we now turn our attention to recent techniques used by gender and youth researchers and outline the research methods we deploy throughout the book.

Methods and Approaches: Biographies, Global Ethnographies and Cultural Studies Analysis

All books are to some extent biographical. This particular study grows out of our own histories, thinking and writing in youth culture. Both of us were postgraduates in Cultural Studies at the University of Birmingham UK, before moving to other institutions to undertake doctoral work in different areas of youth studies and within different disciplines. One of us, Anoop Nayak, went on to investigate the intersections of race, class and whiteness, which became the focus of a community ethnography exploring young people's cultural geographies of identity and place (Nayak, 2003a), while the other, Mary Jane Kehily, explored issues of gender, sexuality and schooling using first-hand observations and in-depth interviews to capture the intricate detail of young people's sexual learning and everyday life (Kehily, 2002). We each, then, are drawn to the value of human experience for illuminating and explicating the use and limits of cultural theory. Throughout this book we engage in a type of theory-led ethnography inspired by recent work in feminist theory, cultural studies, the sociology of youth and the postcolonial geographies of race and migration.

Biographies

One of the most detailed ways of enhancing portraiture in young lives is through the use of biographical research and life-history method. The role of structure and agency in youth biographies has been delicately handled in work of this kind and is particularly insightful when it comes to documenting youth transitions and critical incidents (MacDonald and Marsh, 2001; Henderson *et al.*, 2007; Thomson and Taylor, 2005; McLeod and Yates, 2006). Connell's exemplary exposition of life-history method to an understanding of masculinities is testimony to the value of personal accounts of gender and youth. Indeed we actually deploy a life-history account in Chapter 5 derived from a study of gay Skinhead youth (Healy, 1996), which acts as a prism to shed light upon and refract a range of different gender power relations located across the axis of ethnicity, class, masculinity and generation. This approach is extended in Chapter 9 when we consider the mercurial sexed biography of former tennis star Renee Richards. In the following chapter we explore the complex biographical insights generated by Valerie Walkerdine (1990) to a reading of class and gender. As each of these testimonies will go on to reveal, the personal is polit-ical. For the sociologists of risk and individualization discussed previously, biography is a late-modern 'technology of the self' (Foucault, 1988), a type of reflexive project through which we come to make and understand our place in the social world.

There is a sense in personal accounts that an individual's life is often so much more than theory and words can describe. Using follow-up biographical methods Williamson (2004:41) has remarked upon how even the more soph-isticated approaches to youth transitions, which have focused upon complex trajectories, navigations, niches and pathways, remain imbued with 'a sense that one can somehow dissociate aspiration and experience in relation to training and work from the wider context of individual lives and then dissect this in glorious isolation'. Williamson's British-based work on 'Milltown Boys' is an evocative example of longitudinal biography, in his attempt to recon-nect with the lives of the 67 males he first interviewed 25 years ago in the 1970s. Remarkably, Williamson locates around half of the respondents only to discover that six of the original sample are dead, though none of natural causes. The life trajectories of those remaining are testimony to the remarkable unpre-dictability of individual lives, which refuse to be bound by mechanistic theories of class transition and trajectory. Interestingly Williamson also recounts how occupational pathways can further alter in the later parts of one's life course and cautions against assuming 'success' or 'failure' based on youthful presentations of self that are not open to the possibility of future change and circumstance. There are, then, a number of advantages to interconnected biographies, neigh-bourhood ethnographies and community studies which may span decades of social change and personal transformation.

While biography and life history offer penetrating insight into the lives of individuals it has been argued that the role of mutual experience and collective belonging can occasionally become sidelined through these techniques. There may also be a sense that life histories produce a seamless narrative recon-struction of the past that places discursive order over what is in actuality a more complex 'bricolage' of events and doings. Thus, in their work with young Turkish German break-dancers Bohnsack and Nohl (2003:367) proclaim 'reconstructive research on youth should not be confined to the employment of a biographical method in which the individual constitutes the focus of data collection and interpretation. Such an approach conceals more subtle forms of collective cultural practices and patterns of orientation as well as the collective contexts and practices of action into which distinctively individualized youth biographies are integrated and unfold'. We would suggest that the role of mutual experience is particularly important when it comes to exploring the broader impact that ethnicity, social class, gender or sexuality may have upon groups and individual actors and the ways in which these structural relations intermesh with personal biography. In refusing to isolate biographies we can achieve a fuller picture of generational cohorts, their attitudes, beliefs and ways of life. Locating biography within place-specific relations also enables us to view the contexts that give rise to the landscape of emotions, opportunities and constraints that shape personal histories. The value of an emplaced, collective approach that can yield interconnected biographies is soundly evidenced in Weis's (2004) exemplary ethnography of gender, race and class in 'new times' neo-Liberal America. Revisiting respondents she first interviewed in the mid-1980s, 15 years on, Weis not only captures how individual lives may change but the context within which communities are restructured and former steel towns are 'recast'. We return to this account in Chapter 6 where we discuss place relations in the multi-ethnic neighbourhood. Our appreciation of collective longitudinal methods is seen in the following chapter where we include a detailed discussion of anthropological reports pertaining to East African and Brazilian communities.

Global Ethnographies – Mobile Subjects and Objects

As an early anthropological mode of enquiry ethnography is a powerful anti-dote to abstract theoretical accounts of gender relations that rest unanchored from the grit of human experience. Although the work presented here does not mirror the longitudinal, 'classic' ethnography of anthropological tradition (see Chapter 5 for examples) it maintains what we could describe as a rich 'ethnographic sensibility'. By this we mean the work uses participant observation and interaction with young people as an empirical base not only to try out theory, but also to generate new ideas and reflect upon questions of youth. In many ways ethnography fuses together theory and practice, working through description and analysis. The value of an ethnographic sensibility lies in its ability to put young people centre stage with a focus upon 'doing' and action. This allows us to look in closer detail at the performative dimension of youth practices through an array of gender presentations, displays and exhibitions.

Recently there have been a number of debates concerning the status of ethnography in an interconnected world and the possibilities for developing what Burawoy and colleagues term a 'global ethnography' (Burawoy *et al.*, 2000). It is because globalization is associated with the social, economic, political and cultural transformation of people and place – along with the widening, deepening and quickening of worldwide interconnections – that the value of ethnography is being called into question. Where traditional ethnographies may focus upon a particular site – a prison, steel plant, school, healthcare centre or elderly people's home, *global ethnographies* tend to explore different spaces, often by way of a multi-site analysis that may include observations and reflections upon the variety of arenas individuals inhabit (see Nayak, 2003a). If much early ethnographic research had been relatively 'bounded', focusing upon the detailed anthropological construction of a 'tribe' or the depiction of a street-gang through expert urban sociological excavations, place can no longer be seen as a neutral spatial container within which human actors perform. A more 'progressive sense of place' recognizes the interconnections between the local and the global (Massey, 1994), and the ways in which diasporas, migrations and cultural 'flows' permeate and so pull apart the idea of place as securely bounded. Appadurai's (1990) preference for writing about 'scapes' rather than hermetically sealed places has particular implications for ethnography in articulating the flows of culture, ethnicities, technology, finance, media and ideas that cross the boundaries of the nation-state.

It is our contention that a form of global ethnography which allows theory to 'travel' and operates at different scales from the body to the local, regional, national, international and global is a highly valuable means for accounting for the contemporary conundrum of place. We are struck by the imaginative appeal of global ethnography as a concept that allows us to think beyond the local and examine the worldwide transformations of gender and youth in late-modernity. But how exactly can such a global ethnography be achieved, and does this opening out inevitably mean that some of the finest qualities of ethnography – its close attention to detail, the 'thick' description of locality, the rich characterization of individual lives – are lost? While there is certainly a danger in abstraction, we feel that there are many ways in which a globally sensitive ethnography can yet transpire. The critical readings discussed in Chapter 5 and the themes of risk, postcolonialism and global change discussed above gesture towards understanding the potential of ethnography as a global project.

Rather than view ethnography as an outdated and spatially bound practice, we argue for the overall flexibility of the ethnographic method and its potential for illuminating a range of *mobilities*. More recently writers such as the sociologist Urry (2000) have argued for the need to recognize spaces, flows and the diverse mobility of people, objects, money, information and images within particular places. In this way Urry has urged sociologists to draw inspiration from geography in a bid to 'register the geographical intersections of region, city and place, with the social categories of class, gender and ethnicity' (p. 186). These points of connection between place, space and identity are thus the focus of Chapters 6 and 7 where we respectively consider spaces of production and consumption. But what are the implications of a 'spatial turn' in the social sciences, of the type advocated by Urry (2000) and other social geographers, for an understanding of subjectivity? As Lash and Urry proclaim in a discussion of mass tourism, 'mobility transforms people's identities' (1999:9). While international tourists may be amongst the most mobile, cosmopolitan and to some extent reflexive subjects in late-modernity, even those living more parochial lives are unlikely to be immune to the hyper-mobility of everyday life. This is seen in Doreen Massey's (1998) observations of Yucatan youth in Mexico who live in thatched houses with earthen floors and open fires, a dwelling where corn-bread tortillas are thought to be made in traditional ways. And yet stepping out of the huts Massey encounters a rather different form of Mayan youth culture as she comes into contact with a virtual world of computer gaming, 'Electronic noises, American slang and bits of Western music floated off into the night-time jungle' (1998:121), she recalls. For Massey this is part of a 'geographical constitution of cultures' (p. 123), where cultural interconnections between different places and across different sites and scales are in evidence. Everyday cultural flows and the mobility of objects are then transforming young people's identities in complex ways as they come to interact with and reconfigure processes of globalization.

The tropes of 'flow', mobility, migration or movement may suggest a disembedding of traditional social relations such as class, ethnicity and gender from everyday life. However, the relative freedom of movement enjoyed by global tourists starkly departs from the restricted experiences endured by asylum seekers, refugees and other displaced subjects. This indicates that the art of mobility is itself a locus of power formative of particular geographies of exclusion. Ethnography is invaluable in helping us explore these contradictions by engaging with the intersecting textures of lived experience and connecting this to a world in motion. It discloses, in a thoroughly embodied way, how global transformations are being negotiated in local spaces and within the microcosm of young people's habitual relationships. Thus, while our own accounts are inevitably limited to particular sites and spaces, we continually make reference to the influence of global media, markets, cultures and economies and the role they play in constructions of gender and youth relations. We have been influenced by studies of youth across time and place and the points of connection they make with our own work. The book makes a concerted effort at 'crossing continents' to show how globalization and youth formations are constituted in other times and places. Above all, ethnography is a key to unlocking social processes and is able to reveal what may lie beneath the everyday surface of people, objects, action and landscapes in late-modernity.

The ethnographic research for this book grew from a number of studies carried out during a series of intermittent, but nevertheless intensive stages of fieldwork undertaken between the years 1993 and 2003. As with the previous work discussed, we regard the time-span and opportunity for reflection as strengths of the insights generated. There are occasions where young people's conversations refer to passing cultural icons such as Madonna or older British soaps such as *Brookside*, which is no longer running. However, we have included at least some of these discussions here, as the insights remain highly relevant to our understanding of changing gender relations in late-modernity today. As Skeggs's (1997) acclaimed study of class and respectability illustrates, oscillating between the past and present can be a highly productive manoeuvre which provides a critical distance from which to rethink subjectivities. At some points the ethnography involves narrative recollections and 'well-worn' stories, while at others it is caught in the dramatic immediacy of the moment. In this sense all ethnographic accounts are a partial and selective reworking of action. We developed our ethnographic interpretations in dialogue with respondents, one another and the global literature on gender, youth and cultural studies. This makes for a reflexive, inter-textual account that speaks through and across other ethnographies, theories and representations of gender, to form a multilayered and colourful tapestry of young lives.

The ethnography forms part of a multi-site analysis that took place in four English State Schools, extending into different neighbourhood spaces. It began with our collaborative research on gender and sexuality in the early 1990s, when we went into two large comprehensive schools in the West Midlands conurbation, interviewing and observing young people aged 14–15 years and 16–17 years (see Nayak and Kehily, 1996; Kehily and Nayak, 1997). It also includes data we gathered independently from one another, again in the post-industrial region of the West Midlands (14–15 years) and also by way of a further school in London (14–16 years). Our approach involves participant observation and interaction with young people, thick description of people and events and recorded interviews conducted with teachers and students, complimented by field diaries and local sources pertaining to these areas. The conversation with young people is carried out using a number of small discussion groups who we successively spoke with on a number of occasions and got to know over a period of time. The research with teachers is derived from daily interactions and face-to-face semi-structured interviews that are designed around their biographical testimonies and topical issues related to gender and youth.

The difficulty that ethnography may have when it comes to straddling the local–global nexus remains a source of debate. Brewer (2002[2000]) has intimated that ethnography still has a future in global times. Specifically this is to:

- chart the experience of people in a local setting to demonstrate how global processes are mediated by local factors;

- address the persistence of traditions;

- describe how traditional identities interface with globally structured ones (p. 176).

While we recognize the limited and highly selective ethnography we draw upon throughout this book, we envisage that the above points can be met and indeed elaborated upon through our focus on discourse, representation and media texts as described below.

Cultural Studies Analysis

As part of our research method we also deployed a cultural studies approach to youth, including the use of semiotic, materialist, discursive and psychoanalytic tools of analysis. The cultural studies methodology develops our concern to take popular culture seriously as a dynamic relationship and central locus through which young people's social worlds are formed. In doing so we have been attentive to textual analysis, representation and visual methodologies. Throughout the book we use these techniques to bring meaning and under- standing to film, music, magazines, literary fiction, television and other media that have become part of the global web of technologies around which youth identities are situated. Ethnography and filmic representations are each texts imbued with meanings that can be deconstructed and distilled. While we appreciate the open-endedness of meaning-making processes, this need not depart from a critical cultural studies analysis. As Hall (1980) explains in an early essay on the textual practice of 'encoding/decoding', texts may well be polysemic and multi-referential but they remain historical products structured through relations of power and dominance within which 'preferred' mean- ings are signified. Not least for these reasons a cultural studies analysis of visual texts and popular culture may have a great deal to say about the chan- ging world in which we live and the types of gender identities that are being envisioned.

Our desire to take popular culture seriously rather than relegate it to the margins as frivolous is, we feel, empathetic to the lives of the young respond- ents we spoke with who continually mentioned the significance of music, text-messaging, fashion or video games to their everyday activities. Accord- ingly Couldry (2000:1) authoritatively asserts, 'cultural studies is an expanding space for sustained, rigorous and self-reflexive empirical research into the massive, power-laden complexity of contemporary culture', a remark which certainly affords good reason for in-depth considerations of the popular. Storey (1997[1993]:202) is equally emphatic postulating how 'popular culture is a concept of ideological contestation and variability, to be filled and emptied, to be articulated and disarticulated in a range of different and competing ways'. He solemnly concludes, ' "studying" popular culture can be a very serious business indeed – serious political business' (p. 202), a point neatly illustrated in Hebdige's (1979) eloquent account of post-war British youth subculture and the ideological struggle that may ensue over a variety of signs and signifiers.

In this way, as our subsequent discussion will illuminate, popular culture is the bedrock upon which ideas of gender crystallize. Film, television and popular media showcase how gender is continually made and remade. Thus while some of the characters in popular hit series such as *Sex and the City* remain shallower-than-a-teaspoon and frothier than your average cappuccino, they remain *culturally meaningful* to the contemporary portrayal of gender relations in late-modernity – even, darling, at their most *fabulously* excessive. As these texts show, popular culture is an arena where fantasy, power and gender ideologies come into play but it is also the space within which we attempt to produce our imaginary 'selves' in ever incomplete ways. As Hall (1992:22) expresses in a discussion of black popular culture, we would be mistaken in believing culture is the arena where we uncover the essence of 'who we really are', rather 'It is there that we discover and play with the identifications of ourselves, where we are imagined, where we are represented. Not only to the audiences out there who do not get the message, but to ourselves for the first time'. It is these plastic *gender imaginings* and their accompanying forms of identification and mis/recognition that we feel are both personally significant and globally pivotal to the contemporary gender order and the global information and media superhighway. In this way popular culture and the 'mediascapes' Appadurai (1990) identifies, form a cultural 'space of flows' (Castells, 1997) through which new engagements between gender and youth occur.

When it came to interpreting the material we gathered this activity remained a shared process where we had jointly undertaken fieldwork and cultural analysis within a particular site. Where one of us had been the principle researcher, that person took the lead when it came to making sense of experiences. This reflects our belief that an engagement with the intimate cultures of young people is a valuable form of meaning making. Surprisingly, given the longstanding popularity of collaborative research within many disciplines, little is ever said about the constructive act of collaborative write-up – for example, how do authors reach agreement on ethnographic meaning, what happens when they disagree, and what are the benefits and shortcomings of collective interpretation? Thus one reader who knew our work independently, detected the different intonation of our voices playfully distinguishing a 'girly sensibility' (Mary Jane), from a theoretically 'queer sensibility' (Anoop) attuned to the accent of contemporary scholarship in the field. We too recognize our differing approaches and subject positionalities which are bound together by a commitment to young people, cultural ethnography and improved gender relations. In doing so, we regard the bringing together of different perspectives, knowledges and literatures as formative of the type of transdisciplinary cultural studies that is becoming an invaluable method from which to engage with the fragmentation and multiplicity of meanings associated with postmodernity. A major problem of collaborative research is that we found ourselves continually working and reworking the structure and approach to accommodate the different readings, perspectives and insights we accumulated. Overall we found shared discussion and mutual critique a highly productive means of advancing our thinking and writing. The process of negotiated meaning is further developed as we decided to send each of the chapters to specialist readers for feedback and comment. This tight 'circle of involvement' included youth writers, feminist thinkers and academics with a particular interest in aspects of our work.

3

Gender Relations in Late-Modernity: Young Masculinities in Crisis

This chapter and the following one examine how gender relations are restructured, reconfigured and, on occasion, recuperated in late-modernity. Focusing first on masculinities (Chapter 3), then femininities (Chapter 4), we document and illustrate the ways in which contemporary gender relations can be seen as a site of fissure with the past while simultaneously holding onto many features of continuity. In some examples the gender values and norms of the past haunt the present in mournful ways, while in others gendered styles are reworked in a creative fusion of past and present. We identify two dominant themes that have come to characterize debates on young men and women in 'new times' – first, that masculinities are seen to be economically and culturally displaced, so are in 'crisis'; second, feminine subjects are the flexible beneficiaries and accomplished protagonists of a neo-liberal agenda that has enabled a 'new girl order' to develop, centred upon office work, sexual relationships and heady consumerism. While recognizing the widespread impact of a global restructuring of gender relations our attention is drawn to the limitations and contradictions of these repertoires for a richer understanding of young lives. In doing so we discuss film and popular media alongside feminist cultural theory and new approaches to working-class studies. Reflecting upon these polarized representations of masculinity and femininity enables us to explore how gender is being economically situated and culturally understood – however obliquely – in late-modernity. In order to discuss the different dimensions of young masculinities in crisis, the chapter is organized into the following sections: young men and labour market transitions; inside-out; *Falling Down*; the limits of crisis.

Young Masculinities in Crisis: Rethinking the Dominant Paradigm

I see all this potential – and I see it squandered. God damn it – an entire generation pumping gas, waiting tables: slaves with white collars. Advertising has its taste in cars and clothes, working jobs we hate so we can buy shit we don't need. We're the middle children of history, man. No purpose or place. We have no Great War, no Great Depression. Our Great War's a spiritual war. Our Great Depression is our lives. We've all been raised on television to believe that one day we'll be millionaires and movie gods and rock stars, but we won't. We're slowly learning that fact and we're very, very pissed off. Fox, 1999, *Fight Club* (USA dir. David Fincher, 20th Century)

The above oratory, uttered by Hollywood actor Brad Pitt cast as Taylor Dent the dark overlord of an underground fight club, epitomizes a number of recent concerns regarding the place of young men in Western society. Stripped of an industrial heritage and shorn of the heroic accolades attributed to men of war, contemporary masculinities can appear as displaced subjectivities, alienated and ridden with insecurity about their purpose and role. In *Fight Club* these 'slaves with white collars' throw off the starchy rigmarole of polite bourgeois society. In doing so, they engage in the undiluted bodily practice of spectacular bare-knuckle fighting. In this chapter we consider changing notions of masculinities in the late modern period.

As a cultural text Fincher's film is sophisticated and intricate enough to surreptitiously expose the hollowness at the heart of much modern experiences of young white masculinity. But to an uncritical reader it may appear that the film is reflective of insecure times in which gender roles are not what they once were, where much armed conflict takes place at a technological remove and where globalization is restructuring labour markets beyond recognition. The triumph of global capitalism in late-modernity has only served to intensify the blizzard of signs, dreams and fantasies endlessly circulated through technologies of consumption. It may also seem that modern masculinity has somehow lost itself, forgotten what it once was or at least had struggled to be. Certainly the fantasy that white-collar workers – and other, alienated young men – should 'discover' their masculinities through the embodied acts of acute violence witnessed in *Fight Club* is deeply problematic. On one hand, it implies that masculinity is a tangible essence that once unbuttoned from white-collar lifestyle will spring forth, hell-bent on exerting violent fury. On the other, it suggests that such acts not only afford pleasurable release to young men but are an entirely natural part of their coming-of-age. We argue that these ideas are ultimately little more than the *myths of masculinity*.

Notwithstanding these remarks, we are reluctant to dismiss Fincher's engrossing film out of hand, for it probes what has become a key sociological concern. It asks how do 'boys become men' in a post-industrial world filled with table-waiting jobs, public administration, bar work, call-centres and humdrum service sector employment (Nayak, 2006). Moreover does it follow, as the film suggests, that young men are tortured subjects, bored, listless, frustrated, angry and ill at ease with themselves and nearly everyone else around them? Disembodied from the world of war and work (for it is manual labour that is 'real work'), are young men little more than pale shadows, haunting the de-industrial landscapes which are a constant reminder of their true embodied heritage in years gone by?

A cursory glance at the endless newspaper prose, talk show discussion and popular writing on boys and young men in recent years has provided culturally resonant answers to these seemingly opaque questions. They have suggested that the 'problem with boys' can be put down to a competing and occasionally conflicting amalgam of factors: for example unemployment, absent fathers, working mothers, the break-up of the nuclear family, the decline of military service, the erosion of corporeal punishment, the unabated rise of feminism, video-game violence, the academic success of young women, poor literacy rates, drug culture, rap music, lack of school discipline and a host of real or imagined contemporary dimensions of social change. Amidst the multiple symptoms and numerous proscribed remedies that accompany the 'trouble with boys' thesis there is at least one issue populist commentators seem to agree upon. In late-modernity young masculinities are, self-evidently, 'in crisis'.

The idea that young masculinities are in crisis has been given further credence with a heavy sprinkling of recent self-help books, social and psychological literature written in the field. Indeed it would be very tempting at this point to blitz the reader with a series of statistics to support the crisis theory. Young men are, after all, massively overly represented in figures for violent crime, poor literacy, domestic abuse, house burglary, racist violence, sexual abuse, car crime, drinking to excess, truanting, drug abuse, dangerous and unlawful driving, anti-social behaviour orders (ASBOs), suicide rates, redundancy, prison sentences and gun crime. And if this is not enough the picture does not appear any less gloomy as young men grow older. Here statistics indicate men are more prone to coronary heart disease than women, suffer high rates of stress, deal less well with marital break-up, are less likely to see their children and die younger than their female counterparts (see Beynon, 2002:77–79). So 'is the future female?', to paraphrase a question raised by Segal (1987). As with all dominant paradigms, the idea that young masculinities are in crisis is nothing if not a good story: a compelling narrative which seems to 'tell it like it is', but one we ought to subject to analytic scrutiny. If we are to sketch out the contours of this supposed crisis it can be said to be occurring across key nodes in the body politic of the nation-state and in particular within the social and cultural arenas of education, labour, crime and health. However, rather than rush to personify how the crisis is manifested in each of these arenas, we offer a critical interrogation of how this crisis is constructed and sustained; how is it being articulated and for what purposes; and ultimately we question if a crisis exists at all. We begin by contextualizing the economic changes that have impacted upon young men in late-modernity, examining how this crisis is culturally represented and finally considering the discursive limits of these gender productions.

Young Men and Labour Market Transitions

For young working-class men residing in the Western hemisphere, the transition to manhood was once inextricably linked to the movement from school to work. In the British post-war period, manufacturing employment was seen to offer viable, if restricted, opportunities for working-class males. However monotonous this work was, it was seen to provide the material benefits of regular pay, stability, security and a 'job for life'. Within the complex registers of masculinity, industrial employment also accrued its own type of cultural capital, forged through notions of the patriarchal 'breadwinner', physical 'hardness' and a strict sexual division of labour that split the public 'masculine' world of work from the private domestic realm of women's unpaid labour. For many young men the financial independence ascribed to earning a wage enabled them to vacate household duties and instil a pride in identifications of 'craft' or 'graft' – a theme we develop in Chapter 6. As de-industrialization continued apace throughout the 1980s and beyond young men were increasingly less likely to be 'learning to labour', as the title of Willis's (1977) enduring ethnography had previously suggested. Instead working-class boys were soon caught in the uncertain transition that accompanied ill-paid, poorly structured government training schemes or, quite simply, were left 'schooling for the dole'. For many working-class youth this was to leave a stark choice between what Coffield (1986) matter-of-fact identifies as 'Shit jobs and Govvy schemes' (p. 86). It appeared that young men whose cultural worlds would once have been educationally shaped through a prism of schooling, training schemes, modern apprenticeships and hard labour were soon finding themselves viewed as unskilled, unemployable, redundant youth.

Recently the dearth of manufacturing jobs in Western nation-states has in part been supplemented by an expanding service sector economy and the urban regeneration of old industrial quarters. Whilst this has seen an increase in youth participation in the labour market this new shift is characterized by more casual forms of labour, marked especially by part-time working hours, fixed-term contracts, more 'flexible' patterns of employment along with pay scales that barely hover above the minimum wage. At structural and cultural levels, then, the 'pathways' open to young men as they attempt to make the transition to adulthood and the world of work are rapidly changing yet increasingly individualized. Chatterton and Hollands reflect upon the range of new, sometimes unaccomplished, transitions: ·

> The post-Fordist labour market has not only worked to delay and interrupt traditional youth transitions, but it has also worked to complexify them. Young people today make a bewildering array of labour market transitions, including moving through various training and educational routes through to temporary, contract and part-time work, and in some cases to secure employment. (2003:81)

Thus, while young working-class men are more likely to be 'learning to serve' (McDowell, 2002; 2003) rather than 'learning to labour', this has given way to new masculine subject positions that are highly contradictory. Gender processes are embedded within the discursive repertoires of economic restructuring, thus the growth in a 'soft economy' centred upon services, catering and call-centre work has been interpreted as the 'feminisation' of labour. In a culture where the supposedly 'feminised' attributes of 'deference and docility' (McDowell, 2002:40) are in demand, it would appear that certain white working-class males may be out-of-step with an economy that values flexibility, keyboard proficiency, telephone communication skills and personal presentation. Working-class young men must struggle to find a place in what Castells (1997) calls the new 'network society', a high-wire economy that the sociologist Giddens (1986[1982]: 59) succinctly prophesized in the early 1980s would elicit 'New classes, new technologies'.

As a carrier of signals and a dense economy of signs, it has been stated that 'the body is the most ubiquitous signifier of class' (Skeggs, 1997:82). For if young women are increasingly seen as the 'flexible' neo-liberal subjects of late-modernity, the bodies of working-class young men have long been seen as 'troublesome', non-conformist and marked by resistance (Willis, 1977; Corrigan, 1979; Hebdige, 1979; Cohen, 1997) – in short, lumpen. By inserting themselves into these discursively gendered subject positions it is quite possible that at least some young men are guilty of treating part-time work, customer relations and servicing in a disparaging manner that bespeaks that this is not 'real work' but 'a woman's job'. In the post-industrial period contemporary masculine transitions continue to be marked by opportunity, 'risk', uncertainty and labour market insecurity (Vail *et al.*, 1999). However, rather than leading to the collapse of social class distinctions, theorists such as Beck (1992:35) argue that such 'risks seem to strengthen, not to abolish the class society' in late-modernity. It is within these new times that young men are attempting to rewrite their labour biographies and in doing so are found pursuing multiple, fragmented or unaccomplished transitions. The increasingly individualized biographies include complex, fractured and 'insecure transitions' (MacDonald, 1999:171) mediating across school–work, local–global, boyhood–manhood and so forth.

Inside-Out

It would appear that at the heart of the crisis in masculinity is a crisis of identity. The sense is that young men no longer know who they are in an increasingly post-industrial society where gender roles are rapidly being reconfigured. As Mercer, in a broader discussion on social change, reveals, 'Identity only becomes an issue when it is in crisis, when something assumed to be fixed, coherent and stable is displaced by the experience of doubt and insecurity' (1990:43). Recent psychological and psychoanalytic work has been highly influential in indicating that moments of crisis not only are evident in social and cultural arenas, but also manifest themselves at psychic levels. This work on subjectivity is opening up productive ways of understanding the construction of gender and sexuality through complex psycho-social processes (Hollway, 1989; Rutherford, 1990). In Chapter 8 we elaborate upon the psychoanalytic inflections developed in the writings of Judith Butler, Jonathan Dollimore and Julia Kristeva to explore how the unconscious features in the performance of gender and sexuality in young lives.

An example of a psycho-social approach to gender relations can be found in Walkerdine's essay (1990) 'Video Replay' where she observes a working-class family watching the boxing film *Rocky II* (USA, dir S. Stallone, 1979) starring Sylvester Stallone as Rocky who takes on the 'flash', jive-talking Champ played by Carl Weathers. Walkerdine recounts her initial sense of (bourgeois feminist) revulsion on viewing the battered and bloodied bodies of the boxers as they go toe-to-toe with one another in the final rounds. Her initial reaction is contrasted with the pleasure enjoyed by the Cole family, especially the father. On a second private viewing of the film, however, Walkerdine is tearfully forced to confront her own split class identifications and offer a renewed psychic reinterpretation of *Rocky II* that engages with the affective dimensions of gender and class. The significance of affect and emotion to studies of social class are evident in Kuhn's (1995) personal narrative work on biography, memory and imagination. Kuhn argues that sociology 'too often downplays imagination and understanding, detaching itself from its own ways of knowing and treating its objects – very often in fact the working class – as in some way other, curiously one-dimensional specimens' (p. 101).

In seeking to understand Mr Cole's identification with Rocky Balboa, Walkerdine goes on to recognize the role of class struggle and how 'it is the class-specific aspects of this masculinity that are important' (1990:178). This leads her to reflect upon the working-class significance of the fighter as 'plucky underdog', someone who will not surrender to oppression but will hit back, striking a blow for justice. This reading, Walkerdine argues, resonates with the structural oppression experienced by Mr Cole in the outside world and his psychic desire to present as 'Mr Big' in the domestic setting. Contextualizing *Rocky II* as a potentially pleasurable text within which the regimes of class and gender are struggled over offer alternative ways of rewriting the film, male violence and the subjectivities of Mr Cole and other family members. Walkerdine reveals:

> Fighting can be turned into a celebration of masculinity, but its basis is in oppression. This should also be understood, as in *Rocky*, as the desperate retreat to the body, because the 'way out', of becoming bourgeois through the mind is not open to Mr Cole. (pp. 186–187)

For Walkerdine the fighter identity is less a celebration of sporting masculinity but the desperate resolution of those impossible identifications imaged in *Fight Club*. Walkerdine acknowledges that 'Fighting is a key term in a discourse of powerlessness, of a constant struggle not to sink, to get rights, not to be pushed out' (p. 187). What is important about 'Video Replay', then, is its attempt to locate psychic processes through everyday social relations and the lived material biographies of class and gender. In doing so, Walkerdine revises her previous, potentially pathologizing research opinion of working-class subjects as the 'one-dimensional specimens' Kuhn describes. Walkerdine instead argues that 'The fantasy of the fighter is the fantasy of a working-class male omnipotence over the forces of humiliating oppression which mutilate and break the body in manual labour' (p. 178). The affective dimensions of gender and class and how they are inscribed within the practice of manual labour, fighting or domestic proprietorship are discussed in further detail in Chapter 6 where we explore the emotional intensity of social class relations. The corporeal embodiment of masculinity and labour then resonates through such films as *Fight Club* and the *Rocky* series; it is overtly signalled in the 'dead-end' occupations witnessed in the former and when Stallone is labouring amidst frozen carcasses as a meat packer in the latter.

One aspect which Walkerdine's skilful analysis somewhat underplays is the racialized identifications made available through these films. Indeed manual labour is often portrayed as the prerogative of white working-class masculinity encapsulated in those rooted metaphors and richly emotive histories of being the 'backbone of the nation' or the 'salt of the earth', the authentic emblem of whiteness. Rocky Bilboa, the 'Italian Stallion', comes to represent the hard-working, assimilated new immigrant. In contrast he is continually pitted against other immigrants who are less likely to be easily incorporated as white Americans. These other racially marked bodies include the slick-moving-fast-talking Apollo Creed – the African-American boxer he encounters in the first two films – Clubber Lang, the savage primitive black boxer played by Mr T in

Rocky III whose forename suggests his bludgeoning, undisciplined pugilism and later, in *Rocky IV*, a 1980s Cold War showdown with a giant Russian automaton Ivan Drago portrayed by the blonde and chiselled Dolph Lungren. What these racialized confrontations and the affective qualities they inhabit suggest is that working-class fighting is often an endless struggle for material resources and white respectability that occurs against other immigrants and racialized minorities.

To better illustrate how the crisis of white masculinity is being culturally represented in 'new times' and the complex geography of emotions envisioned, we wish to turn here to another Hollywood film, *Falling Down* (USA, dir. J. Schumacher, 1993). This text epitomizes the processes of global economic restructuring in occurrence and the accompanying crisis of whiteness as an emotive and affective sensory experience. *Falling Down* focuses upon ongoing transformations in the lives of two seemingly ordinary adult white men, offering a very useful illustration of the social and psychic interpenetrations that have come to accompany the masculinities in crisis debate. As Jackson (1990) has shown in an instructive critical analysis of masculinity through the autobiography of former England cricketer Geoff Boycott, such accounts usually function by way of a linear narrative that moves from a base-line of troubled crisis which through struggle leads to resolution and eventual success. Indeed Giddens (1991) suggests that modern subjectivity is characterized by a reflexive biographical reconstruction of self through which we knowingly produce ourselves through narrative retellings. While psychoanalytic methods are generally reserved for patients in a therapeutic situation Tony Jefferson (1996) further reminds us that the materials of dreams, fantasies, memory work and personal diaries are also texts awaiting interpretation. Jefferson employs the secondary sources relating to the boxer Mike Tyson to provide a psychoanalytic reading of black masculinity. But in contrast to the familiar race readings of black subjectivity, such as that undertaken by Jefferson, the lives of white men have only recently been subject to racialized scrutiny. Our analysis develops work in this vein by focusing upon the affective qualities of whiteness and its relationship to changing gender–class relations. We consider the multifaceted form of 'fighting' undertaken in the film, where the lead character in *Falling Down* spars against economic and personal depression, as well as the new rights seen to be attributed to women and what is portrayed as entrepreneurial or dangerous immigrants. We have selected this filmic text as it neatly illustrates how the crisis of masculinity is culturally represented at a structural level and endowed with affect and emotion made manifest in the inner dramas of the psychological. Centring upon a divorced man's desire to attend his daughter's birthday, the film is emblematic of the break-up of the modern family and the new practices of intimacy we discuss in Chapter 4 that must stretch across time and space. Within this displacement and scattering of emotions the marketing material for the film poses a key concern of late-modernity, '*Are we falling apart?'* This is the central question that Giddens' (1991) understands as the 'ontological insecurity' of late-modernity, Beck (1992) regards as a matter of consequence when living in a 'risk society' and Appadurai (1990) senses to be relevant to the manner in which difference and disjuncture appear as a consequence of globalization. Our analysis further suggests that changing gender and work relations strike at the heart of fears that traditional values and the world we once knew are falling apart.

Falling Down

Since its first screening in 1993, the Hollywood box office hit *Falling Down* was an unqualified success. In *Falling Down* Michael Douglas plays the lead character Bill Foster, known as D-FENS (after his car registration plate), and is cast as an all-American 'average white guy' – but with one exception. Bill Foster is experiencing family break-up and job loss, an identity crisis which transforms him into a misguided and highly destructive vigilante, coded by the FBI as D-FENS. We argue that *Falling Down* is a polysemic text ripe for psychoanalytic interpretation that, read against the grain, can be said to be symptomatic of a perceived global crisis of white masculinity. Indeed the film's title not only captures the social collapse of Douglas's material status as D-FENS, but also reflects the psychological disintegration experienced when a white male subject encounters redundancy, marital break-up and restricted fathering rights to see his daughter. The film takes us on a meandering apocalyptic journey, in which it is reiterated at nearly every turn that D-FENS is only trying to 'go home for my daughter's birthday'. Indeed the split portrayal of this everyday 'Bill'/D-FENS illustrates the schizophrenic relationships masculinity forges with the public and the private, hinting strongly at the psychological trauma that ensues when structural and deep personal changes occur. The perplexed, pained sense of masculine injustice which Douglas has become expert at portraying (think *Basic Instinct* or *Fatal Attraction*) rings out in reverberating fashion when in disbelief he beseeches, 'So I'm the bad guy here?'

Once in charge of national security, through his old day job working at a missile plant, Bill has gone from being a 'good guy', the 'D-FENS', to becoming obsolete in the new post-Cold War relations underscored by perestroika and glasnost. The crisis of masculinity portrayed is also deeply inscribed within a further global racialized crisis of whiteness, vividly apparent when D-FENS picks an uneasy path through the rambling chaos of the racially encoded Los Angeles city. Here he encounters a 'tight-fisted' Korean shopkeeper, a black protestor deemed 'not economically viable' by the banking corporation, the pedantic rule-abiding plastic-smiling staff of a burger bar, dangerous bandana-clad gang members, honest construction workers, an obnoxious neo-Nazi army surplus dealer and a pair of wealthy golfers. The journey traces a path delineated by different territories of race and class that in many ways echo early British Victorian 'slum literature' of metropolitan expeditions which decried the urban interior to be a foreign zone where strange primitives and unruly bodies resided. As the promotional material for the film salaciously advertises, in pseudo-anthropological fashion, the narrative marks 'a tale of urban reality' where 'Terror stalks our streets'.

The multiple inflections of whiteness, blackness and Otherness become the defining contours through and against which the director Joel Schumacher is able to constitute a universal and supposedly identifiable white masculinity through the everyman figure of Douglas's lead. This is achieved, as recent scholars on whiteness indicate, when 'White males, by occupying a more strategic position than white females, have been accorded essentially a label-free existence' (Nakayama and Krizek, 1995:302).

So why does the centrality of white masculinity need to be asserted? According to the American labour historian Roediger (1992), being a worker is not only a signifier of masculinity, but 'its actual usage also suggests a racial identity, an identification of whiteness and work so strong that it need not even be spoken' (p. 19). Unemployment can then be read as more than a loss of class status, entailing a symbolic 'slipping back' into the domestic feminized location of non-worker and the racialized configuration of being 'not-quite-white' on account of a loss of white respectability. Indeed the unemployed are often depicted as dirty, unclean, parasitic and evidently 'beyond the pale'. It is plausible to think that as women's rights, multiculturalism and job insecurity increasingly figure in global economies, Douglas's character becomes the embodiment of a white masculinity under siege.

At the beginning of the film, Bill Foster is dressed in a neatly pressed short-sleeved white shirt, dark tie, briefcase and glasses. He is the embodiment of a fresh-minted American whiteness, a deodorized body that has just stepped out of the air-conditioned office into the searing heat and unruly jungle of the city. It is the racialized and class-fractured metropolis that externally leaves its mark upon him as his spectacles splinter and his clothes become dirty with grime and perspiration, while internally he too is transformed into an urban warrior. The transformation of the civilized body is also a means of communicating inner trauma for, as Bob Connell explains, 'the body remains the screen on which the well-launched dramas of power and anxiety are projected . . . depression and disassociation are also experienced in the flesh' (1987:82). The universalism of white masculinity embodied by Douglas/Foster/D-FENS is illustrated in the strap-line accompanying the film. *Falling Down*, we are told, is 'The adventure of an ordinary man at war with the everyday world'. The central motif is one of white rage where 'ordinary men' are culturally estranged from the confusing, 'everyday world' of late-modernity. Like his car which he leaves behind trapped in the sweltering heat of a road works traffic jam, D-FENS is a stalled vehicle who has been discarded on life's highway.

In the film D-FENS occupies an embattled masculinity that is enduring personal trauma through marital, parental and employment losses that serve to challenge the patriarchal order. This is coupled with the daily injustices we see him confronted with, in what we would contend is a narrative constituted through the 'white eye' of the camera. *Falling Down* has rightly been said to articulate 'a complex and inconsistent politics' (Davies, 1995:146), especially when the perceived 'injustice' entails complex negotiations with feminism (father's rights), multiculturalism (various urban encounters) and what is construed as political correctness (becoming the 'bad guy'). There are moments where the film strays into the territory of 'white backlash' only to be reigned in by a leash of liberalism that, rather emphatically, sees D-FENS murder a homophobic neo-Nazi and make fleeting identifications with individual members of the urban black population. In this way white male middle-class resentment is made justifiable. Writing about the gendered media representations of the ultra-Right, Ware (1992) has commented upon the 'deceptive passivity' of images of white femininity which are also silently marked in the film by the birthday girl and her innocent lone mother. As Ware correctly identifies, such images work precisely because they appear in stark opposition to the masculine imagery of Right-wing thuggery encapsulated in 'the tattooed bodies of the young white males who periodically kick their way into the headlines' (p. 82). According to Ware:

> It is no longer sufficient to argue that all white women are born into a racially divided and patriarchal world that they have not helped to create . . . the voices of black women and women of colour both in the US and UK have long since removed any grounds for shock at the idea that white feminists might not be immune to practicing 'female racism'. (p. 69)

In keeping with the 'deceptive passivity' attributed to white women, Schumacher can deploy the neo-Nazi to encourage us to acknowledge that white masculinities are not always the 'bad guy' (if indeed they ever were), an issue poignantly illustrated when at the end D-FENS allows himself to be killed by the white policeman Prendergast (played by Robert Duval) in order that his daughter can benefit from his life insurance. However, this act of disavowal is a means of absenting white power and privilege. In the end this messianic sacrifice only serves to reinstate the authority of masculinity as white saviour, where the baton of white male power is passed from D-FENS to Prendergast. The final scene accentuates the masculine transition when we discover that the gun the redundant D-FENS carries is actually his daughter's water-pistol, a flaccid phallic imitation of the real firepower embodied by the honest public worker Prendergast.

Moreover, if a crisis of white masculinity is occasionally troubling to patriarchal authority it is magically resolved and recuperated into the hegemonic

order in the film. The centrality of white masculinity is then culturally rein-
stated through Douglas's self-sacrificing familial acts, his slaying of a sexist and
homophobic neo-Nazi (an unpalatable whiteness) and the unabated belief that
D-FENS is nothing more than a downtrodden bespectacled 'ordinary' white
man who, somewhere along the line, lost his way back home. The correla-
tion between whiteness and innocence is possibly given further ammunition
through a subtle linguistic slippage, which is a common trope of psychoanalytic excavations of the subject. Could it be that Bill Foster, the emblem of an
all-American, universal, apple-pie whiteness, is exhibiting a righteous white
anger out of (self) D-FENS? If so, the implication is that white men are the new
victims of late-modernity. To achieve this representation white privilege must
be played down (Foster and Prendergast are everyday 'Joes') and should be
set outside the historical oppression of slavery underscored by the belief that
in America anyone who is hard-working can make it. Prendergast is central
to this narrative accomplishment, the quiet deskbound cop who too is going
through a rather different transition as he is about to retire from the force
having never seen 'real action'. Liken Bill Foster, Pendergrast is undertaking his
own personal 'going home' journey as he is about to retire to meet the demands
of his mentally unstable wife who wishes to move to a quiet resort. Repeatedly
rebuked as a 'desk-jockey', the face-off with D-FENS magically transforms him
from the butt of office jokes to the heroic gallant white knight. This reflexive
reconstitution of white masculinity is made possible when Prendergast is seen
as highly supportive of his female Latino colleague, protective of Bill Foster's
wife and child and absolved from the roughhouse culture of masculine bravado
cultivated by other male LAPD colleagues, who fill his desk with cat litter as a
'humorous' final day send-off. The macho portrait of the LAPD was a particularly sensitive issue at the time in the aftermath of the beating and murder of
the black teenager Rodney King by members of the force in an incident which
sparked the LA riots. Pendergrast recuperates his masculinity by refusing this
highly racialized masculine stereotype and substituting it for another: shooting
D-FENS, standing up to his wife on the telephone, deciding to continue his
career and uttering long-awaited expletives to his boss in full view of the
television cameras heralding his success.

Non-representational modes of enquiry and psychoanalytic inflections offer
alternative ways for considering identity crisis (and reparation) beyond the
strictly discursive realm. They enable us to see how white masculinities are
produced through a complex set of inter-subjective and relational processes. In
exposing the effort required not to be the 'bad guy', such Hollywood productions are informative of white guilt, economic fears of ethnic entrepreneurship
and a deeper postcolonial angst. It is these emotions that enable us to understand social change as a felt process in which social and psychic processes
combine to form what Williams (1973) has eloquently styled, 'structures of
feeling'. Bringing together the internal and external world of individuals, as

we have briefly illustrated through *Falling Down*, may enable a reconsideration of the psycho-dynamic interrelationships between race, class and gender formations. This informs us of the role that affect, emotion and fantasy play in the construction of identity and takes us beyond the more structural processes of material and discursive formations. Through this interplay we may come to see that any notion of a crisis of masculinity must now be contextualized alongside the lived experiences of those this predicament is inflicted upon – women, ethnic minorities and sexual dissidents – whom all too often are seen as the cause rather than the victims of this purported crisis. As Beverley Skeggs (2005:63) recently reflects, 'Class struggle becomes not just about the entitlement to the labour of others but the entitlement to their culture, feelings, affect and dispositions. This is a very intimate form of exploitation'.

The Limits of Crisis

At present the crisis of masculinity framework is currently the dominant paradigm for understanding the actions of young men. But it is not without contradiction. First, there is an important conceptual point. In the previous chapter we drew a careful distinction between the sexed bodies of men and masculinity. Here we suggest that masculinity does not exist as an epistemological 'object' but is a sign that has become endowed with an enormous amount of cultural meaning. However, if masculinity is an empty sign, a social construct with no tangible essence, then how exactly can it be in crisis if it cannot 'be' in the first place? And if it is men's roles that are subject to change in late-modernity why is this interpreted as crisis, when it could equally be read as 'a thoroughly good thing' (MacInnes, 1998:55), a long-awaited challenge to the patriarchal order?

Second, the crisis of masculinity as it is portrayed appears a thoroughly Western calamity as manufacturing jobs become relocated in non-Western and developing areas. This leads us to ask if what we are talking about is really part of a 'white crisis' as India and the tiger economies of Far East Asia outstrip their Western counterparts, most notably with the rise in manufacturing in China and recent predictions that it will become the new economic powerhouse on the world stage. Thus some writers have pointed to the way in which debates surrounding boys' poor educational attainment for example have become emotive and recurrent discourses in Western nation-states including Britain, the US and Australia (Foster *et al.*, 2001), though this crisis does not appear so striking elsewhere. We may also pause to wonder why young men in less developed countries were previously not construed as living crisis-ridden lives prior to recent global labour market changes.

Third, there is a lack of precision regarding when the alleged crisis of masculinity began. As Pearson (1983) has demonstrated, through detailed historical engagement with 'troublesome' youth dating back to before the Industrial Revolution, the crisis surrounding young men's bodies in particular is part of a larger legacy of youth 'moral panics' that have crystallized around the bodies of teenage gang rebels, Hippies, Hell's Angels and Gangsta Rappers in the US; and Punks, Goths, Ravers and Chavs in the post-war British era. An examination of the post-war literature on subculture, delinquency and youth gangs would appear to suggest that young men are perpetually portrayed as 'in crisis': indeed it is practically a feature of the lives of young working-class men. By the same token, if there is a crisis it has yet to fully impinge itself upon the lives of upper- and middle-class boys who in general continue to benefit from the gender and class privileges afforded to them.

Fourth, there is an assumption that a loss of masculine status in the workplace necessarily results in a crisis of masculinity, but this assumption is not always supported by empirical evidence. The young working-class men we spoke with rarely saw themselves as 'failing', 'lost' or crisis-ridden. In other words, there is a cultural dissonance between how young men are portrayed in popular media and various academic accounts, and how they interpret and articulate their own lived experiences. Moreover loss of work does not necessarily equate with the end of masculinity. As Taylor and Jamieson recount in their cultural analysis of young men in Sheffield, the English 'city of steel', unemployment did not result in 'the sudden and total evacuation of men from the symbolic terrain of work, or the loss of work references in the discursive construction of hegemonic forms of masculinity' (1997:166). This perspective is supported in Nayak's (2003c) research on 'Real Geordies', young white men in the former coal-mining areas of north-east England who continued to present an industrial masculinity in increasingly post-industrial times. Moreover, for young men from long-term unemployed backgrounds who enact a 'Chav' or 'Charver' identity the anatomy of labour could still be invoked in activities such as car crime which they described as 'grafting' or street robbery which they discussed in terms of being 'taxed'. For these young men there is no loss in masculinity, rather this identity – as it is culturally imagined – is recuperated and reiterated in other arenas: crime, the street, the body and so forth (Campbell, 1993). This would indicate that if there is anything approaching a crisis in masculinity it is something that few young men have reckoned with. Furthermore any purported crisis cannot be read outside the gendered, Western and class-situated context through which this predicament has been derived.

Conclusion

In this chapter we have considered the ways in which masculinities may be reconfigured in late-modernity. We have explored the economic changes that have had an impact upon young men in the labour market. The chapter explores the parameters of the idea that masculinities are in crisis – a dominant notion that features recurrently across a range of social sites. The discourse of crisis suggests that youthful masculinities are out-of-step with new times, leading to feelings of loss, anger and displacement. Looking at masculinities through a selection of films and popular cultural forms, the chapter explores the notion of masculinities in crisis while also considering the limitations of 'crisis' as a dominant discourse that articulates the feelings and experiences of young men.

4
Gender Relations in Late-Modernity: Young Femininities and the New Girl Order

While a loosely worked consensus of late-modernity views young men through the lens of 'crisis', young women commonly emerge as the ideal neo-liberal subjects for post-industrial times. Young men may be represented as the recently dispossessed, pale shadows haunting a de-industrialized landscape, while young women appear to take centre stage in the reconfiguration of labour patterns, consumption practices and gender roles. It could be argued that late-modernity unshackles women from the patriarchal past. In post-industrial times the 'feminization' of labour holds young women in high esteem as flexible, presentable and capable workers. No longer subservient to the male breadwinner, the new feminine subject is economically independent, liberated from the confines of the domestic sphere and, with the help of new reproductive technologies, can actively realize the possibility of 'having it all' and 'doing it all'. The fuchsia-pink hue of late-modernity can be seen as part of the prevailing zeitgeist, giving young women license to become agentic, assertive and 'out there'. Young women in the contemporary period *appear*; their visibility is part of their unassailable presence in the new girl order.

These representations mark a decisive discursive shift that delineates between how young women were portrayed in the industrial period to how they are regarded in late-modernity. To gain an insight into competing and contrasting representations of gender and youth this chapter engages in a critical dialogue with feminist scholarship and in particular the work of McRobbie. McRobbie is a feminist cultural studies writer whose work has focused on youth culture and in particular the plight of young women over the last 30 years. By entering into a 'critical dialogue' with McRobbie we are able to capture at least some of the shifting contours that come to mark the landscape of young femininities. Here we find that the visibility of girls in the contemporary period exists in marked contrast to accounts of youthful femininities in the 1960s and 1970s. Feminist scholarship of this period was concerned with the marginal and subordinate status of young women. It enquired: do girls have a presence in youth cultures and, if so, why are they largely absent from so many studies (McRobbie and Garber, 1975; Canaan, 1991)? McRobbie and Garber's (1975) consideration of the position of girls in relation to youth cultures in the UK provided a valuable insight into young people's cultural worlds from a gendered perspective:

> Though girls participated in the general rise in the disposable income available to youth in the 1950s, girls' wages were not as high as those of boys. Patterns of spending were also structured in a different direction. Girls' magazines emphasised a particularly feminine mode of consumption and the working class girl, though actively participating in the world of work, remained more focused on home and marriage than her male counterpart. Teddy-boy culture was an escape from the claustrophobia of the family, into the street and the 'caff'. While many girls might adopt an appropriate way of dressing, complementary to the teds, they would be much less likely to spend the same amount of time on the streets. Girls had to be careful not to 'get into trouble' and excessive loitering on street corners might be taken as a sexual invitation to the boys . . . The difficulty in obtaining effective contraception, the few opportunities to spend time unsupervised with members of the opposite sex, the financial dependency of the working-class woman on her husband, meant that a good reputation mattered above anything else. As countless novels of the moment record, neighbourhoods flourished on rumours and gossip and girls who spent too much time on the street were thought to be promiscuous. (McRobbie and Garber, 1975)

McRobbie and Garber draw attention to the ways in which girls have been overlooked or misrepresented in studies of youth subculture. They argue that gender is, like social class, a structural inequality that materially affects the life chances and experiences of individuals. It is from this perspective that they discuss the role of girls in youth subcultural settings. A starting point for McRobbie and Garber is the social space that girls occupy in society generally. They speculate that the relative absence of girls in subcultures may hinge around issues of gender and space, girls being more centrally involved in the 'private' domestic sphere of home and family life rather than the 'public' world of the street where most subcultural activities seem to occur. Looking at girls in youth cultures, therefore, shifts the focus from oppositional forms to a consideration of modes of conformity. There are dangers for girls in hanging around on the streets. Beyond the obvious danger of physical assault, girls' presence on the street could be associated with sexual promiscuity and carried the ensuing risk of a damaged reputation. McRobbie and Garber discuss the significance of mass culture to the lives of young people and particularly the ways in which marketing and consumption are gendered. For girls, new patterns of teenage consumption engaged them in more home-based activities: experimenting in changes of clothes, hairstyles and make-up, often in the confined space of the bedroom. Many studies of the period point to the ways in which young women are frequently defined in terms of their sexuality; their physical attractiveness, sexual availability and reproductive capacities become tropes for the general appraisal of girls as individuals and as a social group (Lees, 1986; Canaan, 1991). McRobbie and Garber conclude that where girls do appear in subcultural writing it is usually as male appendages and that it is important to look at the ways in which young women interact among themselves to form distinctive leisure cultures of their own. Engagements with teenage magazines (discussed in Chapter 7) and participation in 'teenybopper' culture are some of the ways in which young women of the period created and structured their own cultural worlds.

Within Western societies, a wide range of feminist researchers over many decades reminds us of girls' sociability. Studies of girls indicate that they have an immense capacity for affective affiliations manifest in friendships as spending time with each other, talking to each other and supporting one another (Hey, 1997). The other side of female friendship, insightfully documented by Hey (1997), focuses upon intra-gender conflict between girls and the ensuing practices of inclusion and exclusion that mark female friendships. In a study of young women's participation in youth clubs, McRobbie (1978) offered a particular reading of the exclusivity of girls' friendship groups. She suggested that the working-class girls who attended the youth club formed a clique that was zealously guarded and difficult to access. McRobbie described them as huddled together in the margins of the youth club, talking, smoking and reading magazines, while boys played table-top games in the central space. McRobbie's analysis of emergent femininity in this setting points to the importance of the female friendship group as a site of support and solidarity in young women's lives, acting as a buffer-zone in the face of the demands placed upon them by a sexist and patriarchal culture. McRobbie argues that through a shared enjoyment of popular culture and the practice of female friendship, young women prepare for their future roles in the domestic sphere as wives and mothers. From this perspective, young women's friendship networks perform an important preparatory function in enabling working-class girls to cope with the exigencies of patriarchal power and subordination.

Bedroom Cultures

Alongside female friendships, feminist scholars have paid attention to the bedroom as a space within the household that can be personalized. The concept of 'bedroom culture' was developed by McRobbie (1978) as a way of addressing the gendering of space and the attending divisions that existed between what was seen as the public and private. The cultural experiences of young women and their location within the home rather than the street, a space where young men congregated and had fun, epitomized women's marginalization. For McRobbie, young women were more likely to get together in each other's bedrooms where they could enjoy a range of self-consciously girly activities such as experimenting with clothes, hair and make-up, talking about boys, playing popular music. Indeed the image of a teenage girl standing in front of the bedroom mirror singing along to a contemporary hit while using a hair-brush as a microphone is one which has been much parodied in adverts and comedy routines. Lincoln's (2001) ethnographic study of teenage girls in the UK illustrates the many points of continuity for young women today:

> For teenage girls in the late 90s, the bedroom is often the only space within the home that is personal, personalised and intimate. It is a space over which teenagers are able to be private from parents and siblings alike, often displayed on the bedroom door with signs such as 'knock before entering!' It is a room in which unmediated activities such as sleeping, reading books and magazines, daydreaming and 'chilling out' take place. The bedroom also exists as one of the central 'meeting' places in a teenage girl's social life world. It is the space into which friends are invited to listen to music, chat (either to each other or on the mobile phone), smoke, drink alcohol, experiment with hair, clothes and get ready for a night out. The bedroom is a biographical space. The posters, flyers, photographs, framed pictures, books, magazines, CDs and so on catalogue a teenage girl's youth cultural interests, bringing together past and present experiences . . . .
>
> Eve, a research participant indicated in one interview the amount of time she spends in her bedroom when she said, 'I just go downstairs for food'. (Lincoln, 2001:7–8)

The use of the mobile phone and CD player is an obvious point of difference with young women of the 1970s. Lincoln further indicates that the use of music is important to the girls in her study. She suggests that in addition to the posters of pop stars and the mixture of fantasy and chat that surrounds listening to pop music, girls may use music to say something about their feelings and their identities. Different styles of music could be used to set the tone for a night in or a night out and could be seen as a 'constant mediator of the "emotional tone" of bedroom culture' (Lincoln, 2001:12). Bloustein (1998) points to further links between the bedroom space, music and moments of self-expression in her Australian study of the everyday experiences of 10 teenage girls. Her study suggests that girls are connected to a global circuit of youth culture in which the bedroom cannot be seen as a 'private' space, uncontaminated by global merchandizing. Adopting an innovative approach to ethnographic research, Bloustein asked the girls in her study to use video cameras to document their daily lives:

It seemed to me, as I looked at the girls' footage, that music continually served as a cultural thread and an effective link, moving between the worlds that we would popularly designate as private and public. Although the participants sometimes videoed their [bed]rooms without verbal commentary, music was frequently played in the background to provide a particular ambience. In cases where it became a vitally significant component of the mise-en-scene, the music was chosen quite deliberately to match a particular mood or to tie in with a specific poster of a pop or rock star. ((Bloustein, 1998:127–128))

In this example the personalized space of the bedroom and the use of music are used by young women to express a range of feminine identities. For young women in the contemporary period the bedroom remains a personalized space that, with access to multimedia, also serves as a global and techno-cultural space. In keeping with Blackman (1995), Bloustein and Lincoln suggest that the bedroom becomes a site of gender production and represents an attempt to create privacy and exclusivity within the family.

Rave Cultures

In her later work, McRobbie (1994) suggests that the relationship between gender practices and social structures have undergone dramatic change since the 1970s. In keeping with other feminist scholars, McRobbie indicates that 'there is now a greater degree of fluidity about what femininity means and how exactly it is anchored in social reality' (1994:157). McRobbie uses the example of rave culture to illustrate some of the differences in what she terms 'changing modes of femininity'. Here McRobbie focuses upon the presence of girls in the rave scene that flourished in the UK and mainland Europe in the late-1980s and early 1990s. As a point of contrast to the economic boom of this period and the corporate boast of Thatcherism, rave, in its initial stages, eschewed commercial culture and capitalist ethics in ways that Willis (1990) would term 'symbolic creativity'. Rave parties were organized by young people themselves and commonly held in disused buildings in out-of-town locations. New technology was used to inform ravers of the 'secret' location and also as a strategy for deflecting police involvement and dispersal.

Rave dance legitimates pure physical abandon in the company of others without requiring the narrative of sex or romance . . . Dancing provides the rationale for rave . . . in rave everything happens within the space of the party . . . .

What kind of image of femininity, for example, is being pursued as female ravers strip down and sweat out? Dance is where girls were always found in subcultures. It was their only entitlement. Now in rave it becomes the motivating force for the entire subculture. This gives girls a new found confidence and a prominence. Bra tops, leggings and trainers provide a basic (aerobic) wardrobe. In rave (and in the club culture with which it often overlaps) girls are highly sexual in their dress and appearance... [T]he tension in rave for girls comes, it seems, from remaining in control, and at the same time losing themselves in dance and music. Abandon in dance must now, post-AIDS, be balanced by caution and exercise of control in sex. One solution might lie in cultivating a hypersexual appearance which is, however, symbolically sealed or 'closed off' through the dummy, the whistle, or the ice lolly. (McRobbie, 1994:168–169)

There are striking differences between girls' participation in rave culture and McRobbie's description of young women in the Birmingham youth club of the 1970s. The girls in the earlier study existed on the fringes of male-dominated space and did not attempt to play a part in the activities on offer at the youth club. They did their own thing on the margins. By contrast, girls at raves have moved from the margins to the centre. Their participation in the party is that of a full-on reveller, like their male counterparts. There is not a separate role designated to boys or girls, rather there appears to be a common entitlement to the pursuit of pleasure and excitement. McRobbie suggests that this gives young women status and an increased sense of confidence. Within the context of the rave, young women can engage in free and uninhibited expressions of pleasure. McRobbie suggests that the point of tension for girls exists around sexuality. In the era of HIV/AIDS young women may dress in sexually provocative ways, while simultaneously regulating their sexual behaviour. McRobbie's analysis speculates that young women may be symbolically sealing themselves off from sexual activity with the self-conscious adornment of childhood effects acting as a protective membrane around the body. Interestingly the sealed-off femininities McRobbie depicts could link in with the themes of individualization discussed previously as they come to co-exist alongside mass collective participation of the rave scene. For such paradoxical reasons Miles (2000:101) suggests that 'Rave is potentially subversive, but can ultimately only be subversive in a submissive form'. For cultural criminologists such as Redhead (1995; 1997) this potential threat is best symbolized through the governmental response of the 1994 Criminal Justice and Public Order Bill forbidding the assemblage of large gatherings in public spaces where musical sound-systems playing repetitive syncopated beats were present.

What McRobbie's portrait evinces is the unconditional acceptance of girls on the rave scene. Even so, we would subject her account to further analytic scrutiny. As musicologists have shown cultures such as rave are not bounded or homogenous but are infinitely nuanced and diverse, coming to include a spectrum of sub-genres such as techno, trance, ambient house or happy house for example. As Thornton (1995) demonstrates young people are adept experts, distinguishing between these different scenes and developing their own hierarchies of taste within club cultures themselves. This suggests that any readings of rave culture need to be placed within the specificity of particular musical scenes and genres. Young people's voices are notably absent in much of McRobbie's prose. While semiotics remains an important youth cultural studies method (Hebdige, 1979) McRobbie displays a tendency to 'read off' gender signs from the bodies of young people without ever situating these interpretations in the lived contexts in which they appear. As Saldanha (2007) has shown in an ethnographic account of Goan Trance music in coastal India, spatial and temporal dimensions are pivotal to understanding how gender and ethnicity play out, relations that alter across time and place even during a single dance event. We would further suggest that many of the accoutrements McRobbie associates with rave not only reflect a semiotics of gender and childhood, but are *material objects* that may have a particular 'use-value' with regard to youthful pleasure, dance and drugs. For example the plastic surgical mouth masks so popular in early 1990s raves can certainly be interpreted as an embodied act of closing-off identities and presenting a faceless anonymity, but it was also a means to heighten the effects of mescaline through the use of vapour rubs. The tactile effects stimulated by the drug ecstasy also mean that pacifiers, ice-lollies and other paraphernalia are not just ephemeral signs but can have a material place as sensual objects on the scene. Thus Jackson (2000) has argued for the need to 'avoid reducing material objects to social relations' (p. 12), when 'our emphasis should be on when and where the materiality of material culture makes a difference rather than assuming its importance in an *a priori* manner' (p. 13).

Rave – in its diverse and hybrid forms – continues as part of a global scene alongside a resurgence of interest in 'going out' in the traditional sense of a night-on-the-town. Town and city centres across the UK have spawned a range of club-style venues – theme bars, pubs, late-night drinking venues and clubs aimed at young people. For Chatterton and Hollands (2002) this forms part of a new night-time economy constructed by corporate capital that ultimately leads to a highly regulated and increasingly similar set of going-out experiences. In previous work on the night-time economy Hollands (1995) identifies a shift from *production* to *consumption* where young people's identities were once formed primarily in relation to the labour market, but in the present era the emphasis is upon new patterns of consumption and identity formations through the market. 'Binge-drinking' and the ensuing social problems associated with excess alcohol consumption has become a feature of night-life in these locations leading to commentaries positioning young women as 'ladettes', whose drinking patterns and behaviour emulates 'irresponsible' young men. Widespread public criticism has censored pubs and clubs for promotional offers encouraging young people to drink cocktails and spirits in greater volumes. Alcohol manufacturers have also been accused of targeting the young with 'alco-pops' – sweet tasting drinks in bright colours, laced with vodka or other spirits and also heavily advertised. There is concern among health professionals that young people are drinking heavily, while police and local authorities express concern about rising levels of violence and public order offences. We return to the practice of clubbing when we consider music, dance and cosmopolitanism in Chapter 7.

Post-feminism and Active Girlhood

How do girls feature in the changing landscape of late-modernity? How has the experience of being a girl changed since the 1960s and 1970s? Contemporary research on girlhood indicates that there are different ways of being a girl and that femininity is no longer so rigidly defined or hinged to the domestic. The embracing of pleasure by young women in the 1990s through rave/club culture, television, magazine readership and fashion and beauty has been observed by feminist scholars as the emergence of new forms of femininity marked by moments of celebration, freedom and fun (Hermes, 1995; McRobbie, 1996; Brunsdon, 1997). Terms such as 'post-feminism', 'third wave feminism' and 'new femininities' have been deployed to characterize the changes in young women's experiences and their engagement with the social world. The terms themselves are open to contestation in different contexts, signalling both an anti-feminist backlash and new ways of understanding feminism in contemporary times (Hollows and Moseley, 2006).

At its most simplistic, the 'post' of post-feminism signifies a way of thinking and acting beyond the rubric of feminism and may imply some critique of former orthodoxies. However, as with other terms such as postcolonialism or postmodernism the new moment cannot fully escape the shadow of the past, but grows out of it. As Sonnet (1999:170) declares, 'The current post-feminist "return" to feminine pleasures (to dress, cosmetics, visual display, to Wonderbra "sexiness") is "different" because, it is suggested, it takes place within a social context fundamentally altered by the achievement of feminist goals'. In this respect gender in late-modernity is characterized by a blurring of boundaries between the feminine and feminist. Young women's presence in the night-time economy is equally as visible as young men's as the girls' night out, birthday celebrations and hen parties become a high profile feature of the city centre pub and club scene. The contemporary moment appears to further enhance the emergence of new femininities in its appeal to subjects as agentic controllers of their own destiny (Beck, 1992). This poses complex issues for sexual politics when girls and young women come to regard a right to pole-dance, sport playboy bunny logos or have drunken one-night stands as an expression of autonomous girlhood. Like feminist subjectivities, this 'active girlhood' places an emphasis on the rights of the individual to be an active sexual subject without recourse to moral judgement from patriarchal or feminist discourse.

Active girlhood extends beyond the sphere of leisure, sex and sociability. The processes of globalization have increasingly relied upon the flexible labour of young women. Shaped by the contours of a girls-own success story in the educational sphere, young women appear as well-groomed, well-governed subjects at the heart of neo-liberal reform. The education of girls and their increased visibility in the social domain coincides with the decline of radical sexual politics in the West and particularly young women's rejection of feminism as a political project. There are of course many ways of reading these changes. A well-rehearsed view, sometimes posited by young women them-selves, suggests that feminism has 'eaten itself'. Young women have new-found freedoms as the inheritors of a feminist movement that has successfully made itself redundant. While not necessarily acknowledging the impact of second wave feminism, young women report feeling estranged from publicly available versions of feminist politics; the anti-male sentiment, the language of oppres-sion and feelings of anger, marginality and missed opportunity rarely resonate with their lives or experiences. The legacy of feminism for many young women exists in the mythic and less than glamorous figure of the 'angry feminist' whose militancy is to be both feared and reviled (McRobbie, 2004). An alternative way of reading the individualism of contemporary femininity is to place it within the context of an intergenerational dialogue that young women may be having with their mothers and grandmothers. Bjerrum Nielsen and Rudberg's (1994) study of intergenerational chains of women in Norway suggests that the indi-vidualism of young women in the present period can be seen as both a response to and a conversation with the 'battle of the sexes' style feminism of their mother's generation. Viewed in intergenerational terms, young women may be exploring points of continuity with previous generations in ways that creat-ively rework feminism rather than reject it. Later in the chapter we discuss the possibility that feminist writers on the new girl order may also be working with intergenerational narratives in their responses to the demise of feminism and the proliferation of new femininities in a section entitled 'Back to the future?' where we consider the preponderance of post-feminist makeover programmes.

Walkerdine *et al.* (2001) take a different approach to the contemporary construction of new femininities. They offer a perspective on new feminin-ities premised upon the salience of social class. Providing a counter narrative to the self-invention of late-modernity, they argue that the remaking of girls and women as modern neo-liberal subjects needs to acknowledge the ways in which social class shapes young women's experiences of education, academic attainment and their subsequent life trajectories. Class is commonly viewed as a feature of modernity associated with fixed employment, stable regional identities and meritocratic forms of social mobility based upon educational and economic success. Walkerdine *et al.*'s study of young women in the UK is a salutary reminder of the centrality of class in young women's lives. Their analysis points to the ways in which the regulation of femininity is related to sexuality and crucially works differently upon the bodies of working-class and middle-class girls. For middle-class girls the emphasis is upon educational success and a professional career in which the possibility of early pregnancy is not allowed. By contrast, academic success for working-class girls involves identity rupture, the transformation of self and a move away from family and community. Working-class girls bear the emotional cost of becoming bourgeois subjects in forms of pain, loss and fragmentation. From the perspective of working-class young women, early pregnancy may be an attempt to resolve some of the contradictions involved in the transition to adult womanhood. Becoming a mother disrupts the educational process while affording young women a particular role and status in the local community. Walkerdine *et al.* suggest that working-class and middle-class girls become 'each other's Other' (2001:209) existing as cautionary examples of what you could become by transgressing the regulatory framework.

For middle-class girls, working-class fecundity is represented as 'pramface', conjuring up the stereotypical image of a working-class young mother on a housing estate, while middle-class girls remain excluded from girls' friendship groups as 'snobs' and 'weirdos'. Two further studies generatively explore some of the themes developed by Walkerdine *et al.* Elsewhere Aapola *et al.* (2005) and Harris (2004) suggest that the lives and experiences of young women in the contemporary period can be understood in relation to two competing discourses – 'girlpower' and 'girls at risk'. Girlpower – the active girlhood we discussed above – suggests to young women that they can get what they want and do what they want. In this respect girlpower exists as a seemingly new version of femininity for new times that can be seen in a range of assertive and individualized expressions of power, characterized by third wave feminism (see Chapter 7 for a further discussion of girlpower and new femininities). Girls at risk, on the other hand, articulate a set of moral and social concerns in relation to young women such as: teenage pregnancy and sexually transmitted disease; drug taking; involvement in crime and particularly young women's participation in gangs and violent crime. This is active girlhood becoming too active. As we can see, the notion of 'risk' when applied to youth extends and elaborates the insights generated by the sociologists of risk discussed in Chapter 2. What are apparent in these representations are class-specific productions of femininity, which are each tropes of excess.

Given the life experiences, trajectories and resources available to working- and middle-class girls, this is of course not a relationship of equivalence. Nevertheless some concerns about middle-class young women are evident in the plight and representations of those that delay childbirth, attempt to clamber up the career ladder and feel justified in tasting the fruits of a Chardonnay lifestyle associated with 'ladettes' and Bridget Jones thirty-somethings. Although Delamont is correct to point to durable continuities within new generations by asserting that most people still 'marry, most are close to their families, most work for most of their lives and so on' (2001:111), a closer look at the statistics also reveals some subtle but noticeable changes. The Office of National Statistics indicates that in 2004 the UK fertility rate of 1.77 children per woman is considerably lower than the 1960s peak of 2.95. In Britain 49 per cent of children are now born to mothers over the age of 30 years and it is apparent that new fertility technologies are now playing a greater part in modern life parenthood. Furthermore a recent ICM poll which interviewed a random sample of 1006 adults in April 2006 (www.icmresearch.co.uk) revealed at least some changing attitudes among men and women in relation to childbirth. The careers of (bourgeois) women are now much more highly prised than in previous generations, with only around a third of men (32 per cent) believing that women should put children before career. However, while feminism may be altering traditional patriarchal constructions of motherhood nearly two-thirds (63 per cent) of all respondents felt career pressures are making it harder to have children, thus reflecting the new challenges facing gender relations in dual income households. In the field of education and employment it is also evident that both sexes may now come to value the prospect of a future career. With the decline of manufacturing trades and their accompanying apprenticeship schemes another noticeable change is a growth in the numbers of young people entering full-time Further and Higher Education, a trend which appears set to continue at least in the near future.

New Practices of Intimacy

Sociologists such as Beck, Giddens and Bauman suggest that late-modernity is marked by the emergence of a new relationship between the individual and the social. As the traditions of the industrial order diminish in significance, Giddens argues that self-identity becomes a reflexive project. The onus is upon individuals to take responsibility for producing and maintaining their own biography, 'What to do? How to act? Who to be? These are focal questions for everyone living in circumstances of late modernity – and ones which, at some level or another, all of us answer, either discursively or through day-to-day social behaviour' (Giddens, 1991:70). Through the creation of a set of biographical narratives, individuals tell a story, to themselves and others, of who they are and who they want to be. For Giddens, the reflexive project of self is linked to the sphere of intimacy, 'Romantic love introduced the idea of narrative into an individual's life' (Giddens, 1992). Moreover intimacy has been transformed in late-modern times from a set of social obligations and regulations to a new form of democracy between couples. Giddens suggests that intimate relationships are increasingly based upon personal understandings between two people generated by a bond of trust and emotional communication rather than external norms and values. The changes in intimate relations identified by

Giddens can be viewed as a new and highly personalized form of democracy based upon emotions.

Further commentary on the condition of late-modernity is provided by Bauman:

> Everyone has to ask for himself the question 'who am I', 'how should I live', 'who do I want to become' – and at the end of the day, be prepared to accept responsibility for the answer. In this sense, freedom is for the modern individual the fate he cannot escape, except by retreating into a fantasy world or through mental disorders. Freedom is therefore a mixed blessing. One needs it to be oneself; yet being oneself solely on the strength of one's free choice means a life full of doubts and fears of error . . . Self construction of the self is, so to speak, a necessity. Self confirmation of the self is an impossibility. (Bauman, 1988:62)

Bauman's contribution to the individualization thesis appears pessimistic in its emphasis on the limitations and inherent uncertainties of individual freedom. The charge of pessimism is further fuelled by Bauman's analysis of consumerism as a form of control that seduces individuals with offers of a 'fantasy community' of freedom and security.

Beck (1992) occupies some of the terrain covered by Giddens in his concern to characterize the late-modern period and articulate the relationship between individuals and society in contexts that have been changed and reshaped by the processes of globalization and new technologies. Beck suggests that Western societies have been reshaped by a process of individualization marked by three distinctive features: dis-embedding; loss of traditional security; and re-embedding. Dis-embedding refers to the individual's break with traditional ties of family and locality, while loss of security points to a pervasive 'disenchantment', produced by the demise of traditional values associated with the past. Re-embedding, by contrast, indicates the emergence of a new mood found in the creation of re-imagined forms of social commitment. For Beck, this is a paradox of the late-modern condition:

> On the one hand, men and women are *released* from traditional forms and ascribed roles in a search for a 'life of their own'. On the other hand, in the prevailing diluted social relationships, people are *driven into* bonding in the search for happiness in a partnership. The need for a shared inner life, as expressed in the ideal of marriage and bonding is not a primeval need. It *grows* with the losses that individualization brings as the obverse of its opportunities. (1992:105 emphasis in original)

Beck and Giddens' working of the individualization thesis has been open to critique, particularly in relation to matters of social class and gender. Skeggs (2004) points out that individualization and the demise of class as articulated

by Beck and Giddens can be understood as a reflection of their social position as occupants of a middle-class habitus and members of a professional
intelligentsia. Adkins (2002) focuses upon the gendered inequalities that may
be reconfigured in late-modernity. Adkins suggests that there has been a re-
traditionalization of gender relations in the late-modern period as men take up
positions as individuals while women are positioned as members of a social
group. We would further suggest that while the writings of Bauman, Beck
and Giddens provide much food for thought, these theories of (post)modern
subjects can appear theoretically abstract and cut-off from everyday lives in
real contexts.

Even so, young people's place in the family has changed with the modern
nuclear unit superseding the large extended families of previous generations.
And while the nuclear family may still exist as the ideal version of familial
relations in the West in essence, it is giving way to what we might call
'new practices of intimacy'. The break-up of the traditional family unit or
rather its reconfiguration is seen in an increase in single-headed households,
same-sex couples, unmarried co-habiting parents and post-divorce couples
who may each bring their offspring into new relationships. For example, while
the symbols, ritual and ceremony of marriage remain popular amongst new
generations, in Britain two-thirds of marriages end in divorce. This suggests
that the move towards 'pure relationships' in which new generations relinquish state practices and develop individualized choice biographies based on
their sole commitment to one another is still not fully accomplished. The
practice of in vitro-fertilization (IVF) by which infertile couples, single women,
lesbian couples and mature women can have children is itself a reproductive
technology that is extending the project of self, individualization and choice in
late-modernity.

Rather than eradicating the stalwart nucleus of the family it could be said
that this new molecular structure is actually serving to rework what is meant
and understood by the term 'family'. Modern work relations that today include
footloose industries, branch plant economies, subcontracting practices and the
expectation of mobility are encouraging a more dispersed set of employment
patterns. Many white-collar workers, professionals, business people and those
working in information technology often have to leave their hometowns in
order to find work and achieve successful careers. This mobility, as described in
the Introduction, has been said to lead to more porous, fluid societies that may
include more spatially 'remote' relations with parents, grandparents and other
kith and kin. The fragmented nature of work relations may also involve couples
living apart where telecommunications, e-mail and other 'space-shrinking' technologies are used to facilitate communication and maintain bonds of intimacy.
As the modern family is restructured in late-modernity affective work relations
and friendship circles can themselves perform as a new practice of intimacy
that, if enduring, may act as a surrogate family as best exemplified by the US

comedy series *Friends* or shows such as *Sex in the City*. As one popular cliché recalls, 'friends are the family we choose'. Although new practices of intimacy may be occurring as a consequence of new work and living arrangements, we suggest that it is premature to speak of the demise of 'blood relations'.

Practices of intimacy vary across cultures and it is evident that global cultures may enable hitherto hidden identities to come to the fore. In Islamic countries, which are often considered to be highly conservative in their attitudes to gender and sexuality, a more complex mosaic can be discovered. North African countries such as Morocco have historically been resorts for Western and non-Western men to engage in homosexuality as sexuality permeates the colonial contact zone. Declan Walsh, an international correspondent in Pakistan, recently paints a colourful portrait of the 'hot boyz' of Lahore:

> 'Under a starry sky filled with fireworks, about 150 gay men clambered to the roof of an apartment building for an exuberant party. Bollywood music spilled into the streets as dress-wearing men twisted and whirled flamboyantly'. (*The Guardian*, March 14, 2006, p. 22)

However, permissive sexual practices are not always routed through Western global 'flows'. In India sari-wearing transvestites with painted faces and nails are culturally permissible as they occupy a sacred, if aberrant, space in religious rites and traditions.

This parallels the acceptance of illicit sexual practices during Brazilian carnival where everyday taboos are transformed in acts of ritual. These small, but increasingly visible changes are revealing of the ways in which gender and sexual subversion may be enhanced through an increased global awareness of an interconnected world. The thriving sex tourism embedded in areas of Thailand and parts of Far East Asia or the way in which particular countries such as the Philippines are becoming renowned for mail order brides are testimony to changing gender relations and the development of a global sex economy. The way in which contemporary life intersects with the global sex economy is evident in British comedy shows such as *Teachers* and *Little Britain* where Thai brides feature as exotic appendages to the otherwise bland lifestyles of white middle-aged men. Inevitably it is in the virtual world of cyberspace that global sex fantasies most densely proliferate in a seemingly endless circuit of cultural production and high-technology sexual performance.

The intensity of modern work and the speed-up of individual lives are also impacting upon established cultures and ways of life. A familiar cultural theme in Japanese theatre centres upon the trauma faced when young women fall in love with one man but must marry another. Where young women had previously been assigned marriage partners by way of familial networks the new economy is reshaping intimacies. Recent changes have enabled women to be more independent and shape their sexual futures more directly. However,

Japan now has one of the lowest birth-rates and to counteract this, the government has actively supported heterosexuality, procreation and the family, for example through state sponsorship of heterosexual 'speed-dating' between single business men and unattached young women. These new transformations may appear quite different to the older, closeted ways by which intimacy was expected to transpire and reflect changes in late-modern ideas of romance, gender, sex and the family.

At least some forms of gender rearrangement are also in occurrence in developing countries where economic and cultural globalization impacts. In India marital break-ups are for the first time becoming known with more couples living beyond the network of the extended family. The rise in a segment of urban middle-class working women with the means to become financially independent and provide for any offspring they may have is also resituating patriarchal power and giving rise to some new gender relations in the post-colonial workplace, as discussed in the following chapter. Already working outside of the home, a growing number of women are no longer willing to carry the sole responsibility for the heavy domestic chores that had once been expected of previous female generations. Although divorce rates in India are still barely comparable with those in the West, standing at around 1.5 per cent, this figure is double what it was a decade ago. While divorce still remains a taboo topic in most Indian households the globalization of the media, the spread of music cultures and in particular the production of Asian soap opera have provided new spaces in which these issues are being wrestled with. For liberals global media enables individuals to have a greater sense of independent agency outside of the nation-state, though for conservatives these new cultural representations are said to only serve to encourage divorce, extra-marital affairs and homosexuality through the uprooting of older family values. Our concern is not with placing heavy emphasis on either of these perspectives, but to recognize the tensions, contradictions and spaces of 'betweenness' that appear in late-modern transitions and the consequences these bear for youth and gender relations.

The uneasy relationship between Western capitalism and consumption in developing countries can be seen in the city of Tehran in Iran. A lack of knowledge on sexual health and perceptions that Iran's strict sexual codes are loosening among its predominantly younger population is said to be giving rise to an increase in HIV/AIDS. It is estimated that around 300,000 Iranian women work as prostitutes and some of these target boutique clothes shops where designer-wear, mini-skirts and skimpy tops are sold. By targeting male shopkeepers the women hope to gain a discount, as reported by Robert Tait:

> Ahmed Reza, 23, admitted having accepted such offers. 'I was sitting outside the shop when two women came and said they wanted to try various manteaus [overcoats]', he said. 'They asked for a bargain and I offered them the standard discount. But

they said, "We cannot pay that – if you give us a good discount and your mobile number, we will serve you". So I gave them more discount and got their numbers.' (*The Guardian*, January 3, 2007)

This article, entitled 'Sex and shopping bring HIV crisis', shows how economies, gender practices and sexual cultures are brought to bear in the act of consuming goods. Although Islamic countries are often depicted as existing outside modernity, this more likely reflects the imaginative geographies of Western 'othering' (Said, 1995[1978]). It is worth noting that in places like Iran mobile communications are powerfully reconstituting sexual relations as seen above. A popular activity amongst young couples, who are expected to abstain from sex until marriage, is the use of 'phone sex' as a new practice of intimacy to traverse distance and the bed-hopping hazard of getting found out. The interface between new technologies and gender is further discussed in Chapter 7 in our account of 'virtual youth' and electronic media. The growth of Internet dating in many countries as a response to the atomized societies and time-constrained lifestyles of modernity suggest new ways of forging social and sexual relations. The virtual worlds of the Internet and mobile communications indicate remote relations and 'plastic sex' to be a feature of the new practices of intimacy and non-intimacy. The way in which new generations are creating new sexual practices is evident in Shahidian's (1999) research on immigrant Iranians in Canada. With eye-opening astonishment, a 65-year-old Iranian woman recalls how Western media led to a new sexual awakening:

All my life I lay underneath and my husband was on top. A while ago, I was visiting some relatives and accidentally watched a video which showed a couple making love. She was on top and he was lying under her. So it *is* possible to do it another way. (p. 204)

In Chapter 7 we discuss the relationship between global media, youth and gender relations. What our examples from Europe, South East Asia and the Middle East demonstrate here is that gender cannot be set apart from the economy but is thoroughly embedded within and spoken through forces of production.

Back to the Future? Contemporary Representations of New Femininities, Women and Girls

McRobbie (2004) suggests that young women are newly positioned in contemporary culture as subjects of consumption, a status congruent with the agentic individualism of new times. Fluid and ever-inventive market practices incorporate feminist and feminine themes into consumer culture while aggressively seeking out girls as consumers. A feature of consumer culture is the increased hyper-sexualization of girls; soft porn images, playboy logos and lewd slogans exist alongside 'girlpower' messages and feminist themes. McRobbie (2004) argues that the neo-liberal shaping of female subjectivities based upon the pursuit of pleasure, hedonism and sexual freedom marks a re-segregation of gendered worlds in which young women are managed and regulated by regimes of consumption. The 'I'm a princess' spending power of girls energetically embraces desires for self-improvement, pampering and indulgence in ways that reinscribe young women within the disciplinary power of gender subordination.

In a cautionary discussion of feminist scholarship and cultural forms, McRobbie (2004) suggests that feminists may have over-celebrated the pleasures of consumption and underestimated the market's appetite for innovation. In an attempt to celebrate young women's engagement with consumer culture as agentic and pleasure-seeking, feminist scholars may have overlooked the tensions and pain of 'doing' girl. Furthermore McRobbie asserts that the emergent codes of sexual freedom and hedonism associated with new femininities should be understood as new technologies of the self rather than celebratory expressions of changing female subjectivity. The renewed emphasis upon the regulatory world of femininity and gendered forms of oppression conjures up, once again, the image of young women in that Birmingham youth club in the mid-1970s. Sitting on the margins while young men occupy the main space, these young women passively awaited their place in the patriarchal order, the oppressive demands of their over-determined futures mitigated only by the solace and support found in female friendships. More recently McRobbie (2006) suggests that the fashion and beauty industry, in particular, punish young women through a self-imposed drive for complete perfection. While the new social contract of late-modernity offers young women political subjectivity in exchange for the evolving capacity to work, consume and be sexually independent, McRobbie indicates that there is a 'new sexual contract' taking shape in which women conform to the regulatory powers of the fashion and beauty industry while simultaneously renouncing any critique of patriarchy. Has the experience of being a girl seemingly changed while the regulation of femininity takes on newly pernicious guises or has feminist scholarship come full circle? The conceptualization of young women as neo-liberal subjects caught in the double-bind of consumer culture and late-modern governmentality may bespeak some of the investments feminist researchers make in girls' subordinate status while articulating some key features of the new girl order.

In an elaboration of her analysis of new femininities, McRobbie (2002; 2004) turns to popular culture and particularly to representations of femininity in television programmes such as *Sex and the City*, *Ally McBeal* and *What Not to Wear*. Feminist scholarship has long been concerned with matters of representation as both a reflection of the social world and a constitutive feature of it.

Feminine identities can be mediated and negotiated through popular culture in circuits of cultural production (Hall, 1997) that promote dialogue between media texts and audience. In broader terms, cultural struggles over the multiple significations of femininity can be seen as expressions seeking recognition or endorsement through social change. As a post-feminist text, *Sex and the City* explores the many-faceted relationship between female sexuality and consumer culture. Zeigler's (2004) reading of *Sex and the City* suggests that the programme constructs the feminine citizen as the 'shopping citizen', thus amplifying the commodification of feminism as a white, middle-class affair. The irony and ambivalence of contemporary femininities is documented across several series that have been likened to a televisual version of glossy women's magazines (Arthurs, 2004; McRobbie, 2004). Arthurs (2004) claims that the popular appeal of *Sex and the City* lies in the successful take up of a woman-centred and sexually explicit discourse in television drama format, a more muted version of which exists in *Desperate Housewives*. Hermes (2006) suggests that the success of *Sex and the City* can be read as indicative of feminist concerns having resonance with a wider audience. Hermes poses the possibility of a new status quo that allows for a new type of woman to be profiled. Central to the show is a countercultural brand of female humour frequently invoked by Carrie and her friends that 'offer glimpses of another sexual economy' (Hermes, 2006:80).

Reflecting upon the sexuality displayed in the show, Skeggs (2004) suggests that *Sex and the City* can be seen as an example of the excessive sexuality usually associated with white working-class women being reworked in a middle-class domain. Hermes (2006) concurs with this point in her analysis of *Sex and the City*, concluding that 'talking dirty' may be the only transgressive feature of the programme and that, in turn, is open to patriarchal recuperation in the unfolding of each series. From this perspective *Sex and the City* represents a re-valuation and re-coding of the relationship between morality and the feminine. However, this new and seemingly liberating configuration cannot be seen entirely in positive terms, as Skeggs, echoing Zeigler (2004), points out that it is middle-class women such as Carrie Bradshaw and her friends who retain the ability to appropriate and transform working-class style at the expense of working-class women who remain fixed by their class position and the negative associations of earlier meanings. Commenting upon the critical attention the programme has received from feminist scholars, McRobbie (2004) is disapproving of feminists who position themselves as fans and indulge in the glossy contours of the programme at the expense of critical engagement with the broader political and economic context from which it has been derived. Sarah Jessica Parker in her role as the central character, Carrie Bradshaw, is generally celebrated as the exemplary post-feminist and style icon, successfully merging the feminine and the feminist in moments of humour and pathos. Independent and needy, fluffy and serious, consistent and contradictory, Carrie epitomizes the slim and successful girl who 'has it all' – a dream job, great mates, enviable New York lifestyle. Carrie is the consummate consumer; she has a wardrobe to die for, shops 'til her nose bleeds while having endless fun. The only aspect of her life that isn't as perfect as a pair of Manola Blahnik shoes (Carrie's much adored signature accessory) is her personal relationships – a recurrent theme in representations of contemporary femininity, played out ad nauseum by characters such as Ally McBeal and Bridget Jones.

McRobbie (2004) points to the largely unexamined ways in which normative femininity is inscribed in the *Sex and the City* text. Her harshest words, however, are reserved for the character of Carrie, especially her 'cloying girlie infantilism'. There is, she asserts, little focus upon Carrie's negative qualities:

> her desperation to win male approval, her self important but painfully talent-free and quite banal writings and voice-overs . . . her wooden self consciousness and tedious narcissism as she skips down the street wearing an ill-chosen hat and stupendously expensive shoes not made for walking. (McRobbie, 2004)

McRobbie suggests that what Carrie Bradshaw and Ally McBeal really fear is 'womanhood, adulthood and the world of seriousness and responsibility'. While we are broadly in agreement with the tenor of McRobbie's critique, it is worth paying attention to the *emotional tone* of her critique. The round condemnation of Carrie and all signifiers associated with her is laced with irritation and exasperation. Far removed from the voice of maternal approbation, the critique can be seen as a condensed moment of intergenerational conflict. Reminiscent of mother–daughter clashes couched in the seemingly innocuous but potentially explosive realm of *appearances,* this form of intergenerational conflict is commonly expressed in phrases such as 'what on earth does she look like?' and 'you're not going out looking like that'. The surface appearance of things encodes more fundamental differences. In appearing to be vain, silly and ridiculously impractical, Carrie is, of course, letting down herself and other women. Ultimately McRobbie feels that Carrie's embarrassing assemblage of femininity represents a refusal to embrace and inhabit womanhood, the key signifier of adult femininity and feminism for previous generations of women. As the representational 'daughter' of a fading feminism, Carrie's fears can be read as a rejection of the identity politics that made post-feminist subjectivity possible. Carrie's extended girlhood and fearful evasion of womanhood is presented as painful and problematic for both herself and those who encounter her.

Gender Makeovers

The theme of appearance has been taken up by a number of reality television programmes specializing in the personal 'makeover'. The makeover frequently centres upon the feminized world of the domestic home, the family or women's bodies. The latter programmes centre upon the idea of bodily transformation and the ways in which this is linked to emotional transformation. The burgeoning of programmes such as *What Not to Wear, Ten Years Younger, Would Like to Meet* and *You Are What You Eat* take non-celebrities out of their everyday worlds and, with the help of 'experts', set them on a path towards personal transformation. Within the bubble of this hyper-commodified media world everyone has the potential for dramatic change, to look great and feel like a star through the experience of full immersion in consumer culture.

Such programmes depend upon ordinary people submitting to the rules of the show, while suggesting that the boundary between celebrity and non-celebrity is permeable. Do these programmes platform the ordinary person's fifteen minutes of fame as promised by Andy Warhol or do they signal more widespread changes in the democratization of commodity culture and media forms? Largely, though not exclusively addressed at women, these programmes assume that successful transformation lies in the adoption of appropriate fashion, beauty and dietary regimes. The aim of each programme is to encourage the chrysalis-style rebirth of the 'new you' from the tired and worn-out exterior of the 'old you'. A recurrent feature of the genre and a compelling 'hook' for audiences is the many televisual moments of emotional instability as individuals are taken apart and put back together again in the course of their transformational journey. The route to the 'new you' is strewn with tears amidst expressions of guilt, shame, anger, frustration, resistance and realization. The closing minutes of each show parades the new look individual as thoroughly rejuvenated: seemingly younger, prettier, slimmer, more stylish, confident and happy, basking in the approval of friends and family.

McRobbie (2002) focuses on *What Not to Wear* as an example of the reality makeover genre. She suggests that the programme reflects the changing identity of women as individualized subjects whose liberation from patriarchy now enables them to compete with each other. McRobbie interprets the programme as an expression of newly reconfigured class–gender relations, played out in the domain of the *cultural*. In the late-modern era, she claims, social class reappears at the level of the body through the vectors of transformed gendered individualization. Consumer culture occupies a key site of normative femininity in which programmes such as *What Not to Wear* construct a new feminized social space defined by status and body image. *What Not to Wear* provides an opportunity for legitimate forms of class antagonism as the upper class presenters of the show, Trinny Woodhall and Susannah Constantine, humiliate women for failure to conform to middle-class values in speech and appearance. Trinny and Susannah use a combination of tactics, gently and not so gently, shaming, prodding and instructing their charges into changing their mode of dress. McRobbie suggests that the presenters exercise cultural capital as they express bodily disgust and distaste for the woefully misguided dress sense of their makeover subjects. Similarly she claims that working-class subjects given the Trinny and Susannah treatment are aware of their subordinate class status and know their place – a realization that produces tears of joy and gratitude at the end of the show.

While empathetic to McRobbie's class-inflected analysis of *What Not to Wear*, we would like to suggest that there may be other factors at play in the emotional rollercoaster of the makeover. First, it appears that women participants in the programme are also competing with the ageing process rather than with each other. Alongside ghastly clothes, what is absolutely not allowed is to look old and frumpy and not caring about looking old and frumpy. Flattering, fashionable clothes as recommended by Trinny and Susannah become the hallmark of an emergent femininity that is youthful, vibrant and 'in touch'. Moreover a successful makeover commonly reconnects individuals with their former (younger) selves, an identity that has been lost, spoiled or buried amidst the cares of middle age. Participants report feeling renewed, getting their identity back and finding themselves again. This part of the programme frequently prompts tears as women look in the mirror at their newly styled selves. Such displays of emotion are interpreted by McRobbie as forms of gratitude and class deference. However, they can also be read as productive of the affective domain of femininity. Here external appearances and feminine subjectivity collide in powerful ways. Feeling like *who you think you are* and feeling *like a woman*, or even the *woman you used to be*, produce highly charged feelings in the women who undergo makeovers. While class may be a feature of these interactions, such intense emotions are not entirely reducible to class relations, rather they bespeak strong investments in forms of femininity and gendered identities that literally move women to tears. As Hall (2000) points out, the link between identity and identification, 'the thin man inside the fat man' as he expresses it, can become a site of powerful emotional investments for individuals, in this case played out at the level of the body. Successful recipients of the Trinny and Susannah treatment can be seen to engage in acts of mimesis which mediate between representations of their inner and outer worlds. Through a mimetic makeover women become complicit in interpreting and creating a version of themselves that links a rediscovery of self with the person they want to be in everyday social encounters.

Second, it is worth revisiting Trinny and Susannah's approach to matters of embodiment. McRobbie characterizes the bodily relationship between presenters and participants as an exchange premised upon the exercise of cultural capital over aberrant and unruly working-class bodies. Trinny and Susannah do breach the bodily boundaries of participants and do indeed express disgust at style disasters that reveal the ugliness of bodily parts. However, it may be helpful to see these interactions as driven by a ubiquitous aesthetic that appraises femininity in particular ways rather than a blanket expression of class disdain. Contrary to McRobbie's claims, we would like to suggest that Trinny and Susannah for all their high-class haughtiness are actually quite respectful of bodies and accepting of bodily imperfections. Unlike some other makeover programmes, Trinny and Susannah never suggest that participants lose weight, have cosmetic surgery or take up a gruelling exercise regime. Rather they appear to work with an economy of the corporeal, acknowledging good and bad points, the aim being to disguise the bad and enhance the good. As such their approach has many points of continuity with fashion advice for women across many generations. From the high-water mark of Hollywood glamour to the present era of eclectic and ironic adornment, magazines, fashion houses and cosmetic companies have said to women – be who you are but dress to account for it. Within popular culture it is generally assumed that what you wear says something about you; the careful selection of clothes and accessories constitutes a form of self-expression and care of the self.

In mapping out the terrain of new femininities, commentaries may have a tendency to emphasize fissures with the past at the expense of continuities. The seemingly different new girl order may present a reshaping of normative femininities that provide many points of connection with the past. Looking at feminist scholarship across several decades suggests that young women in the contemporary period live the contradictions of femininity as in the past. The proliferation of femininities and the extension of girlhood can be read as further manifestations of a contradictory feminine condition that engages young women in ever more artful ways of managing the inconsistencies inherent in identifying as young and female. An abiding feature of this body of literature is the recognition that femininity works on and through the body and is linked in a myriad of ways to sexuality. In the final section of this chapter we point to some of the changes in the sexual sphere and their impact upon young people. The concluding chapter of the book considers some of the ways in which the body can challenge prevailing notions of gender.

Gender and Sexual Economies

While gender relations have been restructured at the economic and cultural level there has also been some restructuring of sexuality. Many Western cities have invested in the development of cultural quarters through the regeneration of gay spaces and the marketing of pink triangles and gay facilities that extend beyond clubbing and night-life. In these cities gay space has been transformed from marginal and dilapidated city zones to becoming associated with bohemian charm and an urban chic that encourages modes of gentrification and what has been described as the rise of the 'pink pound'. Most famously the gay space developed in the Castro district of San Francisco is integral to the cultural milieu of the city. In Britain the cultural marketing and embedded aspects of gay space in Brighton, London and Manchester have enabled these areas to become part of the fabric for a new cosmopolitan identity steeped in the meterosexual. As Zukin (1991) reveals in her analysis of New York, the fashion for 'loft living' organically derived from artists and bohemian residents who formed coalitions to rent the few small spaces they could afford in poor urban neighbourhoods, unwittingly transforming these spaces, at least in the bourgeois imagination, from socially obsolete to acquiring the status of 'funky' and 'hip' sites of desire. Similarly global celebrations such as Sydney's Mardi Gras and London's Gay Pride also contribute to the increased visibility of gay culture and its newly commodified place in large metropolitan cosmopolitan spaces.

The commodification of gay culture is also evident in popular media shows such as *Queer Eye for the Straight Guy*, the American lesbian series *The L-Word*, the British popular drama *Queer as Folk* and the US television comedy *Will and Grace*. Each of these programmes, though not strictly aimed at a gay audience, place gay identity at the centre rather than the margins of our vision and suggest that, when viewed up close, it is white bourgeois heterosexuality that reveals itself to be lacking in many ways as uncool, tasteless, less knowing or fun. Skeggs (2004) suggests that the development of 'global gay' as a concept of post-industrial times produces both consumers and sites of consumption. The corporate appeal of 'global gay' creates regenerated spaces, new markets and increased flows of capital that can be seen as double-edged. While representing a celebratory display of queer politics, 'global gay' can also be seen as reifying and fetishizing difference. It also involves the rewriting of Western gay subjects into model consumers invested in a politics of pleasure, rather than a politics of resistance. 'Global gay' in these terms represents conspicuous forms of consumption and the exercise of privilege through material, social and symbolic capital.

For many young people sexuality occupies a significant place in their lives and can be seen as a resource for play, a site of humour, playfulness and fun. Crossing the boundary between the domains constructed as 'private' and 'public', Giddens (1993) describes sexuality as 'a terrain of fundamental political struggle and also a medium of emancipation' (p. 181). McNair (2002) expands upon this observation by adding that despite the intimate nature of sexuality, these struggles have taken place in public and are increasingly part of the public domain. McNair's analysis suggests that the post-war period in the West has been characterized by the transformation of desire into commodities witnessed in the increased sexualization of culture across a range of local and global media. Central to McNair's argument is the role of the media and particularly new media technologies. McNair suggests that new media technologies have aided the growth of a more commercialized, less regulated and more pluralistic sexual culture, promoting, in his terms, 'a democratisation of desire' (2002, p. 11). For McNair, 'democratisation of desire' describes the present period in which there is popular and widespread access to diverse forms of sexual expression, the availability of pornography through the Internet for example, and simultaneously there are more ways of being a sexual subject within Western cultures. As an illustration of his argument, McNair documents and discusses the ways in which pornography and homosexuality no longer have subterranean or subordinate status; they now exist as part of mainstream media culture. Thinking about these themes in relation to young people's lives it is possible to suggest that young people are the new sexual citizens of a democratized and richly diverse sexual culture. Our work with young people, however, suggests that within school-based contexts and young people's social worlds there remains a tendency towards sexual conservatism and continued stigmatization of non-heterosexual forms. In subsequent chapters we discuss these themes as a feature of the production of gender in young people's lives.

Conclusion

In Chapters 3 and 4 we have considered how gender relations have been restructured in late-modernity. We have examined the ways in which economic restructuring of labour markets and workplaces has had an impact upon gender relations and gendered identities. The chapters consider two dominant themes in discussions of gender and youth: the displacement of young men and the growing confidence of young women. For young masculinities, the notion of 'crisis' features as a recurrent motif, giving shape and meaning to the experiences of youthful masculinities in the global economy. Through an analysis of film and popular media forms, we explore the contours of this crisis and consider some of the limitations of viewing young men through this lens. In contrast to young men, young women appear as successful and accomplished neo-liberal subjects, keen to embrace the consumerism and new opportunities on offer in post-industrial times. The chapter discusses the emergence of new femininities, the points of rupture and continuity with the past and the (often fraught) relationship between new femininities and feminist scholarship. In the next chapter we focus upon ways of looking at gender and youth in a global context. To discuss the ways in which gender is shaped by time and place, the chapter is organized around critical readings of four texts that provide illustrative examples of gender at work in different geographic and socio-cultural locations.

5
Gender in a Global Context

In this section we seek to provide an insight into gender, youth and culture through a consideration of four different 'critical readings' that exemplify our interests. The readings we have chosen – Parker's (1991) *Bodies, Pleasures and Passions*, Healy's (1996) *Gay Skins*, Pilkington *et al.*'s (2002) account of Russian youth in *Looking West?* and Beidelman's (1997) *The Cool Knife* – are selected for three main reasons: theoretical, methodological and historical.

Theoretically the texts illuminate aspects of young masculinities and femininities *in process*. In doing so, they show how gender is a practice that can be affirmed, transgressed or manipulated. In this sense, they focus upon the 'doing' of gender as opposed to the categorical incitement of gender as the natural accomplishment of what a boy and girl 'are'. The concern here is less with girls and boys as proper knowable objects and more with an understanding of masculinities and femininities as complex and contingent constructions perpetually in the making. This work suggests that gender is a far more precarious, fragile and contradictory set of relations than at first may be imagined and that gender competence is in actuality a highly accomplished performance, even if it abounds with numerous ambiguities. Instead of focusing upon boyhood and girlhood as a taken-for-granted state of being, each of the accounts provides critical insight into gender at work: how it is produced, consumed, regulated and performed in the everyday life-worlds of young people.

This leads us on to the second contribution, one of method and approach. The work we have selected is neither philosophical nor abstract. It is derived from first-hand observation and interaction with young people. This stance differs from a purely discursive mode of enquiry imprisoned within the language of theories of representation, to an approach which begins to reckon with the role of affect and emotion by taking seriously issues of embodiment, action and the sensory geographies of youth. Although we remain committed to the value of discursive analysis we are also appreciative of narratives that place human experience at the centre of their accounts. Not least for these reasons, we have prioritized ethnographic research that draws upon in-depth anthropological modes of enquiry, the rich texture of cultural studies and the material landscapes outlined in the geographies and sociologies of youth. We see this approach to youth subjectivity as very much in keeping with the spirit of our book as part of a reflexive, theoretically informed ethnography.

A third feature of our critical readings is that they focus upon issues of transformation: that is, they pay heed to continuity and change at macro- and micro-levels. This includes, for example, the impact that large-scale transformations such as postcolonialism, post-industrialism, glasnost or globalization are having upon the life-worlds of young people. As these youth accounts demonstrate these changes are not lived and experienced simplistically, but are frequently negotiated and transformed in their biographical undertaking. Thus when looking at continuity and change at a micro-level, young people's coming-of-age can be signalled through sexual rites of passage, participation in youth subculture, affiliations to seemingly authentic cultures of the nation-state or the undertaking of gender-specific initiation rituals. The worldwide examples we explore incorporate diverse narratives of gender formation from Brazil, Britain, Tanzania and Russia. Although we do not consider the accounts to be representative of youth practices in these nations, it is evident that the different histories and geographies of youth have a profound effect upon how gender is done and the way that different cultures impinge upon our understanding and habitation of gender.

Sexuality, Carnival and the Postcolonial Spectacle

Parker, R.G. (1991) *Bodies, Pleasures and Passions, Sexual Culture in Contemporary Brazil*.

Parker's ethnography of sexual culture in contemporary Brazil offers insights into the performance of gender by bringing together the diverse histories of Indian, Portuguese and African cultures within a postcolonial frame.

Beginning with the myths of origin, Parker documents the shaping of Brazilian culture from the first encounters with Portuguese explorers in the fourteenth century. The earliest known account of this new land south of the equator described it in arresting terms as a tropical Garden of Eden (Caminha, 1943). Indeed the notion of an earthly paradise is a metaphor that pervades many early representations of Brazil. However, the idea of Brazil as a seductively beautiful heaven on earth is mitigated by a European preoccupation with savagery and sin. New World explorers documented accounts of cannibalism and unrestrained sexuality with gusto, projecting European moral values onto Brazilian culture in ways that revealed their fascination and horror in equal measure. Parker suggests that this ambiguous view of Brazil as a mixture of heaven and hell, innocence and depravity has also shaped the ways in which Brazilians view themselves. An influential essay (Prado, 1931) on Brazilian sadness provocatively suggests that Brazilians inherited the melancholia of their discoverers whose lust for gold and sexual pleasure developed into a source of sadness for themselves and others. Within this context the loss of innocence, miscegenation and syphilis become imbued with negative significance as the dark underside of colonial relations. Above all else, Parker asserts that sexual life in Brazil 'emerged as a central issue at a social and cultural level . . . a kind of key to the peculiar nature of Brazilian reality' (p. 28).

Assumptions relating to gender form a central part of the ways in which Brazilians interpret and give meaning to their cultural history. The legacy of a patriarchal past becomes an inevitable part of this self-interpretation. Patriarchal power is commonly viewed as a response to the contingencies of colonialism. While the patriarchal family remains the dominant social unit, it has retained a partial and fragile dominance that is dualistic in nature. During the colonial period the legitimate lineage of the patriarch through marriage coexisted with the illegitimate lineage of mistresses and alternative families who shared the experiences but not necessarily the privileges of plantation life. The sexual double standards of a slaveholding society are encapsulated in a Brazilian proverb that has salience in the contemporary period, 'White woman for marrying, mulatto woman for fucking, black woman for working' (Freyre, 1983:10). Patriarchal authority and control shaped relations between the sexes in familiar ways. While daughters were subject to socialization processes that located them within the domestic sphere and imposed a rigid set of restrictions especially during puberty, sons were active in plantation life and commonly initiated into sex through relationships with slaves. In contemporary Brazilian society gender socialization begins in early childhood. Girls are largely shrouded from knowledge of their bodies especially sexual knowledge associated with menstruation and intimate relationships. Adolescent girls find their movements outside of the domestic sphere further curtailed by the fear of 'dishonour' they could bring upon the family. Boys and young men have a markedly different experience. From the age of 5–6 they are encouraged, indeed coerced, into spending time with other boys and young men outside the home. At the age of 6 or 7, one of Parker's respondents, a bisexual young man, recalls hearing a group of older men comment, 'I prefer that my son be a bandit rather than a Zica or sissy' (p. 60), indicating that the fear of being contaminated by femininity, of becoming sissy or queer, haunts many boyhood experiences. Initiation into the culture of heterosexual masculinity includes sexual learning through pornography and prostitution; many young men reported that their father's bought pornographic magazines for them and took them on their first trip to a brothel.

Within the context of asymmetrical power relations between men and women, ways of thinking about masculinity and femininity become symbolically coded and embodied in particular ways. The phallus becomes associated with an aggressive form of patriarchal power central to notions of masculinity. Women by implication, femininity is characterized by 'the fissure between her legs – the mysterious entrance that somehow defines her entire being' (p. 39). The mystery, however, is not necessarily enticing or benign; the vagina is commonly associated with notions of impurity, a site of pollution through urine, menstrual blood and venereal disease. The costs of masculine domination included the ever-present risk of becoming a victim of women or other men. Typically, the risk is cast in terms of the fear and humiliation of being cuckolded or dominated by a strong woman – *sapatao*, big shoes or dyke. Parker suggests that the female figures of virgin, whore and *sapatao* function symbolically to define the domain of the feminine, articulating both the positive and negative features of a socially constructed feminine role. There is also a risk of being emasculated through homosexual relations. Homosexual men who allow themselves to be penetrated by other men are regarded as queer, passive and weak, whereas homosexual men who penetrate manage to hold onto a masculine identity. Such a stark delineation within same-sex practices suggests that the distinction between active and passive remains pertinent to achieving a masculine identity.

Parker's ethnography powerfully demonstrates that the ideology of gender in Brazilian society was in dialogue with perspectives drawn from organized religion and modern science/medicine as key features in the organization of social relations. He points to the importance of Catholicism in holding together gender arrangements through the relatively informal religious backdrop of a sensuous Catholicism inherited from the Portuguese, placing emphasis upon feasts, festivals of saints and a relaxed form of sexual morality. This cultural context was well suited to the early colonial life of the *casa grande* with its hierarchies, transgressions and sexual double standards. This was disrupted, however, by the arrival of the Inquisition in the 1591. The Inquisition introduced a more punitive form of Catholicism marked by the theatricality of dramatic displays of discipline and public confessionals. The Inquisition provided classifications of sexual practices and sets of formal prohibitions that in Foucaultian terms produced an 'incitement to discourse'. Distinctions were drawn between legitimate and illegitimate sex, with marriage, monogamy and procreation as the trinity at the heart of the legitimate. The dramatic quality of the new Catholicism produced a shift in emphasis from public 'shame' to private 'guilt' with the stress now being placed upon the individual and feelings of inner guilt rather than the dishonour of families. The changes heralded by the Inquisition were marked by a dualistic moral distinction between the flesh and the spirit that conceptualized sex as sinful and dangerous. As Parker notes, sex 'plays across the body but takes root in the soul' (p. 74).

The sexual landscape of the Inquisition in many ways reverberated with the concerns of the social hygiene and modern medicine movement of the mid-nineteenth century. Gaining influence with the middle- and upper-classes, the imperatives of social hygiene and modern medicine coincided with industrialization and widespread social change. Sexuality, though unfettered by religion, is once again cast as a dangerous and uncontrollable force that must be known and spoken. Reproduction becomes the responsibility of individuals to the state, while homosexuality, libertinism and prostitution are viewed as threats to the social order. In keeping with Weeks (1981) UK-based analysis, this period sees the birth of the modern homosexual. Sexuality defines personhood as 'normal' or 'sick', an inner essence revealing the truth of one's self. Within this conceptualization, sex and sickness become ways of labelling and controlling the unacceptable.

In addition to the hierarchy of gender and modern interpretations of sexuality, Parker suggests that an ideology of the erotic offers another perspective for defining sexual meanings in contemporary Brazil. The realm of the erotic explores the diverse possibilities for sexual pleasure, otherwise overlooked or circumscribed by other perspectives. Here the emphasis is upon the transgression of norms and the subversion of established arrangements for gender and sexuality. Within the domain of the erotic, negatives can be transformed into positives, as one of Parker's respondents commented, 'the things that are most prohibited are always the most exciting' (p. 103). Sin becomes pleasurable in the emergence of a new symbolic economy based upon an index of excitement and desire. A common saying in Brazil, 'beneath the sheets anything can happen' alludes to the transformation of sexual life in erotic encounters that do not impose boundaries upon desire or sexual practice. The sensual and erotic potential of the body is central to the erotic frame of reference. The body, especially the genitals, is understood as 'instruments of pleasure rather than markers of power' (p. 112). In the realm of the erotic, sexual pleasure holds the potential to break down the boundaries of the body and unite the individual with the rest of the physical world. The *bunda* (tail), important to notions of masculinity, is an obscene word in childhood, associated with dirt and excrement. Within the erotic, the negative connotations of *bunda* and other bodily functions can be transformed into positive and pleasurable practices with new meaning. The erotic potential of excrement can be realized in the erotic domain where sex and faeces offer the exciting possibility of experiencing the self as integrated with the world around it rather than separate from it. The eroticized self, however, is not a natural state. Parker suggests that erotic possibilities are learned in childhood and adolescence in the games of friendship groups and early sexual encounters. The pleasures of masturbation, oral sex and anal sex – key elements in the repertoire of the erotic – are commonly learned in male peer groups. Many of Parker's respondents describe adolescent friendship groups in which they take turns in masturbating, fellating and penetrating each other. These activities are variously cast as preparation for manhood, an initiation into the pleasures of the flesh and practice for future heterosexual relationships.

The sexually charged nature of contemporary Brazilian society is ultimately associated with the erotic ideology and ritual of *carnaval*. In a globalized post-industrial economy *carnavalization* has become a metaphor for the export of Brazilian culture across the world. A popular proverb in Brazil, 'sin does not exist beneath the equator', suggests to the rest of the world that they too should loosen up, create a little space for themselves beneath the equator and below the waist. The dominant musical form of *carnaval*, samba, also emphasizes bodily freedom; in order to dance the samba, as one of Parker's respondents insists, 'you have to let your body go free' (p. 151). *Carnaval* itself offers Brazilians new definitions of reality, a utopian vision of a world where anything is possible and everything is permitted, if only temporarily. *Carnaval* is usually interpreted as a reversal of normal life, a time when everyday struggle is replaced by freedom, where desires can be spoken and satisfied. The emphasis is upon play and playfulness in which boundaries between childhood and adulthood become blurred. During *carnaval* Brazilians claim play as important for adult happiness and well-being, extending beyond the childhood years to acquire significance across the life course. Adults can legitimately regress into childhood as desirous, pleasure-seeking, orally fixated beings whose needs must be satisfied. The oversized dummy (*chupeta*) becomes the most common accessory or plaything of *carnaval* for all ages, symbolically bringing together, in exaggerated form, the erotic pleasures of childhood and adulthood. This theme is echoed in *Mamae Eu Quero* (Mommy I Want), the most popular of all *carnaval* songs:

> Mommy I want,
> Mommy I want,
> Mommy I want to suckle,
> Give me the pacifier,
> Give me the pacifier,
> Give me the pacifier,
> So that baby won't cry.

Inversion and transgression characterize the ritual of *carnaval*; girls become boys, boys become girls, adults become children, the poor become kings and queens, transvestites move from the margins to the centre, normal rules do not apply. During *carnaval* the erotic becomes the norm, invoking the collective memory of a Brazilian past before the arrival of the Portuguese. *Carnaval* suggests to Brazilians that it is possible to transgress the restrictions of everyday life and indulge in the imaginative potential of a wider social and cultural universe. Parker comments that the 'contradictory capacity for transformation, for the continued search for freedom and happiness, lies at the heart of the whole *carnavalesque* fantasy' (p. 162). As Parker points out, the ability of *carnaval* to hold contradictions within a whole appears as an ironic riposte to a nation in search of a national identity. *Carnaval* offers a cannibalized and comic version of the myths of origin as a way of conceptualizing the present and the future. *Carnaval* presents a utopian vision of the world, an illusion based upon freedom and desire and the possibility of realizing anything and everything for a few days once a year. Though temporary and fleeting, the dramatic spectacle of *carnaval* exists as a metaphor for Brazil itself, a psychologically significant event in which categories such as gender and youth can be played with and transformed. Above all *carnaval* exists as a powerful narrative of self-definition, a story that Brazilians tell about themselves.

Sex, Youth and Subculture

Healy, M. (1996) *Gay Skins: Class Masculinity and Queer Appropriation.*

Youth subcultures are amongst the most influential arena in which young people's gender identities are practised, subverted and brought into play. In adopting the dress codes, music, mannerisms and attitude of a Riot Girl, Raver, Skater or Goth young people are expressing something about the type of masculinity or femininity they seek to inhabit. Subculture, then, offers a very particular way of 'doing gender'. In response to feminist critiques that early studies of youth subculture were in fact accounts of young men (McRobbie and Garber, 1982; Griffin, 1985), since the 1980s a number of studies have been completed on youth culture exploring the lives of girls and young women, in particular their role in music scenes, science fiction, dance, internet chat rooms and the full gambit of consumer cultures (Kehily, 2003; Aapola *et al.*, 2005).

Arguably one of the most outwardly masculine subcultures to have become enshrined in the richly decorated hall of cultural studies remain Skinhead youth. As a number of accounts show, Skinheads appear amongst the most authentically working class, macho and nationalistic of subcultures (Daniel and McGuire, 1972; Clarke, 1977; Cohen, 1997). However, the white authenticity of the Skins starts to blur in accounts that underline the complex and contingent construction of whiteness in many of their lives which entails a perpetual interaction with black culture through participation in reggae, marijuana and the fashionable accoutrements of turn-up trousers and trilby or porkpie hats (Hebdige, 1979) – or more recently with the take up of hardcore Rave music, tracksuits and aspects of patois (Nayak, 1999). Moreover, although masculine dominated, not all Skinhead gangs are comprised of young men. In an exploration of teen friendship groups in South London the anthropologist Wulff (1995) recalls, 'When one of the white girls went out with a Skinhead for a while, she regarded herself as a Skinhead' (1995:72). This would indicate how subculture can be a technique for the performance of gender, class and race as the boy in question, 'was mainly using the Skinhead label as a way to decide for himself and others that he had chosen a white identity' (p. 72). Despite their masculine bravado, Richard Allen's grim pulp fiction series on Skinheads in the 1970s also doffed their cap in the direction of young women with titles such as *Skinhead Girls, Sorts* and *Knuckle Girls* that implied a female subcultural readership, if not direct subcultural participation.

While early subcultural studies were accused of marginalizing young women and minority ethnic groups, themes that have subsequently taken centre stage in studies of youth, with few exceptions, the vast majority of accounts have tended to operate with a heterosexual presumption rarely lifting their gaze beyond dominant sexual norms. Read in this light one of the most eye-opening accounts of Skinhead culture can be found in Healy's remarkable study *Gay Skins: Class, Masculinity and Queer Appropriation* (1996). In what is a multilayered textual analysis combining press reports, Skinhead pulp fiction, subcultural literature and the vivid memories of gay Skins themselves, Healy stitches together a new, if much neglected history of the subculture. While it is some-times presumed that the rise of a gay metropolitan 'butch' Skinhead look is the preserve of recent times, Healy reveals how Skinhead subculture was always a thoroughly Queer tapestry. He points to the fetish for leather boots and crotch-hugging denim, the sweaty bare-chested beery dancing and the ardent dedication to the male gang at all costs as examples of queering, which we can regard as indicative of the fine gauze that slips between, yet cannot fully separate, the homosocial from the homoerotic.

If carefully deployed, life-histories and personal testimonies can act as exemplary case material through which to illuminate interactions between gender and youth. Here, it is worth spending time discussing the biography of Nick, one of Healy's respondents who grew up on a council estate in the city of Coventry in the English Midlands. From an early age Nick adopted the steely, razor-sharp apparel of Skinhead style, 'You'd have a handkerchief with a stud through it in your Crombie and your sharpened comb and Durex – 'cause I was going with girls then' (p. 152). By his mid-teens Nick had dropped out of school, leaving home when he was 16 feeling angry and oppressed. Becoming a Skinhead provided him with an unequivocally masculine gender persona. He reflects, 'the most angry, most aggressive, most violent image I could think of was the skinhead . . . Being a skinhead gave me an identity, values, self-worth, all the things I was lacking in myself' (p. 152). Nick's lack of gender accomplishment and his sense that he was deficient in the credentials to be a 'proper boy' were underwritten by his position as an uneducated working-class male struggling to come to terms with his latent sexuality. Soon he was to leave for London where he remembers, 'Tripping up queens, intimidating them, that sort of thing, especially the really camp ones' (p. 153). Indeed, he recalls how a number of hardcore Skinheads were gay but would indulge in queer-bashing activities in an attempt to expel any sign of gayness from themselves as they viciously carved out their own masculinities against those they so ardently despised. Shaving the head, getting facial tattoos done and adopting an antagonistic posture became a means of authenticating this rough masculinity. The body is then a type of corporeal canvas upon which competing configurations of gender – camp or hardness – can be situated. Noticeably being a gay Skin brings together these apparent dichotomies, holds them in tension and hollows out their intended meanings.

For Nick and some other working-class young men he knew, being a gay Skin meant you were 'a subculture within a subculture' (p. 155). Neverthe-less he recalls his past with eminent pleasure, discussing the hedonistic, illicit sexual relations he forged with other working-class Skins. He fondly remembers different boyfriends: an Asian Skinhead, a long-haired young man whose head he shaved before fucking him and sexy Skins with hard bodies. Even so, these exciting forays into gay subculture cannot hide the material logic underpinning his status as a jobless young man in the capital. To earn a living in London Nick would sleep with middle-class male punters trading sex for money as the lines between 'play boy' and 'rent boy' became increasingly difficult to disentangle. Viewing Nick's time in London through each of these representations offers rather different ways for approaching his sexual biography. In many ways he was engaged in high-risk sex, dangerous work that brought him into contact with those whom he describes as 'alkies' and the 'drug-fucked'. He recounts how a lot of young working-class men would engage in these, occasionally volatile sexual liaisons in order to survive. Moreover, Nick soon discovered that Skinheads are ascribed very particular attributes by their male clients that in turn may lead them to perform a highly stylized sex/gender identity:

> I used to pretend I was straight, because that was their fantasy. These men expected us to be hard. The middle classes associated skinheads with being rough and there-fore they could have rough sex which they craved but which they wouldn't allow themselves to express. The middle classes were more educated, which repressed some things. And you got a lot of these men who wanted to be dominated, or whatever. A lot of them just wanted me to kick the shit out of them, call them queer bastards, that sort of thing. I think back now . . . how could I have done that? But in those days, I needed the money, so I didn't think about it, I just did it. (pp. 155–156)

The complex, shifting relations of power that meander between the transactions of middle-class male punters and gay Skins are as intricate as they are elastic. Nick's account points to the psychoanalytic dimension of these encounters that involved responding to the fantasies and repressed desires of middle-class gay men with an enactment of their imagined Other. Nick went on to explain how he purposely selected older men when he worked as a sex-worker. He described how one man in his mid-forties, 'was like Daddy really we used to hang around him and he used to look after us' (p. 155). For Nick the choice to go with older men was essentially a mode of protection. At a more psychic level it may also have been an attempt to reconstruct his own troubled relationship with his father. Indeed, Nick was to later encounter a wealthy philanderer who took him away from the London rent boy scene and enhanced his cultural education in Europe. Here, he gradually developed new tastes, read literature, met different people and came to terms with his sexuality. It was at this juncture that Nick relinquished Skinhead identifications. 'I didn't have to protect myself' cause I wasn't on the street anymore', (p. 156) he solemnly concludes.

So, what can one brief personal history tell us about the relationships between gender, youth and culture? In the course of his life we see Nick's sexual compass turn through a number of overlapping orientations. He navigates a path that travels from straight sex with girls, to casual sex and long-term relationships with working-class Skins, to paid sex with older middle-class men, through to a belated reckoning with his own sexuality. Amidst this dense proliferation of sexual activity we also discover that gender identifications are equally malleable. Even within the context of homosexual relations Nick can appear to inhabit a 'hard', occasionally 'straight' masculinity that entails beating up the camp queens and middle-class punters he had rough sex with. At other moments Nick wantonly submits himself into the hands of a 'sugar-daddy' taking on the emasculated position of a subservient son. Power is then written through gender identifications. Gender and sexuality appear as mobile and ever-changing patterns in young people's lives. They are the effect of a dense discursive interplay of signs, representation, reiteration and embodiment. They are also material practices. The influence of these relations is seen on Nick's masculinity when he drops out of school, leaves home angry and uneducated, becomes a Skinhead, works as a rent boy and, eventually, relinquishes this lifestyle as he accrues a cosmopolitan cultural capital. Cosmopolitanism becomes a means of rewriting his identity as the angry, Coventry estate kid who once longed to escape.

At a more basic level Nick's sexual biography is also revealing of the important role that subculture plays in young lives. It shows us how subcultures tend to be seen as the preserve of deviant youth groups that operate with their own styles, values and repertoire of beliefs. It is possible to read Nick's account of gay Skinheadism through a subcultural lens, marking it as a class cultural 'ritual of resistance' (Hall and Jefferson, 1977), though this would be to ignore the ways in which gender norms are resisted and overturned. The radical potential of the gay Skinhead lies in the subversion of all hard forms of masculinity. The queering of Skinheads is disturbing precisely because it makes any claims to an authentic, 'real' Skinhead identity a phantasmatic impossibility. The gay Skinhead unzips the category of masculinity and empties it of meaning, an act that renders all forms of maleness fictional. As Healy skilfully explains, 'The relation of gay skin to "real" skin is exposed as being one of copy to copy rather than imitation to original' (p. 188). In other words, the corporeal, 'hyperreal drag effect' (p. 118) of the gay Skin calls all forms of masculinity into question, making any claims to an authentic Skinhead identity thoroughly counterfeit. The multiple iterations of what the Skinhead 'is' transfigures this identity into a site of radical excess. As Healy alludes, the contemporary Skin is no longer the epitome of rooted certainty rather, 'head-shaving becomes a stripping away of social signs which fix the wearers identity' to the extent that the 'Skinhead' has become blank; 'it refuses to situate itself with any clarity within the social' (p. 173). We can regard the postmodern choreography of the Skinhead as a performance of gender that prises open the closed signifier of masculine authority, turns it inside out and renders it obsolete.

Local-Global Youth Cultures

Pilkington, H., Omel'chenko, E., Flynn, M., Bliudina, U. and Starkova, E. (2002) *Looking West? Cultural Globalisation and Russian Youth Cultures.*

Pilkington *et al.*'s (2002) empirical study of Russian youth points to the place-specific impact of cultural globalization. Their study was conducted at the historical juncture towards the end of the twentieth century when the West became dislodged as a model for political and social emulation while political transformations in Russia following the post-Soviet era saw the emergence of newly negotiated East–West relationships. Focusing upon how Russia's opening up to the West has been reflected in the cultural practice of young people, their study provides a rich illustration of Russian youth as discerning, critically aware and media literate with an ambivalent relationship to the West. The steady withdrawal of the 'iron curtain' is particularly interesting as it enables us to gain an understanding of globalization from a non-Western perspective. This is particularly revealing as a good deal of work has adopted a Eurocentric vision concerned with an understanding of how global change and difference is negotiated within Western nation-states. In Chapter 3 we witnessed the impact that the end of the Cold War had upon US security workers, where characters such as Bill Foster in *Falling Down* suddenly became redundant and found themselves positioned as the bad guys of perestroika. Pilkington *et al.*'s text by contrast, offers us insights into Russian culture, focusing on the views and changing experiences of young Russians.

Cultural globalization in the West has been theorized as a series of 'flows' from the Western 'core' to the non-Western 'periphery' bringing a stream of ideas, products and practices to non-Western locations. The idea of a 'global community' remains a largely Western conceptualization associated with the Americanization of local cultures. Cultural globalization provides new channels of information for young Russians, reflected particularly in new youth magazines presenting a global youth culture that is inclusive of Russian youth. In general terms, youth cultural texts in Russia reflect the globalized cross-fertilization of youth cultural formations and are particularly available to young Russians living in cities. Respondents commented on the ways in which Moscow and other large cities could be regarded as part of the West, having affinities with London and sharing youth identities based upon lifestyle, music and culture. As one respondent expressed it, 'Young people in the West do not differ from those in Moscow, only from provincial [young people]' (2002:80), indicating that differences between young people are more likely to be based upon urban and rural locations rather than national boundaries. Many young people, when asked about their image of the West, referred to ideas of a developed world, marked by progress, freedom and choice – 'Everything there is the very best, highly polished, of the best quality and the latest fashion' (2002:82). The West offered young people rights of citizenship, an 'easy life' and an abundance of fun and pleasure. Despite this, however, many young Russians were also critical of Westerners as selfish and superficial, consumption-fixated individuals with no sense of fun. By contrast, young Russians saw themselves as having a strongly developed sense of collectivism and community, a commitment to core values and the ability to party.

A feature of Western life that appeared different and intriguing for young Russians was the contrasting approach to gender and sexuality in the West. Russian youth noted that, unlike their Western counterparts, their relationships were bound by moral and social norms, which proscribed gender roles and sexual relationships in traditional ways as a legacy of 'Soviet upbringing'. Young people reported feeling 'inhibited', as one young man expressed it, 'In this sense, of course, the West is ahead of us. While we still have these limits on our behaviour, these restraining bonds, in the West people are becoming more and more uninhibited' (2002:85). A further respondent, commenting on the relative freedom of young women in the West says, 'Girls don't have to get married between the ages of seventeen and twenty there. They are more full of the joys of life there at twenty-five or even thirty-five' (2002:89). While ideas on gender and sexuality may be changing among some young people, especially in urban areas, the notion of gender appropriate roles and behaviour was largely held in place by social conventions that appear more relaxed in certain contexts.

Pilkington *et al.* demonstrate that taking a Russian perspective on globalization rather than a Western one points to the inadequacy of the core-periphery model and particularly the absence of 'nation' in much Western theorizing. Their study, based in three Russian cities with differing demographic and social trajectories, suggests that the idea of nation and nationhood is important to the ways in which young Russians think about themselves in relation to the West. A sense of Russian identity and cultural practice becomes a significant mediating influence in young people's practices of engagement with the *flows* of cultural globalization. As one respondent expressed it, 'Everything here is always shared, people are always trying to pull together, we celebrate all of our holidays together, and everyone tries to pull together all the time' (2002:83). The spoils of choice and privilege available in the West may appear seductive at certain moments but for many young Russians they did not compensate for the poverty of feeling that they regarded as endemic to Western experience. Their research with Russian youth suggests that far from being vulnerable to Western influence, young people's relationship to the West is 'filtered through the critical lens of family, teachers and peer group' (2002:xv).

Sociological conceptualizations of youth have a markedly different history in modern Russia. While notions of subculture and post-subculture have been influential in Western theorizing (Muggleton and Weinzierl, 2003), in Soviet Russia the concept of subculture was resisted by sociologists as an ideological construct that only had salience in capitalist societies. Soviet sociologists critiqued ideas of subculture and counterculture as bourgeois diversions that promoted intergenerational conflict at the expense of class struggle. They were critical of modes of analysis that focused upon the cultural sphere as if cultural practice in itself had the political power to effect economic change. Studies of Russian youth in the Soviet era favoured structuralist–functionalist accounts that emphasized the importance of youth cultural practice as a socializing force in young people's lives, facilitated through formal activities and settings that served to create bonds and commonalities between generations. Pilkington *et al.* document the decline of state socialist structures and the emergence of alternative forms of youth groupings from the mid-1980s onwards that became known as 'informals' (*neformaly*) rather than subcultures. By the 1990s young people's cultural groupings had proliferated into a diverse and shifting youth scene, interestingly explored by the authors as a sophisticated and discerning set of strategies that young people draw upon in different ways to forge a range of life positions. Pilkington *et al.* suggest that their study of the youth scene in Russia in the late 1990s offers a panorama of youth cultural practice that is not helpful to read as forms of 'Westernization' or incorporation into global youth culture.

In matters of style and music, young people's various levels of engagement with the West and their locale produces a diverse range of local narratives inflected by global cultural forms and locally produced meanings. Pilkington *et al.* identify two broad youth cultural strategies defined by young people in contemporary Russia through their identification as either 'progressive' or 'normal'. These loosely structured umbrella categories are defined in relation to each other and can be seen to forge distinctly different approaches to global and local resources. The authors point out that these affiliations, while influenced by broader social formations, cannot be attributed to class positioning or consumer practice. Neither can they be regarded as examples of postmodern subculture selected at the 'supermarket of style' (Polhemus, 1997:150). Rather, they exist as complexly constituted agentic strategies for negotiating the present and imagining the future. 'Normals' and 'progressives' draw upon a range of resources such as music, style and local space to define their identity as a group while distinguishing themselves from other groups. 'Progressives' take up a subcultural identity with links to the West through music and new technologies; they look beyond the locality to create new and inventive ways of being young and Russian. Progressives blur boundaries between work and leisure, aiming to forge 'lifestyles' premised upon the exercise of agency and individual choice. Identifying as a progressive involves paying attention to matters of identity, narratives of self and reflective modes of self-definition, as articulated by this young man:

> I like clothes which create a mood, I like clothes that are accessible to me . . . sometimes I want to create a character for myself . . . but I rarely wear things that would place me in a concrete *tusovka* [youth subculture] . . . I just like things that are style. (2002:168)

Progressives regard themselves as individuals seeking to express themselves through music, style and outlook. They eschew 'following fashion', going with the crowd and unthinking forms of social conformity. Their emphasis on individuality stresses the importance of personal choice and lifestyle in ways congruent with late-modern notions of the self as a project. Significantly, progressives seek to challenge normative gender relations considering themselves to have a more relaxed, Western-style approach to gender, treating young men and women as active, reflective individuals with free choice and equal participatory rights. Among normal youth, approaches to gender are imbued with traditionally defined notions of masculinity and femininity. Normals appear reluctant to comment upon gender relations, which they regard as self-evident 'essences', rather than process 'relations'. Pilkington *et al.* point out, however, that the relaxed approach of the progressives did not extend to sexuality, in this respect progressives and normals remain bound by normative heterosexual values and assumptions.

'Normals', as their name implies, blend into local cultures more readily and do not occupy a subcultural space. 'We don't like to stand out . . . so that everyone looks at you' and 'I don't try to dress as anything' (2002:173) can be seen as examples of an affiliation with the 'normal'. Unlike progressives, normals do not want to be different. They voice some distaste for the expressive cultures of the progressives and are opposed to their non-traditional attitudes in matters of gender and lifestyle. Normals are more at home in their locality, tending towards stable friendship groups within the locale and do not look to travel beyond the area in which they live and study. The expression of individuality so important to the progressives does not feature in the 'normals' lexicon. They are guided by group norms and expectations rather than notions of personal choice and individual agency. Normals are more likely to engage in organized leisure pursuits and a diverse range of cultural consumption. Paradoxically, progressives are more critical of the West than normals despite being more Western orientated and in touch with Western influences. As the West has become mainstream for Russian youth, progressives seek to further differentiate themselves from the normals by embracing domestic culture, placing renewed value upon its authenticity and meaningfulness. This is particularly the case with musical preferences where clear binaries emerge to create differences between 'meaningless' and 'meaningful' music. Western music is constructed as meaningless, insubstantial and for the body, while meaningful music is constructed as non-Western, substantial and for the soul. Progressives position Western culture as fun but superficial in contrast to Russian culture, which they regard as imbued with spirituality, authenticity and meaning. For progressives, looking to the West prompts a positive reappraisal of local and national values.

Gender, Ethnicity and Ritual

T.O. Beidelman (1997) *The Cool Knife: Imagery of Gender, Sexuality and Moral Education in Kaguru Initiation Ritual.*

Within the discipline of anthropology it is not uncommon for researchers to make the study of a particular community their lifetimes work. This can enable a very rich longitudinal set of data to emerge derived from field observations, interviews, diaries, story-telling and first-hand experiences of critical incidents. Beidelman's ethnography of the East African Kaguru people in Tanzania involved two eighteen-month fieldwork periods in 1957–1958, then again in 1961–1963, and two three-month stints in 1975 and 1976. In addition, the author continued to correspond with informants (1963–1978), whilst writing a series of articles and books documenting their everyday lives. In focusing upon a particular book of his – *The Cool Knife* (1997) – for its explicit engagement with gender and sexuality, we aim to disclose one of the most spectacular 'rituals of initiation that transform children into adults' (p. 2). Beidelman's account is of particular relevance to this volume as it brings together the lives of young men and women to show how gender and ethnicity are fashioned through cultural rituals.

The Kaguru are named after the highlands from which they descend and thus differ from other outlying communities within East Africa residing in different spatial and temporal zones. The primary way in which they maintain their identity and sense of cultural difference is through the initiation ritual of circumcision. Circumcision at adolescence is a pivotal youth transition, Kaguru young men must endure if they are to become responsible adults and active sexual citizens. For young women adult status is achieved primarily through menstruation and any future onset of childbirth. However, some girls also undergo circumcision or some form of cutting to affirm their ties to the community and the preservation of Kaguru initiation rituals. Inevitably these practices may seem antiquated and even barbaric through Western eyes (although male circumcision is a feature of many major world religions). Colonial anthropology with its endless fascination with 'tribes' is also littered with dark tales of head-hunters, cannibalism, voodoo and sexual fetish, all of which have sought to construe developing nations as uncivilized and Other to the West. But as Beidelman implores, 'To understand how Kaguru characterise gender and sex we must approach these concepts with sympathy . . . It is by addressing the ambiguities and complexities, not by trying to rise above them, that we may appreciate how gender and sex work for Kaguru' (pp. 17–18). It is necessary then, not to measure up Kaguru practices against a familiar white norm. Thus the surgical scalpel of Western science that facilitates breast implants, face-lifts, buttock enlargements and tummy tucks is less likely to be viewed as the harbinger for horrific modes of body mutilation of the type conducted by the Kaguru 'cool knife'. The description that follows of ceremonial initiation is also designed so as not to 'rise above' non-Western cultures and pronounce in God-like status upon them, but rather to explore what they may tell us about our own norms and values on gender and youth within a postcolonial context.

The initiation of Kaguru adolescent males takes place in the bush well away from the settlement under the scrutiny of male elders. When Kaguru males first undergo circumcision they are said to have died, having killed their maternal and childhood ties with the shedding of blood and foreskin; on return to the settlement after a period of recuperation they are regarded as reborn into adulthood. In Kaguru culture the foreskin is considered dirty (*mwafu*) and intimately linked to the construction of gender since, 'the uncircumcised, moist penis makes a male unclean because this makes boys resemble women, whose moist genitals, especially during menstruation, are sources of pollution' (p. 117). The notion of femininity as a polluting influence in the West is explored in Chapters 1 and 6 when we discuss the work of Thorne (1993), and later in Chapter 8 when we extend this particular construction of gender to the perception of homosexuality as a vilified, contaminating Other. The anthropological work of Mary Douglas (1966) has been especially influential here in distinguishing the boundaries of what she terms *Purity and Danger*, the eponymous title of her most famous account.

The initiation of Kaguru young men and women is an elaborate ritual that is accompanied by the dissemination of sexual knowledge by male elders and matriarchs through the deployment of folklore, riddles, jokes and songs. Having undergone surgical excision, through a period of convalescence young men are allowed special access to sexual knowledge. They can ask whatever questions they wish on sex and are repeatedly informed about carnal matters through the medium of narrative, song and riddle. It is through these story-telling forms that initiated Kaguru young men and women learn what it means to become 'apprentice adults' (p. 232). They are told that they will acquire new responsibilities, will gain a certain amount of respect from younger uninitiated children and must learn to speak and act in ways becoming of adulthood.

But what does it mean to perform as an adult, to act as the fully sexed-up subject of masculinity or femininity? As we will find this is, above all, an *embodied display* of knowledge.

> Kaguru rituals, and especially initiation, emphasise bodily comportment and develop a sense of facility and security by putting initiates through various routines of movement: stressing polite comportment; encouraging proper tone and rhythms of voice, especially in responsive songs and riddles; and providing further instruction about dancing and singing. Kaguru novices emerge from initiation with new gravity and poise in their demeanour. There is no other period in a Kaguru's lifetime when her or his every move and word are so likely to be scrutinised and criticised as during the weeks of indoctrination as a newly initiated novice. (p. 245)

The transformation that is undergone is both mental as well as physical and it involves the competent performance of what is culturally imagined as an adult masculinity or femininity, substantiated through the enactment of socially recognized signs, gestures and bodily iterations. These actions must be practised and ceaselessly rehearsed if they are to achieve the semblance of appearing 'real'. Adult gender performance involves holding oneself differently and speaking in a dignified, measured tone that is distinguishable from 'childish' idle chatter. The performance of gender in Western contexts and the matter of the body are discussed in detail in Chapter 8 where we consider gender conformity and its transgression.

The centrality of circumcision to a boy's coming-of-age is repeatedly emphasized within Beidelman's ethnography. Once again we are drawn to the social construction of childhood and adulthood as liminal practices that cannot be pinned down to age or biological development. 'Kaguru manhood's most crucial social sign is physical, a cut penis', declares Beidelman. 'No matter how old he is, a Kaguru male cannot become a man (jural adult) without undergoing circumcision. Emergence of pubic hair, change of voice and musculature, and physical growth do not suffice' (p. 133).

Initiation is the spark igniting the process of cultural maturation from which sex, marriage, fatherhood and proprietorship follow; eventually it will enable boys to become male elders and in death ancestral spirits. Circumcision is a cultural practice of material value as it will later permit young men to have access to women, land and the sacred knowledge and information monopolized by authoritative elders. As *The Cool Knife* cuttingly reveals gender may well be a cultural construct, but it must be embodied and sculpted from the tissue and sinew of fleshy acts if it is to retain any meaning. In this way, 'The body provides a powerful and ready tool for introducing imaginative thought. It is both an object of cultural attention and a means of cultural communication.

Kaguru sensibly make it the focus of ethnic memory and identity' (p. 251). Evidently Kaguru are living testimony to what Judith Butler (1993) has termed 'bodies that matter'.

However, we would be mistaken in presuming that initiation ceremonies are simply exercises in power, carried out solely as a means of securing the gender order. Rather, these corporeal acts are implicated in a broader matrix of social experience. Kaguru live in a shrinking world where modernization and global change have the potential to profoundly alter traditional ways of life. However, traditions are themselves cultural inventions that can be re-imagined and transposed onto new times. Ironically the act of cutting and separation is one of the primary means through which Kaguru are able to bind together tradition, community and ethnicity in the ritual preservation of an identity 'under siege'. The threat posed from global forces and outsiders is muted through the adaptation of these practices. Thus the highland areas of East Africa now contain refugees and people from neighbouring lands who may indeed be integrated; initiation is one of the techniques by which this process is negotiated. In this way initiation is the practice of ethnicity and the basis for what we may consider to be a 'whole way of life'. For Beidelman these acts 'are, at a deeper level, about confirming Kaguruness. They evoke recollections of places, practices, and ways of thinking that create a sense of being and belonging to a land and to a shared cultural life. They form an encyclopaedia of Kaguru ethnic identity' (p. 133). In Tanzania highland communities may then preserve their ethnicity through elaborate bodily rituals designed to symbolically separate culture from the external contamination of modernity and to combat the threat posed to tribal living in global times.

Interestingly, bodily mutilation of the type undergone in adolescent initiation is an act unsupported by the nation-state. The nation at once looks to modernity at the same time as it celebrates what it romantically construes as a traditional African cultural heritage. Of course tradition, customs, ethnicity and culture are not monolithic entities preserved in the fossilized moulds of the past. Cultures are interwoven, dynamic and promiscuous processes that are continually made anew. Kaguru are not a homogenous community but are the internally diverse, resourceful mediators of a past, present and still uncertain future. They emphasize tradition in response to the challenge of modernity. In an age where gender roles are said to be more blurred in the West, the practice of initiation is a bodily spectacle that emphatically splices sex into its socially recognized components of male and female. The complexity of these rituals is encapsulated in the ambiguous instrument that is the circumcision knife, from which the study derives its title.

[A]t initiation a knife expresses ambiguous or ambivalent powers and responsibilities. It hurts and kills in order to heal and perpetuate; it heats (disturbs) in order to cool (stabilise); it separates in order to link; and it transforms in order to facilitate a never-ending cycle that embodies permanence. (p. 3)

It is these contradictory tensions at the heart of gender processes and cultural identity that we aim to reckon with. As each of our ethnographic critical readings shows gender, youth and culture are mutually constitutive relations that produce and inflect one another in ever-meaningful ways.

Conclusion

The critical readings we selected provide useful 'jumping off' points from which to understand how gender, youth and culture vary across time and place. The selected accounts inform us of the power that global transitions play in individual and collective biographies. Postcolonial reconciliations, post-industrial negotiations, post-Socialist transitions and tribal resistances to globalization are seen to be lived out in the practices of everyday life. These accounts demonstrate the value of anthropological modes of ethnographic enquiry and the role that discursive representations of gender and youth play. In Part II of this book, we use these critical readings as valuable reference points for further discussion and as useful reminders that gender is above all a global project.

Part Two

Performing Gender and Youth: Production, Regulation and Consumption

6

Producing and Regulating Gender

technologies of production...permit us to produce, transform or manipulate things

(Michel Foucault, *Technologies of the Self*, 1988, p. 18).

When the French feminist Simone de Beauvoir (1972) famously declared in 1949, 'One is not born, but rather becomes, a woman' her insights were to have far-reaching repercussions for the future of gender theory and politics. If the category 'woman', or for that matter 'man', are contingent and forever in the making how, we may wonder, do we become gender subjects? What are the sites and spaces in which this activity happens? How is gender produced and reproduced? Why do so many of us seek to claim a place in the gender order, and if gender is not natural but made can it yet be unmade in the way Foucault suggests?

This chapter seeks to shed light on some of these issues by exploring the multiple ways in which gender is produced, reproduced and lived out in the everyday lives of young people. It looks at how the idea of gender is communicated through the circuits of everyday life – the family, neighbourhood, nation, workplace, bodies and media. In this way we examine how spaces of production are being reworked in late-modernity and how this impacts upon gender relations. We are also interested in the ways in which gender relations are forged in institutional settings and as our concern is with young people, a primary focus is with the Western state institution of compulsory schooling. We maintain that schools – like workplaces for the adult community – are important public sites where young people spend a good deal of their time and are further disciplined into becoming modern-gendered subjects. Moreover, school arenas are also spaces in which young people produce their own gender identities which are negotiated not least through education, popular culture and peer relations. Throughout we maintain that schools, colleges and universities are connected to a web of local and global flows.

The chapter begins by looking at the way masculine spaces are being 'reworked' through post-industrial transitions. It goes on to consider issues of embodiment, affect and emotion in an age where hard labour, craft and graft are on the decline. We then turn to an exploration of neighbourhood spaces as sites for the production of gender, ethnicity and class. Here, we are interested in how schools are situated in relation to local cultures including neighbour-hoods, homes, shops and the local political economy. Connecting institutions to the wider circuit of lived material relations is our attempt to avoid isol-ating schools and young people from other social networks, processes and relationships. In exploring schools as sites for the production of gender we consider the relationship between schooling and the nation-state to investigate how gender and sexuality is subject to a form of state governmentality. Here we discover that young people resist, challenge and overturn their allotted positions and the implied meanings of formal state sex education by drawing upon popular culture and personal experience. In the final section we turn to the role of informal cultures and the struggle for gender power between students and teachers. The informal arena comprises the underground economy of student life where ideas about gender are configured through such items as teen magazines, television soaps, computer games, pop stars and footballers which figure as the motifs of popular culture addressed in finer detail in Chapter 7. This 'hidden curricula' is a space where ideas about gender learning are dynamically processed, contested and culturally re-imagined. These acts are fashioned through or against, but always in relation to, the official cultures. We regard schools, workplaces, neighbourhoods and other spaces as sites where particular technologies for gender production are in occurrence. In this sense, if gender is a production it is one that is continually in the making.

Workplaces Reworked

The women stare almost disbelievingly, wide-eyed and open mouthed. We hear their cheers, raucous laughter and screeching whistles of approval. In front of them, backs to the camera, are standing an ensemble of naked men who we have gradually seen peel of their garments to the strains of popular music backing tracks. This is the closing scene of the globally successful film *The Full Monty* in which – 'for one night only' – a group of unemployed men strip down and get butt-naked for their female public. The film ends with thunderous applause and appears a fitting resolution to the bare reality seen at the beginning, profiled through depression, despondency and male redundancy. Set in post-industrial Sheffield, a northern English steel town with a powerful past of coal-mining, the film provides a telling twist to gender relations in late-modernity. In the restructured economy the workingmen's club is still the site for strip-tease, drink and music, but now it is men's bodies that are disrobed and transformed into a new sexual spectacle. The act of undressing is a potent metaphor for the ways in which masculinities have been stripped of an industrial heritage and must come to perform a different type of bodily labour, tailored and gift-wrapped for the service sector. In the rapturous, humorous, conclusion to the film, it is perhaps all too easy to ignore the awkward question: what happens to these men after their one night of fame (or shame)? Can they adjust to a jobless future and continue to support their families?

While pondering these questions it is worth pausing and rewinding to a previous exchange in the film. Here the central protagonist Gaz (Robert Carlyle) chances upon a poster for The Chippendales, male strippers who are performing in the Workingmen's Club. The following interaction between Gaz, his unemployed mate Dave and Gaz's young son Nathan who he aims to keep seeing and assert father's rights for, vividly captures the impotence of industrial masculinities in the modern era.

Gaz [*Starring at poster*]: – 'Women only?' Cheeky buggers. It's a bloody Workingmen's Club. I mean, look at the state of that. [*To Chippendale figure on poster*] I don't know what you've got to smile about. I mean he's got no willy for starters, has he? There's nowt in the gym that'll help you there mate! No decent woman wants to be seen dead in there [a strip club]

Dave: [*Referring to his wife*] Jean does.

Gaz: Oh Dave, what's going on?

Dave: It's her money, isn't it?

Gaz: Fucking hell. You gonna just stand there while some poof's waving his tackle at your missus? Where's your pride, man? She's already got you hoovering. I saw it and I let it go. But this? No, no, no. You get her out of there and tell her what for.

Nathan: He can't. It's women only.

The above extract is highly revealing of changing gender relations in the workplace, in the domestic arena and in everyday leisure spaces. Other popular British films such as *Brassed Off*, *Kinky Boots* and *Billy Elliot* are similarly characterized by dark humour, post-industrial transformation and gender restructuring in 'new times' that reveal a complex interplay of economies, signs and motifs in late-modernity. However, what we wish to draw attention to here is the manner in which the break-up of an industrial community is portrayed as a deeply *gendered* affair. Women are taking over men's leisure spaces, they behave indecently in strip joints, male strippers are poofs with maggot-sized genitalia, men are having to do hitherto feminized domestic chores and now find themselves barred from what was once a male-only club. Things come to a head when Gaz later reflects on seeing a woman urinate while standing upright in the men's toilets. It is the final occupation of male space and phallic demonstration of female equality. 'A few years and men won't exist', proclaims a wounded Gaz. 'Except in a zoo or something. We're not needed no more are we? Obsolete. Dinosaurs. Yesterday's news, like skateboards', he muses.

The context within which these remarks take place is in the job centre, at which point Gerald his former foreman who sees himself as a cut above interjects, pointing out that he is skilled, marketable and employable. However, Gaz brings him back down to earth, reminding Gerald that he is no longer occupationally superior, 'You're just like the rest of us: scrap'. Through an economic and gendered configuration the crisis of industry and the crisis of masculinity are conjoined where both steel and men are effectively surplus by-product, scrap. Although films such as *The Full Monty* are fictional they bring to the surface key issues on gender, work and class. The film is a useful starting point for trying to understand the production of gender as a material, discursive and embodied form that is lived out in different ways by different men and women.

However, it is not only industrial spaces of production that are being restructured in the new economy. As Halford and Savage (1997) demonstrate in their research on building societies (discussed in Chapter 2), new working cultures may give rise to new gender practices but do not necessarily lead to the end of gender regimes. This work on the restructuring of the finance sector compliments research undertaken by Linda McDowell (1997) in an exploration of gender and labour in the London banking system. McDowell investigates the types of masculinities and femininities made permissible by 'capital culture'. Her interviews with bankers and city workers identify the multiple ways in which men and women must perform gender in order to establish themselves within the corporate testosterone-fuelled world of banking. Each of these accounts points to the power of workplace cultures as sites for the production and making of gender typologies. They also inform us of how middle-class sectors of the labour market are implicated in forms of gender production. This is further evident in Massey's (1999[1993]) study of high-technology scientists and engineers in Cambridge, England. For Massey, Cambridge is envisioned as a space for educated elites, 'with hardly a smoke-stack or blue collar in sight' (p. 399). The world of Cambridge science is overwhelmingly masculine with over 90 per cent of the high-technology labour force men. Massey notes that this produces particular gender stereotypes that associate masculinity with intellect, 'reason' and logic. The power of this discourse, as Massey discovers, enables men to delegate the majority of domestic and childcare responsibilities to their female partners in favour of work they palpably enjoy. This is perhaps an example of the way 'individualization . . . strengthens masculine role behaviour' (Beck, 1992:112).

So what does it mean to connect the production of gender to forms of globalization, family practices and the local political economy? In the old manufacturing period Western communities were often closely knit and tied to the local steel works, shipyard, colliery or mill. These labouring sites produced generational histories of masculine work practices as sons would invariably follow fathers down the pit or into a skilled apprenticeship. It was expected that young working-class men would get a 'job for life', marry, start a family and take up their anticipated role as 'breadwinners'. Clearly, the deeply symbolic masculine codes embedded in manual and mechanised labour had material impacts on the expectations, prospects and opportunities of young women whose roles lay firmly entrenched within the domestic arena. Moreover, the way in which these traditional industries were rooted in local communities meant that a host of cultural activity came to surround them. This includes the development of sports clubs, miners' galas, workingmen's clubs, financial services, leek shows and so forth that enabled work, leisure and lifestyle to be fashioned together. The rise of service sector economies and the fragmentation of human relations is said to be a feature of the compression of time and space in the move to a globalized infrastructure. At the same time, family and kinship relations become increasingly distanced and there is a sense that monetary and non-monetary exchanges are coated in a superficial sheen. The 'hollowing out' is evident when Lash and Urry proclaim how, 'This accelerated mobility causes objects to become disposable and to decline in significance, while social relationships are emptied of meaning' (Lash and Urry, 1999[1994]:31). Throughout the UK this 'hollowing out' is seen where processes of urban regeneration transform factories into sleek designer apartments, flour mills into art galleries and churches into neon bars that make for a new site of worship and community.

For many young people personal development, retraining and extended periods in education are becoming increasingly common in the late-modern era. Increasing reliance on parental support, financial debt and an inability to penetrate the housing market are changing and extending conceptions of youth. Recent years have witnessed profound economic, political and cultural change in young people's life experiences, employment aspirations and gendered expectations. Such has been the scale of these transformations that the story no longer concerns what academics once portrayed as a lifelong 'drudge' through the conveyor-belt of restricted schooling opportunities, poorly paid government schemes and 'dead-end' factory jobs. The increasingly post-industrialised economy is generating an increase in 'footloose' industries that have the mobility to move where labour is cheapest and invariably where workers' rights and union practices are not so well established. The new global economy is no longer tied to localities, giving rise to an expansion of the service sector and the dis-embedding of social relations. This is seen with the growing number of part-time workers, fixed-term contracts and more 'flexible' patterns of employment that are a feature of much of the globalized West (see Chapters 3 and 4). These 'casual' forms of labour give rise to greater risk, insecurity and individualisation. However, as we shall now consider, the changing material landscape cannot easily erode the emotional connections to manual labour, felt, practiced and understood ways of life.

Bodies, Affect, Emotion and the Anatomy of Labour

Although affect, emotion and experience have been much debated within philosophic enquiry, more recently these ideas are taking centre stage within contemporary social science theorizing concerned with the sociologies and geographies of emotion. Of particular interest here, is the ways in which emotion registers with gender and work-based practices to produce a class-specific anatomy of labour (see Hochschild, 2002). In the old industrial heartlands young men, in particular, may still feel compelled to invoke the anatomy of labour through a 'curriculum of the body' based on physicality and a muscular exhibition evoked in the absence of manual work. In a recent study in north-east England (Nayak, 2006) this 'structure of feeling' (Williams, 1973) can occasionally be seen to transpose itself into street violence and car TWOCing (taking without owner's consent) as performed through a socially recognized template of hard labour. Here, particular young men may embark upon an intricate cultural apprenticeship of crime from an early age and compare their illicit activities to a form of 'grafting'. The romantic symbols of 'craft' and 'graft' fuse together a highly localized geography of emotions based on industrial skills, masculinity and the loss of social class privilege. 'Working with emotions' as Walkerdine *et al.* (2001) remind us, reveals that 'The transformations of class and labour in Britain have not only occurred at the economic level', but 'social changes are crosscut by fiction and fantasy, which resonate and implicate subjects at the personal level' (p. 83).

In our ethnographic research in the English West Midlands, a district once renowned for its heavy 'metal bashing' industries and skilled craft work in specialized techniques such as the art of jewellery making, we were also struck by the powerful, affective qualities of labour culture. A vivid example of these emotive structures and the crafting of subjectivity is evident in remarks delivered by a Craft, Design and Technology teacher we spoke with, who made direct links between his subject and the process of moulding young lives.

> Mr Carlton: My subject, making things, playing with things in the right way, develops the kids natural abilities [. . .] They're the most important thing, they're the raw material that we've got to work with, and you've got to work with that raw material. And it's something that I've always done, taken a material and made something out of it whether it be a piece of wood, piece of metal or a piece of person, you've got to get the kids to work and enjoy what they do.

The affective resonance of labour and craft is not only detectable through the discursive mode of metaphor, simile and representation. It also abounds in the non-representational practices of body posture, accent and attitude. For example, Mr Carlton describes himself as, 'At heart a big kid', he never wore a jacket, his shirt pocket bulged with the necessary requirements for a break-time fag and he carried a biro behind his ear in an action reminiscent of a factory foreman or manual worker on the job. He is engaged in what Lash and Urry (1999:45) term 'bodily-technical action' wherein the body is itself the primary instrument. Mr Carlton's labouring identifications are further revealed when he reflects upon current changes in education. 'Eventually we'll have a two-tier system', he recalled, 'they won't be called teachers, they'll be managers and teachers'. The heartfelt emotional connections to local culture are evident in this evocative statement, underscored with affective claims to authenticity.

> Mr Carlton: I'm from here right, from this part of the world. I grew up in this part of the world, went away and came back and taught here ever since. And I've never been to another school – which could be a mistake – but the kids here I've always managed to relate to. And I treat them probably the way their parents treat them and I think that's what it comes down to. They know that if I tell them something then I tell them from the heart, not from what other people are telling them. I try to always tell them the truth even if the truth hurts, you know, tell them the truth.

Such remarks form part of the inner drama and 'psychic landscape of class' (Reay, 2005:912). As Reay argues it is important to engage with these dimensions as the 'affective aspects of class – the place of memory, feelings of ambivalence, inferiority and superiority, visceral aversions and the markings of taste – have traditionally been ignored or downplayed in UK analyses of class' (p. 913). Certainly, the role of memory ('I'm from here right'), ambivalence ('I've never been to another school – which could be a mistake') and so forth, underpin Mr Carlton's account from which we have cited but a tiny fragment. The emotional histories and geographies of class can also be traced in Hoggart's (1957) experience of class displacement after winning a scholarship to become a grammar school boy. They are written through Raymond Williams' notions of feeling and belonging and are played out in *Landscape for a Good Woman* (Steedman, 1986), the social and psychic terrain upon which Steedman and her mother cultivate their femininities. Such accounts remind us of the insights achieved through biographical methods and the significance of working-class experiences. As Annette Kuhn remarks, 'social class is actually lived on the pulse' where 'it informs our inner worlds as it conditions our life chances in the outer world' (1995:101).

It appears evident, then, that the affective dimension of manual labour continues to leave a cultural and psychic imprint upon people and local landscapes long after industrialization has all but deceased as the major dynamic in national and local economies. This is carefully demonstrated in Taylor *et al's* (1996) exemplary account of global change and local feeling in the post-industrial English cities of Sheffield and Manchester. They reveal:

> We are particularly aware of the specific and local forms of hegemonic masculinities that have been dominant in these old industrial cities, as in other North of England cities and industrial regions, which carry enormous weight for many local men, with their powerful continuing mythology and imagery about the value and the community of industrial men. But we are also aware that these are contested definitions, which are now so firmly located and legitimised in local labour markets or industries. (p. 32)

As Taylor *et al.* (1996) disclose, the local landscape of Sheffield had once provided an industrial arena in which skilled labour and masculine prowess could be forged when boys became 'Little Mesters' by taking up apprenticeships in the steel and cutlery industry. Without this material curriculum the benefits afforded by the take-up of a hegemonic masculinity continue to remain elusive. The opening sequence to *The Full Monty* canvasses a tourist information film from the 1970s which encapsulates the antiquated 'other-wordliness' of these times. It stridently asserts:

> Welcome to Sheffield – the beating heart of Britain's industrial North. The jewel in Yorkshire's crown . . . is home to half a million people and thousands flock here daily to shop and work. All this is built on Sheffield's primary industry – steel. The city's rolling mills, forges and workshops employ some men and state-of-the-art machinery to make the world's finest steel, from high-tensil girders to the stainless steel cutlery that ends upon on your dining table. (*The Full Monty*, 1997)

Sheffield, like many other British cities has been undergoing rapid de-industrialization. This is evidenced in ethnographic research on young masculinities and the emotional pull of class in 'new times' within the former coal-mining districts of the Tyneside area of north-east England (Nayak, 2003a). This compares with MacDonald and Marsh's (2005) biographical accounts of young people in the nearby Teeside district where chemical and steel industries had once prospered and continue to preside. Here, it was found, respondents in poor neighbourhoods were 'united by a common experience of economic marginality' and that 'individuals remained tied to locally-rooted, social networks' (p. 876). So as not to obscure the role of affect and emotion so far we have reflected upon empirical accounts as well as the bodily techniques practised in *Fight Club*, the affective resonance Michael Douglas achieves in

Falling Down, the identifications with the white labouring body of *Rocky*, the emotional body-work of 'makeover' shows and the felt intensity of Valerie Walkerdine's essay 'Video Replay' to an understanding of class and gender relations in the Cole family. We now turn our attention to the way in which race and class feature in the cosmopolitan local–global spaces of multi-ethnic neighbourhoods where industrial work is in decline. This backdrop is used to frame the following sections which consider how gender is produced in the formative cultural arena of schooling.

Neighbourhoods: Race, Class and Spaces of Production

A wealth of research has been conducted on gender and schooling including work on teachers lives, the gendered responses of boys and girls to academic learning, the different playground games they may play or the violence occasionally committed through a wilful assertion of masculinity. However, with a few notable exceptions, much of this work has tended to focus on the microcosm of the school in ways that may disconnect schooling from other social processes. Delamont has indicated that there are at least four other important spheres in young lives which may include, 'the family, paid employment, leisure and the search for a sexual identity' (2001:42). Connell, one of the leading cultural theorists on gender and masculinities has similarly reflected how, 'Research on schooling is usually confined to schooling, and thus has difficulty seeing where the school is located in the larger process' (1989:282). An invaluable exception to this is Willis' (1977) enduring ethnography *Learning to Labour* which intertwines work, family and schooling and is the subject of discussion towards the end of this chapter.

The resilience of local cultures and the affective dimensions of social class are revealed in Charlesworth's (2000) moving description of post-industrial Rotherham, an area in South Yorkshire, England, with a past tradition of coal-mining. In view of widespread pit-closure in the 1980s Charlesworth fittingly depicts Rotherham as a 'dead man's town' on account that we are witnessing the dying embers of a way of life, 'the extinction of a kind of people' (p. 1). The impact is the end of a particular 'way of life' and the fragmentation and atomisation of the working class. Within such 'ghost towns' the spectre of the industrial past continues to haunt the immediate present. For example, there is a scene in *The Full Monty* where Gaz and his mates are in a disused factory auditioning for male strippers and discover that the old brass band continue to rehearse and parade through the factory site. Notwithstanding the fading away of an industrial culture, as Savage *et al.* (2005:111) discuss in their case study of British social class in Cheadle, Greater Manchester, one can still trace an 'embeddedness in locality, training in practical, manual skills, and a culture of "hard graft"'. Drawing upon in-depth interviews with 43 residents the authors draw attention to a culture of neighbouring, pub rituals and what is identified as a strong, practical culture of manual labour in which a number of participants are skilled in a trade.

Place, labour and locality continue to exert an important influence upon social relations and the formation of gender identities in global times. What Lash and Urry (1999) term the 'economy of signs and spaces' are evident in local neighbourhood cultures and daily spaces of habitation. In an exemplary exposition of what she terms 'ethnographic longitudinality' Weis (2004:2) revisits the young people she first interviewed in 1985 to see how the American white working class have negotiated post-industrial global change in 2000. Through a painstaking comparison of past and present biographies, Weis reveals how a few young people can be 'catapulted' across class borders but many do not escape the dark 'shadow of the mill'. In the former US steel town of Freeway, gender relations have been reconfigured to the extent that many working-class men and women's lives have been the subject of gender arrangement. She reports how in the new economy certain 'Freeway High white girls strut forward' (p. 113) but at the same time can remain tied to class-bound forms of patriarchal power exhibited through domestic violence, male drunkenness and abuse. Weis tellingly reveals how this 'newly minted class fraction' (p. 92) come to produce and reproduce 'white living space' (p. 157) through shared bonds of whiteness that deliberately position them against, and privilege them above, black, Yeminite and Puerto Rican communities wherever possible. This 'racial border work' (p. 105), an entrenched feature of US society, can be detected in other spaces of production where it may also be corroded or creatively reworked by new immigrants.

An example of this is pursued in Archer's (2003) school-based research in north-west England, derived from interviews with 31 British Muslim boys aged 14–15 years. Archer found 'a more specific notion of "local hegemony" is developed and utilized to account for the ways in which particular discourses may be powerful, or hegemonic, within highly localized instances' (p. 16). The Muslim boys interviewed by Archer and her colleagues are in the process of reconstructing their gender through reworked notions of race and religion. The local and global backlash against Islam enabled these boys to vacate older racialized stereotypes of Asian youth as weak and feeble. In turn, some Muslim boys were embracing their newfound public notoriety as 'deviant' by investing in racialized forms of 'hard' masculinity. Archer expands upon the different ways the competing discourses of race and religion interact, and their gendered implications.

> Muslim boys did not reconstruct these masculine identities in simple or straight-forward ways. They creatively fused 'rude' and 'gangsta' discourses with religious and racialized identifications. As such, their identifications can be read as 'culturally entangled' and diasporic (yet locally grounded). (pp. 62–63)

Global events such as the destruction of the Twin Towers in September 2001, war in Iraq, the Bali bombings and the later London bombings in July 2005 have led to the production of new 'imagined geographies' (Said, 1995[1978]) giving racialized meaning to particular people and places in late-modernity. Each of these events hold specific meaning for the US, Australia and Britain as they mirror back fragmented images of the Other that are cut, pasted and circulated anew within popular local and national discourse. While it may occasionally be tactically useful to enact what we could describe as a 'dark and dangerous' masculinity, as a long-term strategy this subject position is imbued with an uncomfortable amount of racialized baggage. This baggage is carefully unpicked in Alexander's (2000) study of young Asian masculinities in inner-city London where she found Bengali youth were particularly likely to be marked out as a 'gang' despite engaging in practices not dissimilar to other young people. This racialized demarcation is seen to impact upon how Asian youth are treated in school by teachers and the education establishment, while having a powerful bearing on how Bengali boys come to be perceived within their local communities. The production of race and gender categories across the material circuits of institutions and neighbourhoods is then an effective means of embedding the globally available racialized and religious myths of Asian masculinity within the meaning-making arenas of the local and the bodies of those that lie therein.

Such neighbourhood accounts are enmeshed within the networks and cultural flows of a 'global sense of place'. Massey's (1994[1991]) rich descriptions of wandering along Kilburn High Road in north-west London, where she encounters Sari shops, Punjabi Bhangra Music and a newsagent selling Irish newspapers come to situate London as a global city with multiple connections to the world beyond the local. Alongside this colourful portrait of urban living a more prosaic interpretation of the cosmopolitan may also be found. Vibrant ethnographies of south London conducted by Hewitt (1986), Back (1996) and Cohen (1997) are further testimony to the importance of neighbourhood cultures as sites upon which multiculturalism is understood and worked through in fashion, music, dance, language and style. Thus Back describes south London as involved in the making of a new heritage through the production of a creative and locally specific, 'neighbourhood nationalism':

> The notion of neighbourhood nationalism that states 'it is out of order to talk about people's colour' is not an empty gesture but the product of a long struggle over the inclusion of black people within this parochial identity. It is not a benign ideology facilitating cross-racial 'harmony' but a product of lived struggles between black and white young people over belonging. (1996:66)

These new dynamics are also present in other empirically detailed accounts of south London. For example, in an exploration of the influence of dance hall music culture amongst teenage girls, Wulff (1995) describes how the culturally hybrid texture of the local community is further impacting upon gender relations for new generations. Referring to the race and gender articulations of her young respondents, Wulff suggests, 'it is likely that the idea of ethnic equality will stay with them as they grow up to be young women' (p. 17). The studies presented here are each effervescent examples of what Stuart Hall (1993) has termed 'new ethnicities'.

Byrne's (2006) recent book, based on qualitative interviews with 25 white mothers in two areas of London, further exposes how gender and whiteness are communicated in the multi-ethnic metropolis. Byrne remarks upon the way in which a number of her respondents adopt a position of 'colour-blindness' in relation to race: a location premised upon absenting white privilege by choosing not to 'see', 'hear' or acknowledge the opportunities afforded by whiteness or indeed the injustices meted out to those who exist outside its borders. As Frankenberg (1993) lucidly explains when discussing 'the social geography of childhood' it is evident that 'white people and people of colour live racially structured lives... any system of differentiation shapes those upon whom it bestows privilege as well as those it oppresses' (p. 51). In her interviews with 16 university African-American students in suburban USA, Windance-Twine (1996) also reveals the importance of social class and place-specific relations for the constitution of racial identity. Her respondents 'argued that they had been white because they had the same *material* privileges and socio-economic advantages of their suburban peers. Hence, a white identity became inextricably linked to a middle-class economic position' (p. 212). The micro-geography of the neighbourhood, and the real and imagined divisions and meeting places it contain, are then key to understanding the making and unmaking of identities through the complex interplay of race, class and gender formations.

Contemporary representations of the working class suggest growing cleavages between workers and non-workers, between established citizens and new migrant labourers, between an upwardly mobile working class and a supposedly sinking 'underclass'. There is also strong evidence to suggest that gender is a class-ridden terrain for young women whose opportunities in the job market are thoroughly patterned by social class relations. In Britain young women who have benefited from a middle-class upbringing, university education and social networks are delaying transitions into motherhood as they attempt to establish their careers and independence. However, alongside this portrait of 'protracted pregnancies' underlies a stark reality that the UK still has amongst the highest numbers of young teenage mothers in Europe, an issue that various government-sponsored health promotion schemes have unsuccessfully tried to tackle. Strong class differences, then, continue to shape and inflect gender practices on such key modalities of transition as child-birth and employment. This has led Delamont, in her survey of gender and post-industrial change in Britain to conclude, that 'Women's opportunities have widened, but class differences between women are more powerful than any gender-based similarities' (2001:111).

In addressing spaces of production and their ties to the material curricula we are suggesting that gender is produced, embodied and occasionally transfigured in material configurations experienced through the nexus of local–global relations. For example, the changing times of late-modernity have also been characterized by significant transformations in the domestic sphere. This includes the 'feminization' of certain aspects of labour and at least some disintegration of a traditional sexual division of labour, once orchestrated around a solitary patriarchal 'breadwinner'. In discussing the 'feminization' of labour, we are referring not only to the ways in which jobs that were once the preserve of young men are now beginning to employ a greater number of women, but also to the ways in which mechanical work is increasingly being replaced by new technology with a greater demand on keyboard skills, public relations and customer services. These skills have been in particular demand in a recent growth area of employment, that of telesales and telecommunications. The communication and inter-personal skills that many women may either acquire as a consequence of gender inequality, or are simply attributed to have, has enabled employers to perceive them as a highly useful source of cheap labour. Women have also found the allure of office work and flexible hours an attractive option that may fit with the child-care responsibilities and the domestic roles they may continue to shoulder in familial relationships. However, the footloose nature of call-centres has seen a number of international corporations relocate their branches from America and Europe to the East and developing countries where the costs of labour can be kept to a minimum and workers rights may be non-existent. The ways in which gender, class and race feature in post-Fordist economies is then highly uneven, complex and contradictory. In the following sections on official and the informal curricula we draw more deeply on our ethnographic research to illuminate the complex production, reproduction and reconfiguration of gender in young lives.

Schooling and the State: The Production and Regulation of Sex and Gender

> sexuality is not just discursive or a representation, but also a materiality which is institutionalised. (Skeggs, 1997:118)

One of the most formative arenas in which young people experience and contribute to the production and reproduction of gender is through the institution of schooling. Compulsory education is a prerequisite in Western nation states and now a feature of many children's lives in developing countries. Children and young people spend a good deal of time in schools. They learn what it is to be a 'proper' girl or boy. They learn about friendship, fashion and fear; what it is to be liked or disliked. In a multitude of different ways they are implicated in forms of *gendered learning*. Our approach in this section is to explore how schools produce gender identities. These relations also work through sexuality, class and ethnicity, for example in imperial Britain public schools were widely acknowledged as 'nurseries of empire' (Rutherford, 1997:15), implicated in a very particular 'making of men' (Mac an Ghaill, 1994) that was manufactured through whiteness, Englishness and upper-middle-class masculinity. We ask, how then is gender made and reproduced in institutional environments such as the school, what is the relationship between gender and power and how are these relations reconfigured in daily interactions?

In order for nation-states to effectively articulate gender ideals they have to be communicated and mediated by teachers, parents, religious leaders and so forth. As Kehily's (2002) analysis of sex education classes reveals, even within one school institution teachers may operate with a different philosophical ethos, for example using traditionalist, feminist, pupil-centred or liberal models of teaching. Furthermore, despite this individual steering, it would appear that within youth cultures many gender productions tend to be resisted, transfigured or simply go unaccomplished. In our focus group discussions with young women we found that Personal and Sex Education (PSE), an official part of the UK national curriculum, to be one of the most striking technologies through which gender – and ideas about what constitutes appropriate gender behaviour – is produced. Here, in our discussion with Sixth Form students, Melissa remarks on the current techno-sex practice of using video material to disseminate information on sex and gender relations within the classroom.

> Melissa: We had this video about sex and that and it made it all very perfect. And you know, it all went right the first time and they had this couple making love and there was like music in the background [*all laugh*]. And there was a couple of people in our biology class who have [sexual] partners and they said, 'Oh, don't believe all that!' And it was very perfect and very straightforward and, 'You know you love someone' or 'When you marry', teachers tend to refer to it as when you marry you see. We've got a particular biology teacher and we were doing genetics once and he's going, 'When a man and his wife . . . ' – it wasn't a man and a woman – it was *a man and his wife*.

The French philosopher and cultural historian Foucault (1976) has provided a thorough examination of sexuality and discourse in modern society. Discourses, as ways of knowing and understanding the social world, generate values and particular ways of being. They form patterns and function as 'regimes of truth' combining the cumulative power of a host of institutional know-ledges and procedures. From a Foucaultian perspective sex education can be seen as a 'discursive field' in which particular techniques regarding appropriate sexual performance proliferate. The above account reveals how gender as a discursive practice is officiated in pedagogic discourse. The assumption, iterated in numerous ways, is that sex is a practice between couples, is about 'making love', is natural ('very straightforward'), is reserved for married citizens, is strictly an adult practice, and, above all else, that it is *heterosexual*.

Ironically, the citation of this norm also gives rise to a plethora of illicit sexual activity between young people, lesbians, gays, unmarried partners, casual singletons, those who are not 'in love' and those who have no desire for procreation. The production of sex and gender occurs through what Butler (1990) identifies as a 'heterosexual matrix', that brings to utterance such foundational categories as imparted in the citation 'a man and his wife'. The discursive enactment of such terms as girlfriend, wife or mother, accrue greater intelligibility as they come to be defined and institutionally iterated through the repetition of these norms. These words condense an encyclopaedia of cultural understanding and knowledge about sex that is ideological and powerful. As Foucault states, 'The family was the crystal in the deployment of sexuality' (1976:11), precisely because it provided an invaluable framework through which state norms about sex, procreation and gender could be envisioned and reproduced. This metaphor of production is eloquently captured by Weeks who describes the making of modern sex as 'a transmission belt for a wide variety of needs and desire' (1986:11). In the extract the discursive production of sex and gender is now occurring through the intermeshing technologies of video and pedagogy where a multitude of words, images and even music combine to present an ideal high-resolution future vision of appropriate gender behaviour within the intimate spectacle of sexual practice. As Skeggs notes, 'sexuality and gender are the product of representation and reiteration produced through various technologies, institutional organisation and discourse, epistemologies and practices. They are material practices' (1997:120–121). These images are also endowed with powerful imaginary tropes of identification. For the French philosopher Baudrillard (1983:51), the image of the family is inevitably 'hyper-real'. It is an effect of the dazzling glare of the American Dream refracted back to us in the consumer spectacle of car and house ownership, having the 'right' number of children and possession of what he describes as an 'ornamental housewife'. Baudrillard regards the flawlessness of these images as an effect of the 'precession of simulacra'; however, not unlike the impossibility of Butler's heterosexual matrix, 'it is this statistical perfection which dooms it to death' (1983:51).

The disciplining of sexual practices is a key theme in Foucault's volumes on the 'history of sexuality' where he mines what amounts to an archaeology of social production. He claims that since the seventeenth century there has been a 'discursive explosion' in the field of sexuality, as the state attempts to incorporate the irrational excesses of the sexual into the rational order of the state. Foucault reports on the administration of sexuality where, 'Through the political economy of population there was formed a whole grid of observations regarding sex' (1976:26). This regulation was based on the notion that sex is 'precocious, active and ever present' (1976:28) in society. However, we would be mistaken in believing that this process of policing is entirely repressive. For Foucault discourses are *productive* with subjects embedded in the strictly relational character of power relationships. He ascertains that 'points of resistance are present everywhere in the power network' (1976:95) and distributed in irregular fashion across a dense capillary of nodes. This 'multiplicity of force relations' (1976:92) is evident in the extract where power, though present in the teaching of sex education, simultaneously enables students to divulge in what is a highly sophisticated critique of gender relations. The Foucaultian impulse that 'power-is-everywhere' is apparent when young people with sexual partners extrapolate the video images from the perfect context of sexual bliss; when students giggle at the faux music in the video used to convey an ambience of sexual ease; and when they undertake in critical reflections on the teacher's wilful assumption that sex is a practice that occurs only within the discursive regime of an adult loving marriage.

Furthermore, ideas about gender and sexuality are inscribed into the built environment of the school. Gordon *et al.* (2000) provide a detailed discussion of how time and space in school is carefully regulated where entrance into this world immediately submits citizens to becoming bound by a disciplinary regime. But despite these considerations subversive activity is not so easily contained. One Head Teacher we spoke with openly admitted, 'There's unlimited scope for delinquency isn't there? Whether it's smoking behind the gym or bullying or stealing or vandalism'. Schools are also part of the gender order and may move towards the regulation of sexuality as Foucault (1976) shows in his analysis of eighteenth century secondary schools. Here, he considers the space of the classroom, the shape of the desks, the seating or sleeping arrangements of institutions and the broader panoptical modes of surveillance embodied in the architecture of schools. This leads him to remark how 'one only has to glance over the architectural layout, the rules of discipline, and their whole internal organization: the question of sex was a constant preoccupation. The builders considered it explicitly. The organizers took it permanently into account' (pp. 27–28). However, despite this excessive spatial regulation there is also much that goes unsaid in the production of gender and sexuality. As we have seen this includes the resounding silence surrounding sexual practices amongst young people and the ways in which unmarried sex and homosexuality are discursively bracketed out of the teaching of much PSE. Foucault explains how such silences and absences constitute 'an integral part of the strategies that underlie and permeate discourses' (p. 27).

One of the most patent recurring absences identified to us by Year 9 students (age 14–15 years) in the teaching of sex education was the lack of *emotional* content. 'They just warn you about pregnancy', complained Susan, 'how it all works inside', before going on to add that teachers, 'don't tell you if it hurts or bleeds or anything'. For many students sex education was a disembodied unemotional experience, often reduced to what Libby flatly describes as, 'The sperm and the egg and that'. As another young woman, Sam, went on to comment, 'It's mainly if you want to get pregnant, and they tell you all about what happens and everything'. This discourse forms part of what Foucault describes as the 'medical technologies of sex' (p. 119), that serve to construct (hetero)sexual norms through reproduction and the regulation of the body. It is a discourse that absents pleasure, emotional uncertainty and desire. As Melissa, the Sixth Former we heard from above reflects, 'They didn't go into feelings and responsibilities and misunderstandings and confusions and things like that. It was basically "take precautions!" '

The production of sexual practices can then have particular regulatory effects upon the activities and spaces which young women can inhabit, warning them of pregnancy and impinging upon their social relationships. Thus Emma explains how in her class, 'We got shown all sorts of contraceptives and we were told by the Head Teacher that we should never, ever, set foot in a pub!'. The limits of sexual pedagogy and its complex relationship to popular culture and lived social experience are further elaborated in discussions with this cohort.

> Anoop: How would your experiences of relationships compare with what you learnt in the classroom?
> Sam: It doesn't.
> Julie: What they teach us, we already know. It's just a waste of time.
> Emma: I think it depends on which teacher you have.
> Anoop: What they teach you at your age now, how do you get to know that then?
> Julie: Like Nicky says, from magazines and everything, television.
> Nicky: I think we probably know more than our teachers do [. . .] Like all the new stuff that's coming out.
> Julie: She's like asking us questions and we're saying things back to her and she goes, 'God, you know more than I do!'.

The discursive absences on gender and sexuality evident in the official curriculum meant that nearly all the students we spoke with regarded popular culture and friendship groups as vital arenas for sex-gender learning. As Claire explained, 'Some of the teachers don't know how to approach it [sex education], they're not sure how they should approach it, so it makes it difficult for us to approach them'. 'I wouldn't be able to ask a teacher', Julie concurred, 'I'd have to ask a friend who'd experienced it because teachers are so difficult to talk to'. While some young people were able to seek sound parental guidance on sexual issues, usually from mothers, a number maintained that they would avoid asking questions as they feared parents would immediately equate this curiosity with impending sexual activity. As Lucy commented, 'They might think that I'm *doing it* or something!' Recalling one conversation with her mother she went on to remark, 'When I was going out with my boyfriend she goes, "Just remember you're only fifteen. When you're sixteen [the legal age for consenting adults in the UK to have sex] a lot of older boys will want to go further"'. Although the official doctrine on sex is invoked, its discursive limitations become apparent. The suggestion is that young people below 16 years will refrain from sexual intercourse on grounds of legality (an unlikely scenario) or that once this watershed is reached a sudden explosion of sexual activity may occur (a source of moral panic). At the same time, Lucy's gender is constituted as that of a passive young woman at risk from predatory males fuelled by testosterone: 'She said to just beware, just be careful, you know what they're like'. Despite a host of media-saturated images related to women's sexual fulfilment – going for it and getting it – many teenage girls remained only too aware of the personal costs engendered if this sexually active role was adopted at an early age. 'I wouldn't do it anyway', opined Nicky, 'because I know that you get a reputation here like – I don't know. It's just that girls get called slags, boys get called studs. Boys get a pat on the back and girls get abuse'.

As previously noted one of the most poignant absences in the official curricula of gender production concerns the ever-abject identity of homosexuality. Following Foucault, Weeks (1985), a leading British historian on sexuality, has painstakingly shown how the making of the 'homosexual' is very much a modern invention. This was not because same-sex practices between men – for it was men that the term initially encompassed – was not already in occurrence, but, rather, that the incitement to discourse was part of the project of modernity to classify and designate all sexual activities in order to establish sex-gender norms. For Foucault the 'persecution of peripheral sexualities' (1990:42) has the effect of enabling the diverse proliferation of sexual acts to become located onto the locus of the individual, marking them out through a new vocabulary, a scarlet letter, as 'perverse'. Thus he famously declares, where 'The sodomite had been a temporary aberration; the homosexual was now a species' (p. 43).

The idea that homosexuality can be 'spotted' commonly features in young people's accounts (see Chapter 8), but is occasionally expressed by teachers.

> Miss Green: I remember one lad I taught, name was Malcolm. Became a hairdresser. I always knew where I could find Malcolm. He'd be smoking at the back of the school on his own, but he was isolated. I knew why he was isolated, the other kids had some gut feeling he was different. I suspect that Malcolm at the earlier age didn't know why he was being

isolated. Well, he wouldn't know why he was different, but there must be kids here [that are also gay].

The manner in which Malcolm is identified as 'different' suggests that homo-sexuality is defined against a prevailing normative version of heterosexuality. As Rasmussen recently affirms, 'Rather than striving for equal recognition of diverse sexual identities, it might be preferable to continue to problematize the privileges associated with heterosexual identities and to examine further their relation to the subjection of homosexual identities' (2006:14). Above, there is a powerful sense that teachers and students can 'spot' gay individuals at an instinctive level based on 'gut feeling'. Strangely enough, there is a belief that although Malcolm may have not 'worked out' his sexuality, those around him already have done so. Malcolm's isolation is blamed on his difference, a discourse which serves to absent the school and the actors therein as culpable of homophobia. For writers on sexuality such as Foucault, Dollimore (1996[1991]) and Weeks (1986) it is the context and meanings that surround sexuality, rather than sexual practices themselves, that are of political and theoretical interest. This approach offers a useful framing device for interpreting the absence of discussion around non-heterosexual practices in school.

> Melissa: It's one thing that's never been discussed, we had a lady from the council come in and do sexism – discrimination against the sexes – and we were saying, 'Why can't we talk about homosexuality?' And apparently teachers are not allowed to talk about it, there's some government rule or something, they're not allowed to discuss it in class because they're not allowed to promote homosexuality [. . .] And cos you talk about it doesn't mean you're going to turn into a homosexual does it? A homosexual is something that you are, something you've developed not cos you've talked about it – but apparently you're not allowed to talk about it. We'd just like to know more about it you know, just understand it more. People use it as a term of abuse because they don't understand it.

The government ruling described above refers to the, now repealed, Section 28 of the Local Government (Amendment) Act which came into force in Britain on May 24, 1988. The Act states that local authorities shall not 'intention-ally promote homosexuality' (1 a), before further adding, that homosexuality should not be discussed as an acceptable 'family relationship' (1 b). Although this carefully worded ruling, imposed by the Conservative government did not specifically apply to the teaching of sexuality in schools many education institutions felt impelled to avoid the topic altogether for fear of state and media reprisals (see Watney, 1991; Smith, 1994; Epstein and Johnson, 1998). This is something that has not gone unnoticed in student cultures with Emma commenting, 'I think you need to be educated about gays and lesbians. I really do. But you're not. I think the people need to know'. That non-heterosexual kinship relations should be set outside the nexus of 'the family' once again invokes the powerful symbolic and material value of this unit. For Foucault this exclusion, this 'frozen countenance of the perversions is a fixture of this game' (p. 48). And yet, as Melissa remarks above, the silencing of homosexuality from the official curricula only acts to intensify the discursive power of sexuality, willing homosexuality to life and bringing it to bear on the gendered field of student relations often by way of abuse, as we shall now consider.

Informal Cultures: Teachers, Students and the Struggle for Gender Power

Through meticulous observations of gender practices amongst elementary school children (aged 9–10 years) in North America, Thorne's (1993) ethnography provides a fertile base from which to view the production and reproduction of gender (see Chapter 1). In recognizing that boys and girls were not perpetually engaged in the enactment of opposite 'sex roles' Thorne challenges convention by focusing, instead, upon the variety of situated relationships between students in classrooms, playgrounds and school corridors. Thorne develops the term 'borderwork' to explain the different situations in which gender boundaries are deployed and consolidated through single sex alliances. She regards borderwork as an incessant process in which gender boundaries may become demarcated through dress, sport, chasing games, jokes and a host of discursive cultural activity. However, there are also points where gender-appropriate behaviour is transgressed resulting in what Thorne terms, 'border crossing'. So, though gender difference is always in the making, it can also be reshaped, devalued and unmade. This work points to the gender-bound limitations of sex role theories. 'In this sense gender', observes Bob Connell, 'even in its most elaborate, abstract or fantastic forms, is always an "accomplishment"' (2002:55).

A further exploration of the accomplishment of gender is provided by McLeod and Yates (2006) longitudinal study of 26 young Australians from diverse backgrounds across four different schools. Interviewing the young men and women over a seven-year period from age 12–18 years, their study illustrates the ways in which schools become sources of biographical meanings, values and trajectories over time. Taking a longitudinal perspective allows McLeod and Yates to look forward and back, to explore the temporality of young people's self-narration across time and in relation to their contemporaries. Focusing upon the impact of two decades of feminist and gender reform on Australian schools and students, McLeod and Yates are mindful of schools as sites of reproduction and rupture as the ripple effects of de-traditionalization and globalization are felt in everyday life. Their empirical story finds that aspects of both change and reproduction characterize gender relations and gender identity in Australian schools. McLeod and Yates explore young people's subjective approach to gender as a generative account of 'being in the world' (2006:191) in which gender may remain acknowledged or not consciously spoken. Pursuing this approach points to the unevenness of social change in young lives, the difficulties for some of accessing 'choice biographies' and the emergence of new forms of traditionalization. Most young people in their study agreed that gender discrimination was no longer prevalent and that gender was not necessarily an indication of future possibilities, however, normative narratives of gender and traditional modes of dominance such as 'males are just normal' (2006:215) persisted.

In keeping with McLeod and Yates (2006) our own observations in English secondary schools also suggest that while the production of gender is a formative part of children's and young people's lives, it can only be made sense of when situated in the context of the variety of relationships they engage in. We found that one of the devices through which the current of gender power could be transmitted is in the combative arena of 'cussing matches', what was locally known as 'blowing competitions'. 'Blowing competitions' are hotly contested verbal duals that tended to occur usually between two male protagonists, in break periods, at the edges of the official school, away from the gaze of teachers. Based on the 'dozens', the black vernacular word-play and rhyming games of urban America, these forms of ritualized abuse are a means of displaying a masculine dexterity with words to humiliate an opponent. Moreover, gender power is inscribed into a number of the insults which may be carefully rehearsed, elaborated or invented for the immediate context. A feature of this game-play is the deployment of family insults and sexist language frequently directed at an opponent's mother. Comments we heard included, 'Your mum's been raped so many times she puts a padlock on her fanny [i.e. vagina]' or 'Your mum's got so many holes in her knickers, you can play Connect Four'. As Lyman's (1987) study of an American male fraternity demonstrates the 'dozens' perform a number of functions. In the all-male context, sexist banter operates to consolidate the bonds of an 'in-group' through the mutual hostility of an 'out-group'. In these exchanges the ability to keep control of your emotions in the face of a barrage of abuse is a means of achieving group acceptance through the demonstration of a competent, socially validated masculinity.

Whereas 'cussing matches' may perform a specific role in the context of British mixed Secondary Schools, it is also evident that the production of gender power is a vital component of these interactions. Here Mr Carlton, a teacher we heard from previously, reflects on the venom of these exchanges and their impact upon masculinity.

> Mr Carlton: We get things like, we use to have, 'Your mum's a dog'. What does that mean, y'know? [laughs]. 'Your mum's a sweaty armpit'. It is

purely an insult and kids had competitions here called 'blowing competitions' to see who could give the worst insult, right. Now, we've managed to stamp it out, but my God, you should have heard some of the things that were said. And it was always about their mother right, because this is the one thing that everyone has in common. They all know their mother and that's very personal. They know where they come from, very personal and it hurts. And you get all these brash kids who've been reduced to tears by some of the comments that have been thrown at them.

As Mr Carlton indicates, the blowing competition is a stage for the production and enactment of gender power. It involves the performance of masculinity through the ability to absorb 'very personal' comments with seeming indifference and to respond sharply by drawing upon an arsenal of insults for successful verbal jousting. The term blowing competition is a metaphor for the manner in which masculine status can be inflated or punctured in these routines. This entails an ability to reduce 'brash kids' to tears by rupturing an opponent's ego whilst simultaneously asserting one's own superior masculinity. As with fighting, blowing competitions have the effect of creating clear-cut masculine identities, crystallizing who is 'hard' or 'soft' through the public exposition of power and vulnerability. As Tolson (1977:32) recognizes these exchanges form a part of the 'complex boyhood culture of mutual challenge'. They are also embedded within the institutional apparatus of schooling and shaped in the architecture and relationships between teachers and students. Although Mr Carlton spoke of the institutional attempt to 'stamp out' these volatile exchanges it appeared that milder versions of the game could still have a place within the official culture of the school.

> Smithy: Some teachers treat you like a mate, dayn't ay?
> Shane: Like Carlton. Me and Carlton 'ave cussing matches.
> Smithy: And Mr Wilson . . . .
> Jason: He [Mr Carlton] calls me mum a slag he does. Me and Carlton, we 'ave a laugh man.
> Anoop: He called your mum a slag?
> Jason: Aye. We 'ave big arguments, mess about like.
> Clive: He's a bugger.
> Jason: We take the mickey out of him.

A more subtle form of 'borderwork' may then operate within the classroom when deployed by male teachers who seek to establish bonds with other male students through the strategic use of 'wind-ups'. This shared male discourse enables certain teachers to elevate their masculine status in the classroom where they are occasionally seen as 'mates' and people who 'ave a laugh'. This serves to distinguish them from women and other teachers who may be less competent at male banter. An example of this shared banter occurred during a conversation about an impending school trip to France and the sexual opportunities the excursion could afford to male staff and students alike. Jason remarked that this year Mr Carlton would be attending, adding, 'He thinks he's gonna pull while he's over there, so I says, "I'm gonna tell your missus". He says, "You can't tell my missus nothing, she already knows!" ' This type of masculine camaraderie was something Mr Carlton himself recognized as a feature of his teaching, a form of gender work that earned him respect from at least some male students. The 'wind-up' is also an established part of apprentice work-based cultures and connects with this particular teacher's affective class history and biographical self-presentation as seen previously. He admitted, 'I have in the past said something I totally disagreed with. I wind people up quite a lot and I'm pretty good at it. I can get people going and I upset them a bit. I bet most of the people you've spoken to who say they can relate to me are boys'.

However, not all male teachers were as unabashed as Mr Carlton when it came to the performance of a competent heterosexual masculinity. Here, two 15-year-old girls we interviewed on several occasions reflect upon a mythic episode involving another teacher, Mr Smedley.

> Tina: He had a nervous breakdown he did. She – [*gestures to Samantha*] – asked him for a Christmas kiss and she had the mistletoe and everythin'. And he went, 'Bugger off!' and she chased him 'round the classroom. You should 'ave seen him. His little legs was runnin' like this [demonstrating] and Samantha was running after him with mistletoe!
>
> Samantha: He had a bald patch and I was trying to kiss it. Get some lipstick on the top of his head! No wonder he had a nervous breakdown.
>
> Tina: I saw him, y'know, in [name of city] and I went [*sing-song intonation*] 'Mis-ter-Smed-ley!' and he saw me and he shot the other way . . . .
> He was ever so funny he was, he chased Savage 'round the classroom downstairs, Savage and Shane. Oh, he was hilarious he was.
>
> Samantha: He was good he was. It was a shame though [referring to the nervous breakdown].

The Christmas kiss was a mythic tale that, along with a few other choice narratives, was frequently referred to by the student cohort. The story demonstrates how gender and sexuality is interwoven into school life and is a site upon which boundaries are drawn up and tested. It informs us that not only is a considerable amount of 'borderwork' undertaken in schooling institutions, but these borders are regularly challenged and transgressed. This is seen when Samantha invokes the yuletide ritual of mistletoe kissing in the context of the classroom by asking Mr Smedley for a Christmas kiss. The transgression of the public and private is also seen when Tina sees Mr Smedley in town and sings out. In each case, it is alleged, the teacher is forced into evasive action, telling

Samantha to 'bugger off', running away from her and shooting 'the other way' when Tina calls out to him in the city centre. The Foucaultian notion of power as productive and unpredictable is abundantly evident in a situation where young women, whose power should be restricted on the basis of their age, gender and location as students in an institution, are able to temporarily over- turn the male authority of the teacher. The contestations in the Christmas kiss narrative illustrate how complexities of power – male/female, teacher/pupil, adult/child – are struggled over and given gendered and sexualized meaning.

In a British study of white working-class women in a Further Education college Skeggs observes that where sexuality is concerned 'students are not rendered totally powerless' (1991:130). She argues that in a masculinist insti- tution young women may engage in 'a transformative attack on masculine hegemony whereby female students take up masculine subject positions . . . to control male teachers' (p. 127). For Skeggs, it is because female sexuality does not have an institutional basis like masculinity that it can be experienced 'as fun, empowering and pleasurable' (p. 130) in the classroom. The power and pleasure of sexuality were certainly evident in our ethnographic observations. This is seen in the habitual fashion in which Tina and Samantha flout school regulations on the use of cosmetics and jewellery, wearing copious amounts of make-up and donning rings on every finger. The attire is not necessarily a passive acceptance of the sculptural codes of dominant femininity but, as McRobbie and Nava allude, an assertion of a particular type of 'female-ness' (1984:104), that runs counter to the de-sexualized environment of the school. Samantha's style of dress and permed, peroxide bleached-blonde hair worn high above her head, prompted other students to call her 'Barbie' after the doll. It is possible to read this highly elaborate gender performance as a stylized enactment of hyper-femininity. This excessive femininity is deployed when Samantha, in comic Benny Hill fashion, chases Mr Smedley and tries to get some lipstick onto his balding pate in what amounts to a flagrant disregard of schooling authority. Tina also remarked how boys could deploy gender power to humiliate teachers. She explained how Mr Smedley's nervous twitch could be seized upon by male members of the class and ridiculed. 'We sat up the back every lesson', she recalled, 'Shane was up the corner and he was going [*starts to wink*], winking at him, [*saying*] "Queer, he is" '.

These situated interactions disrupt established relations between teachers and students and glaringly reveal the contingent construction of gender power in schools.

In many respects schools are *playgrounds* for the performance of gender and sexuality. They are spaces in which gender power swings both ways, sea-sawing between the sexes, rotating in roundabout fashion amongst peers, sliding down and clambering up the ladder of discursive gender hierarchies in interactions with teachers. In our discussions and observations with students and teachers sexual innuendo, put-downs, mythic stories and in-jokes were common. For example Tina identified one of the 'Snobs' as 'queer' on the basis that he worked hard and conformed to teaching authority, leading others to chime in that he was the teacher's 'bum-chum'. Jason would tease Tina about prostitution and 'doing business' behind a local department store in a district renowned for sex workers. Whenever Samantha's sister in a lower year of the school was mentioned Jason asked us to 'chat now to Shane McGregor', knowing full well that Shane had been in a previous relationship with her. In other words, boys and girls chose to organize around gender relations according to the situation and context at hand. They insert themselves into the prevailing gender order of the school but in ways that are culturally meaningful to local circumstance. These relations are mobile and unfold in ways that go beyond dichotomous sex role typologies that define girls as against boys. Alliances between girls and boys against teachers are apparent, as are similar coalitions against 'Snobs', the term used to distinguish conformist students. While there is no denying the sexist and homophobic tropes available in student forms of gender production, it is also clear that the meanings of these interactions are highly contingent upon local histories and the biographical web of personalities involved in specific situations.

One of the most memorable ways in which these factors came together is seen in a group discussion when Paddy is spotted walking past the room. An immediate link is made between Paddy as a person and an event in his recent past which the students sought to prioritize. Incredibly, the event itself actually occurred in another school so could not have been witnessed by the students we spoke with. However, this particular mythic tale was repeatedly referred to and became a touchstone for student experience. It is difficult to capture the flavour of the regional accents, the speed of delivery, intonation and growing excitement as the tale unfolds. Nevertheless, the relationship between gender and power is starkly evident:

Smithy: There's Paddy!
Jason: He's the one you wanna question – Paddy.
All: [*laughter*] Watch him go red!
Anoop: Why what's he done?
Clive: He's a nutcase!
Samantha: He's a nutter! [*all laugh*]
Jason: You'll have to go and fetch him and watch him go red.
Clive: Ask him about his old school days.
[*Savage enters the room*]
Samantha: Savage, go and fetch Paddy.
Savage: Paddy's just beat me up! [*all laugh*]
Jason: Paddy's beat him up!
Samantha: Is he coming?
Jason: Watch his face. He's going red already! [*all laugh*]

Samantha: Oh, leave him. He's probably doing something for his own house
   group.
[*Swelling laughter*]
Smithy: [to Savage] What's he say?
[*Paddy enters*]
Clive: [to us] Ask him why he got expelled from his old school.
Jason: Say, 'Why d'yow git expelled!', aye.
Mary Jane: We don't wanna embarrass him.
[*More swelling laughter*]
Jason: [loudly to Paddy] Why d'yow git expelled from your last school?
[*all laugh*]
Samantha: Go on, tell 'em!
Jason: Just tell 'em Paddy!
All: Tell 'em!
You've said it before.
Smithy: They're curious.
Jason: Nothing gets said.
Samantha: Go on!
Mary Jane: No we don't embarrass him.
Clive: Jus' say it Pad, go on.
Paddy: I made a cock outta clay an' give it to a nun!
[*Mass laughter ensues*]

What is it about this particular story that has such unbridled appeal for the
young people concerned? What does this powerful mythic event have to say
about the production of gender in school arenas? And what is the role of
performance, audience and narrative in this exhibition of gender transgression?
We would suggest that the celebratory fervour of the story stems from the
dramatic violation of norms produced in the mythic event. Making a 'cock
outta clay' and presenting it to a nun can be seen as the ultimate transgression,
with all its symbolic masculine overtones. Here, the cock as a symbol of phallic
power has the ability to threaten and shock, a means through which Paddy
can use a masculine discourse of power against female teachers in a Catholic
school. The act of defiance is further exaggerated when a nun is said to be
the unwitting recipient of the clay cock. The narrative humour is produced
through seeing the nun as a symbol of passivity and purity, with Paddy's
defiant gesture crossing religious and sexual boundaries.

Paddy's story is also a 'verbal performance' structured through the social
interplay of 'audience' and 'situation' (Volosinov, 1973). The act of storytelling
is reliant upon recognition with others, as the group interacts as both actors
and audience. Within the mobile ethnographic encounter we felt the group was
providing an audience for Paddy, staging a show for us, and one another, while
watching our reactions. Watching Paddy, and watching us watching Paddy,

generated intense excitement in the school context. It also offered the potential that these unspoken religious and sexual taboos could yet again be crossed in the immediate moment of retelling. The students mediated relations between ourselves and Paddy, presenting us as an interested party – 'they're curious' – and a confidential one – 'nothing gets said'. At the same time we are duly informed about Paddy that 'he's the one you want to question' and asked about 'fetching' him in. Paddy is ushered in by the students for comic purposes, to tell his story and 'watch him go red', before being summarily dispensed with. Our role of audience becomes central to the excitement, where our comments about not wanting to embarrass Paddy serve only to fuel the exhilaration. The group operates as a supporting cast and provide the context for Paddy's one-line revelation. Paddy's daring masculinity is continually appraised through the retellings of the narrative sequence and the collective 'remembrance' of his expulsion. In recounting the episode his status as 'mad', a 'scream' or a 'nutter' – a discourse regularly applied to the Irish – is repeatedly consolidated. It is an iteration that 'makes it so'.

However, this type of student humour may also conceal the darker reality of Paddy's biography as a failing pupil who had to be excluded. In an early account of humour Woods (1976) has described laughter as an 'antidote to schooling', claiming it provides a means of escapism through 'transforming the reality of schooling' (p. 179). In this reading humour is part of a survival strategy, a response to being in the oppressive institution of school. For Woods laughter becomes 'the coping agency par excellence' (1990:191), a means of suspending the rules of everyday school life through 'play', resonating with Parker's postcolonial discussions of the carnivalesque (Chapter 5). Here, humour has the potential to heal the emotional scars incurred under compulsory state education.

For other researchers, humour has been understood as part of a class cultural ritual of resistance. For the working-class 'lads' in Willis' (1977) famous ethnography of education and labour in the industrial heartlands of the English West Midlands, having a 'laff' was regarded as preparation for the workplace: the styles and rituals whereby young men 'learn to labour'. Here, humour is not simply an antidote, but a point of class cultural reproduction in school contexts. Consequently, Willis identifies a 'parallelism' (1977:190) between the school counter-culture of humour and the practices of the shop-floor. As a result he suggests that '[w]hen the lad reaches the factory there is no shock, only recognition . . . he is immediately familiar with many of the shop-floor practices: defeating boredom, time-wasting, heavy and physical humour . . . ' (p. 193) and so forth. In this comparative reading of school counter-cultures and shop-floor practices there remains an 'atmosphere of rough humour and horseplay . . . instantly recognisable among the "lads" in working-class schools' (p. 191). The significance of the local cultures we discussed previously is also apparent in the work of Dubberley (1993:88), for example, who writes how humour 'in school shows not simply that pupils will use the local culture to resist teachers, but that the local culture actively resists the dominant school culture by parody and subversion'. Walker and Goodson (1977) have also argued that oppression is a fertile ground for humour and that its emergence in asymmetric relationships is evidence that power is rarely experienced in totality.

The themes of growing-up, social class and gender power is more fully developed by Walkerdine, most evidently in the corpus of essays that comprise her collection *Schoolgirl Fictions* (1990). In 'Sex, power and pedagogy' (1991) Walkerdine focuses upon the way in which two four-year-old boys in a nursery school are able to invoke a bodily 'male sexual discourse' (p. 5) by referring to 'bums', 'knickers' and so forth, to undermine the power of the teacher Mrs Baxter in particular, and women more generally. Walkerdine's analysis is especially generative for a gender re-reading of Paddy's story, taking us beyond class and institutional modes of oppression. For Walkerdine these unexpected power 'variables' (p. 6) can be explained at a discursive level where subjects enter 'into a variety of discourses, some of which render them powerful and some of which render them powerless' (p. 6). The mythic events surrounding the mistletoe and the clay cock suggest gendered forms of power can occasionally rewrite student–teacher relations. For Walkerdine, these trans-formations are possible because teachers and students are not unitary subjects but are 'produced as a nexus of subjectivities, in relations of power which are constantly shifting' (p. 3). The multiple and contradictory subjectivities enacted in Paddy's story contrast the identities of teacher/nun/adult/female and pupil/child/male in ways that are neither unitary, simplistic or in any way straightforward. Consequently Walkerdine indicates that not all acts of resistance against school authority have revolutionary effects, as early heroic accounts of class struggle had intimated, but rather that these acts may also become reactionary when gender discourse is invoked. This would imply that students and teachers are enmeshed in multiple, shifting and sometimes conflicting discourses. That the dramatic exhibition of gender, as witnessed in Paddy's wilful display of phallic masculinity, may also culminate in student expulsion further reveals the material and symbolic power gender signs and gender productions are endowed with in school arenas.

Conclusion

In this chapter we have considered the ways in which gender is produced, reproduced and regulated in society. We have focused our account on particular sites and spaces such as the family, neighbourhood, workplace, body and school. These are the spaces of production in which young people become modern-gendered subjects. The chapter begins by explaining how workplaces are being restructured and the impact this has upon gender relations. We suggest that the material relations of gender are embodied and that these feelings leak out into the affective domain with a long-term impact upon the cultural and psychic landscape of people and places. The chapter moves onto a consideration of local political economies through an engagement with race, class and neighbourhood cultures. Here we profile many studies that have brought these themes into focus and highlight the gendered aspects of this work. We then turn our attention to schooling and the way in which state legislation, textbooks and pedagogy are regulatory technologies for the production and incitement of sex and gender identities. In the final section we shift our gaze to the underground curriculum and the sexual economy of student learning. By inspecting informal cultures as vital spaces for identity production we reveal how gender and sexuality can become a site of power and point of struggle for teachers and students giving rise to humour, drama and rituals of abuse.

7
Consuming Gender

In this chapter we consider the cultural domain of commodities, cultural products and practices of consumption. We consider how young men and women may embody gender as a cultural commodity while simultaneously being positioned as consumers through engagement with patterns of consumption. Second, we look at the consumption practices of young men and women and the ways in which these may shape versions of masculinity and femininity. In keeping with much contemporary research in this field, we acknowledge that young people exercise agency in their interactions with cultural resources and this gives rise to practices which define and structure young people's lives and gender experiences. Within this context young people are positioned as consumers who *engage with* the world of consumption in diverse ways. Finally, the chapter discusses the place-specific sphere of consumption as an important site for the negotiation of communities of interpretation which shape gendered subjectivities.

In the contemporary Western world young people are surrounded by commercial products that are made and marketed especially for them. In economic terms, young people can be seen as an important and influential consumer group. In Western countries the notion of the 'teenager' as a distinct phase in the life-cycle has been coupled with the emergence of a 'youth market'. With the rise in manufacturing industries and the mass production of goods in the post World War Two period, youth have been looked upon in marketing terms as a specific group with a disposable income. The 'teenager' has evolved as part of a generational cohort with a distinct style expressed in the conspicuous consumption of records, clothes and leisure activities. In the globalized economy youth can be seen as the exemplar of a market segment, sharing common patterns of consumption across the world. A diverse range of products aimed at young people such as clothes, television, music, sports equipment/facilities, books, magazines and games are now regarded as part of the staple fare of teenage life. The advent of new technology has increased the range of products available to young people, expanding upon the battery of accessories and paraphernalia that become integrated into the cultural worlds of young lives.

Understanding Consumption

In *Keywords* (1976) Williams explains that earlier meanings of the terms 'consumer' and 'consumption' had negative associations with destruction and waste. From the fourteenth to the seventeenth centuries consumption meant to 'destroy, to use up, to waste, to exhaust' (1976:69). Consumption took on an economic meaning with the growth of industrialization in Western societies during the nineteenth century. In this period consumption came to be understood as the opposite of production – the end point in a process which involved turning raw materials into products to be marketed and sold. In the twentieth century this use of the term grew with the economic boom of the post World War Two period that made mass-produced goods widely available. Consumption is now commonly understood to mean the purchase and use of manufactured goods, though aspects of the earlier meanings still persist. Production and consumption can be seen as social processes that involve individuals in making, using and remaking the resources they have available to them. More recently the use of the terms has been expanded to embrace cultural as well as material products. O'Sullivan *et al.* (1994) offer the following definition:

> The act or fact of using up the products or yield of any industry in support of any process. Production and consumption are terms borrowed from political economy, and they are now widely used to describe the parties to and the transactions of communication. Thus meanings, media output, texts and so on are said to be produced and consumed. Media professionals are seen as industrial producers while audiences or readers are seen as the consumers of meaning. The industrial metaphor is useful and suggestive as far as it goes but there is a danger of taking it too literally. This is especially the case with consumption, which as a concept implies the using up of a finished product by an individual. Meanings and communication, however, are not consumed as finished products. The consumption of messages, therefore, is simultaneously an act of production of meanings. (O'Sullivan *et al.*, 1994:244)

In this definition notions of production and consumption have been applied to the world of culture, cultural products and communication. O'Sullivan and his colleagues suggest that we are all consumers of meanings and messages that saturate our everyday cultural worlds. Furthermore as consumers of messages we also *create* and produce meanings by interpreting them in ways that make sense to us as individuals. Daniel Miller (1997) highlights the significance of consumption in the cultural sphere by pointing out that 'consumption can be a means of creating authentic culture' (1997:19). Miller suggests that consumption may be more important than production or distribution as it is fundamentally a social activity, providing a site for developing social relations. Following this approach to consumption and culture, we suggest that the social relationships engaged in practices of consumption also make subject positions available to young people. From this perspective characterizations of youthful femininity such as 'ladette' and 'can-do' girl are brought into being in the realm of the cultural where identities can be delineated and played out through forms of consumption and lifestyle. The chapter works with this contemporary under-standing of consumption as part of a cultural process involving social activity, identity work and the negotiation of agency.

Early work on consumer culture inspired by the Frankfurt School of Soci-ology in the 1930s tended to cast the practices of consumption in a negative light. Studies from the 1950s and early 1960s point to the many ways in which consumption serves the interests of manufacturers through processes whereby individuals become passive victims of consumer capital. This approach is reflected in the title of an influential study, *The Hidden Persuaders* (Packard, 1957). This study, like others of the time, presents the expansion of mass production as a *bad thing in itself*, creating commodities which lack authenti-city and meet 'false' needs. From this Marxian-inflected perspective, consumer needs can be understood as generated by marketing and advertising agen-cies, which have ideological control over our lives. A common theme of such studies is the emphasis on the power of production and its ideological hold over the individual, placing consumers in a passive position as the manip-ulated dupes of omnipotent and highly persuasive commercial forces. This tendency to cast consumerism as a destructive force is reworked by Bauman who argues that consumer freedom has become a major medium of social control in late capitalism. Suggesting that consumerism has replaced work as the main instrument of social cohesion, 'the hub around which the life-world rotates' (1988:76), Bauman concludes that consumer culture offers individuals freedom at a high price. For Bauman, the power of the consumer market lies in its enduring appeal to those who are controlled by it. Offering individuals choice, pleasure and seemingly endless 'model identities', the consumer market provides 'a substitute for permanently frustrated power ambitions, as the sole recompense for oppression at work, the only outlet for freedom and autonomy' (1988:73). By contrast much other contemporary work on consumption tends to position consumers as agentic individuals, commonly pointing to the ways in which practices of consumption involves the creative reworking of mean-ings, identities and practices. It is interesting to note that in countries where consumption has been regulated and restricted, the ability to consume the products of modern Western capitalism may be seen as a new found 'freedom'. The demise of communism in Eastern Europe, as Pilkington *et al.* (2002) point out, has been marked by the opening up of new markets for Western goods in contexts where the ability to consume has been viewed simultaneously as a form of liberation and a cultural imposition.

An early study of practices of consumption (Veblen, 1899 [1970]) explored the world of the nouveau riche in late-nineteenth century America. Veblen's analysis suggests that this group bought products to impress others and were more concerned with issues of taste, display and status than with function or use-value. Ideas of taste have been further explored in more recent work by Bourdieu (1984) who suggests that identities are produced through practices of 'distinction'. Bourdieu argues that culture is concerned with the processes of identification and differentiation that allow individuals to distinguish themselves from others. Through the practices of consumption individuals and groups exercise cultural capital, express taste and articulate a sense of identity. Such practices point to the potential for consumption to become a 'moral project' (Miller, 1997:47), a vehicle for the expression of priorities, judgement and choice. Bourdieu uses the concept of 'habitus' to capture a sense of the cultural environment that is structured in terms of taste and distinction, learnt in childhood and applied in later life. Discussion of Skeggs (2004) below illustrates the way Bourdieu's theoretical framework can be generatively applied to the cultural production of class and gender. Viewing class and gender as embodied cultural characteristics, Skeggs documents the ways in which individuals may be ascribed class and gender as commodities with varying degrees of use-value and exchange value.

Historical approaches to the cultural provide a complementary account of practices of consumption that pay attention to meanings generated across time. Importantly historical approaches indicate that concerns of the present commonly have historical precedents that can be traced and documented. Kearney's (2005) study of teenage girlhood and telephony illustrates the ways in which the trope of the teenage girl on the phone has been used as a signifier of American girlhood from the 1940s. She suggests that in the immediate post World War Two period teenage girls were presented in media culture as resistant to domesticity and the prevailing gender order in ways that posed a threat to traditional Western values at a time when the US was attempting to reconstitute itself through domestic containment strategies. In this context the telephone worked symbolically as a sign of social progress and social disruption, representing simultaneously girls' liberation and containment within the domestic sphere. Like young people's use of mobile 'phones in contemporary times, the ability to communicate can give individuals greater independence while also subjecting them to increased forms of surveillance and control (Henderson *et al.*, 2003). The image of the teenage girl on the phone was used across a range of media throughout the 1940s, 1950s and 1960s to symbolize an expression of emergent new femininities that could be mediated and contained. This period also saw changes in marketing strategies that recognized young women as an emergent consumer market. The Bell Telephone Company, for example, began marketing the 'Princess Line' as a second telephone for the teenage girl in the house whose long calls and idle chatter could be viewed with disdain and amusement. Kearney's analysis of images of girls on the telephone in the 1940s points to three competing versions of young female subjectivity: 'Junior Mrs'; 'Miss Bobby Sox' and the 'Pratiette'. They represented the concerns and aspirations of young women of the period as: wishing to/about to be married; independent and desirous of change; and nationalistic, committed to the war effort. Images from the 1950s and 1960s pursued the idea of girls' sociability through talk that could be ridiculed as idle, vulgar and frivolous to the point where girls' excessive use of the telephone was represented as a disease, 'telephonitus'. Kearney's study offers an interesting insight into the ways in which femininities are shaped by time and place. Her study creatively implies that new and competing femininities of the contemporary era are not so new if we take a historical perspective. Youthful femininity has been seen as a vehicle for societal concerns in the US at least since the 1940s.

The consumption of cultural products can be seen as an active process through which individuals make sense of the world around them and define themselves and their place within it. The idea of consumption as a form of use-value has been challenged and elaborated, most notably through Baudrillard's (1983) emphasis on 'sign-value' and the 'commodity sign', wherein he argues that the commodity has become the sign. The way in which the McDonald's 'golden arches', the Nike 'swoosh' symbol and other global signifiers appear to have 'a life of their own' is testimony to what Mike Featherstone (1998[1991]:65) refers to as the 'aestheticization of everyday life'. Thus wearing a baseball cap that sports a Pepsi cola slogan may bear no obvious relationship to the consumption of carbonated beverage, but it may enhance the appeal of the headgear (and supposedly wearer) through a sign which has come to popularly symbolize modernity, Americanism and youth 'cool'. Baudrillard's conceptualization of consumption as a system of signs points to the playfully elusive qualities of postmodern culture in which consumption can be seen symbolically as a temporary and quickly fleeting form of self-expression. But in these readings there is a strong sense of media cultures as a site of disappearance through a sensory overload which gives way to endless simulation, image hallucination and a distorted 'hyperreality'. The speed-up of media communication, then, engenders an acute acceleration of the image, but to such an extent that we are now bombarded with a 'blizzard of signs', a cacophony of white noise which threatens to drown out communication and through which we struggle to be heard. Commenting on the increasing velocity and circulation of signs Lash and Urry (1999) state that 'With an ever quickening turnover time, objects as well as cultural artefacts become disposable and depleted of meaning' (pp. 2–3). The feeling is that within the 'eye of the storm' reality and simulation are indistinguishable in a 'depthless' culture where floating signifiers, artifice, affective intensities and simulation pervade in advertising, popular music, Internet websites, film and a seamless plethora of media productions. As Featherstone (1998:83) concedes, 'the end of the deterministic relationship between society and culture heralds the triumph of signifying culture'.

Popular Culture and Consumption

But is youth itself a commodity? Like sex and romance, youth seems to have an enduring appeal to advertisers when it comes to face-creams, fashion or food. So is it necessarily helpful to follow economically derived conceptualizations of youth as if they bespeak a social category that has salience in and of itself? Skeggs (2004) takes an innovative approach to the domain of the cultural by demonstrating the ways in which categorizations of class, gender and race can be ascribed meaning and value through culture. Following Bourdieu's analyses of class, culture and taste, Skeggs develops a rich framework for applying economic delineations to the realm of the cultural. She identifies four processes at work in the cultural making of class: inscription; exchange valuing; institutionalization; and perspective. Crucially these processes work at the level of the body to produce cultural characteristics that fix and constrain some social groups, while enabling others to become resourceful and mobile.

Attention to the workings of these processes entails looking at the positioning of groups and their ability (or otherwise) to move through social space by exchanging their cultural characteristics for forms of social and/or symbolic capital. In an adaptation of Marxian terminology Skeggs uses the term 'use value' to denote an individual or group's sense of self-worth and 'exchange value' to suggest that cultural characteristics can be hierarchically appraised in the symbolic economy of the cultural, in varying measures, as valuable, desirable or worthless. Exchange value, however, cannot be reduced to the economic, rather it is informed by the symbolic value of the object being exchanged and the relationships that make exchange possible. Skeggs concludes that symbolic exchange enables culture to be used as a form of 'property' to be accumulated by (certain, usually middle-class) modern subjects, increasing their value and ability to move across social space. Viewed from this perspective, the domain of the cultural acquires significance as a site of embodied social practice that is imbued with meaning and value:

> What we learn to recognize as race and class are not just classification or social positions but an amalgam of features of a culture that are read onto bodies as personal dispositions which themselves have been generated through systems of inscription in the first place. (2004:1)

Skeggs documents the many ways in which social class can be known and spoken through the cultural. The act of 'reading onto bodies' also ascribes gender, sexuality and race to bodies in ways that can be both productive and negative. She gives the example of black masculinity as a form of racial inscription that essentializes the black subject as cool, hip and glamorously non-conformist. In certain contexts, black cool may be ascribed to black males as a highly prized commodity with exchange value, to be appropriated by white males seeking rebel status without incurring the loss of cultural privilege. The exchange is of course one way as young black men become fixed by an inscription that remains an optional and shifting form of enhancement for white males. In a discussion of cosmopolitanism later in this chapter we shall demonstrate how these exchanges are increasingly more complex and at a global level extend beyond this more familiar black–white binary. A further example is provided in Skeggs' (1997) earlier ethnographic study of white working-class young women in the UK. Here she demonstrated the way working-class femininity was symbolically positioned as morally lacking and worthless. However, unlike the subjects of black masculinity, Skeggs' study pointed to the young women's ability to contest their positioning within the symbolic economy by generating their own alternative systems of value for *becoming respectable*.

An identifiable theme in Skeggs' work is a concern with the negative associations surrounding working-class femininity. Femininity can be understood as a class-based property premised upon appearance – what you look like serves as shorthand for who you are, defining at a glance feminine identity, behaviour and morality. Skeggs argues that appearance operates as a condensed signifier of class in which negative value is attributed to working-class forms of embodiment and adornment. Representations in popular media play a key role in giving symbolic shape to the meanings of class:

> Understanding representation is central to any analysis of class. Representation works with a logic of supplementarity, condensing fears and anxieties into one classed symbol . . . The proliferation and reproduction of classed representations over such a long period of time demonstrates the understated ubiquity of class, showing how it is continually referenced, even when not directly spoken. (2004:117)

Seen from this perspective, class exists as a process that works through evaluation, moral attribution and authorization. Skeggs suggests that representations of the working class are one of the ways in which the middle class create value for themselves. Within the symbolic economy working-class women are commonly assumed to embody a style of feminine excess, denoting an overly abundant and unruly sexuality that places them dangerously close to the reviled figure of the prostitute. The fecundity of young working-class women, particularly, is viewed as excessive and morally reprehensible. Skeggs claims that the respectable/unrespectable binary that served to evaluate the working class in industrial times now works in different ways to construct certain vices as marketable and desirable while others retain no exchange value. Young working-class mothers provide a striking illustration of a group whose embodied vice is not recoupable for exchange. 'Even in the local context her reproductive use value is limited and limits her movements . . . white working-class women are yet again becoming the abject of the nation' (2004:23).

In contrast to theories of individualization, Skeggs suggests that mobility exists as an unequal resource, offering different points of access to different social groups. In Skeggs' analysis mobility becomes a classed and gendered affair that confines working-class femininity to the local, offering little opportunity for movement. Young women, however, are not only positioned by popular culture, but also engage in the representational sphere and produce meanings for themselves. The following sections consider young people's engagement with popular culture and practices of consumption.

Dyson's (1997) generative study of children's culture suggests that children imagine possibilities for themselves by appropriating heroes from culturally available stories. In *Writing Superheroes* (1997) she argues that this form of appropriation may be drawn from the media as well as from written texts and can be seen as one of the ways in which individuals make sense of the world and attempt to create coherence out of chaos. Dyson suggests that superhero stories allow children to experience a sense of power and control in an environment where they often have little power or control. Children use cultural products as *resources* to define themselves, invest products with meaning and also use them to establish hierarchies of power and status. Studies of young people suggest that these forms of engagement with cultural products continue through adolescence. Nilan's (1992) ethnographic study of teenage girls in Sydney, Australia, describes four categories of female friendship drawing inspiration from culture and style: 'kazzies, DBTs, tryhards and originals'. Girls characterized these groups in the following way:

> *Kazzies* – girls from ethnic minority backgrounds, usually Greek, who live in less fashionable parts of town and dress in ways that emphasize their femininity
>
> *DBTs* – Double Bay Trendies – middle- and upper middle-class girls, living in exclusive suburbs, attending private schools and dressing in casual but expensive clothes to achieve an American college look
>
> *Try-hards* – girls in either of the above categories who simply try too hard to possess style and achieve 'the look'
>
> *Originals* – girls who embody a style and a look that is recognized as individual, distinctive and eclectic, setting fashion rather than following fashion

Based on her discussions with these young women, Nilan presents a very particular cultural world – of femininity and adolescence – that provides a way of making sense of everyday experience. All groups can be defined and identified by their *style*. Style in this sense can be seen as more expansive than the appropriation of fashion, make-up and other forms of adornment. In the lives of these young women, style can also encompass issues of social class and ethnicity. Key markers of style can include: ways of talking; ways of dressing and self-presentation; and finally issues of location – where you live and what your neighbourhood is like. Nilan's analysis illustrates the ways in which the intimate cultural world of girls is linked to and shaped by broader social structures in ways not dissimilar to those suggested by Skeggs (2004). The following sections will focus upon young people's engagement with practices of consumption in different fields – magazines; new technologies and electronic media; television, fashion and fandom; local and global consumerism; music and dance. In each arena young people's consumption creates *gendered* meanings and subject positions in relation to these products. As such the practices of consumption involve young people in the creation of a 'habitus' extending beyond the use-value of products, wherein they organize themselves and others into classificatory systems marked by moments of identity and difference.

Magazines, Gender and the Circuit of Culture

The magazine industry aimed at young people is a relatively recent example of cultural production usually located in Western societies from the middle of the twentieth century. Publication of magazines in the contemporary period is aimed at a predominantly female market, offering a range of titles to appeal to girls and women across the life course from pre-teen to middle age. By contrast there are fewer magazines available to men as a social group. Despite the popularity and subsequent decline of 'lads mags' such as *FHM*, *Nuts* and *Loaded*, many publications aimed at a male market remain hobby based or interest focused. We will explore some of the features of this gender difference below.

Feminist scholarship has explored the enduring popularity of magazines for women and the ways in which the magazine can be seen to provide a space for the construction of normative femininity. Through this literature it is possible to trace key themes in feminist scholarship more generally: a concern with issues of power and subordination, a consideration of the pleasures of femininity and, more recently, a recognition of the 'failure' of identity, the 'unfixing' of femininity and the impossibility of coherence at the level of the subject. Early studies of magazines aimed at a female readership pointed to the many ways in which the stories and features of the magazine format could be *bad-for-you*, often directly connecting the femininity presented between the covers with the oppressive structures and practices of patriarchal society (McRobbie, 1978; Coward, 1984; Winship, 1985; Tinkler, 1995). Further work has explored the complexity and agency involved in reading practices where pleasure and fantasy can become strategies for the organization and verification of domestic routines and lived experience (Radway, 1984; Hermes, 1995). Psychoanalytically inflected studies indicate that reading practices involve formations of fantasy where desires take shape and conflicts can be resolved (Walkerdine, 1990; Blackman, 2004).

Teenage magazines can be placed within the broad cultural context of young people's lives as a popular, mass-produced and publicly shared media form, which speak to young people in particular ways. Magazines are commonly regarded as a *cultural resource* for young people that they can, at different moments, 'talk with' and 'think with'. In an ethnographic study of gender and sexuality in the UK, Kehily (2002) observed and spoke with young women aged 13–16 years in schools serving a large, diverse and ethnically mixed urban area. All of the young women and some of the young men were regular readers of magazines aimed at an adolescent female market. Many of the young women were aware that the magazines played a part in a developmental process that was guided by age and gender:

> Sophie: I think that *More!* is for older girls really. Like the younger ones [comics and mags] where you've got, you've got ponies and stuff.
> Naomi: And pictures of kittens.
> Sophie: Yeah, there's *Girltalk* and *Chatterbox* and you go up and you get *Shout* and then you get *Sugar* and *Bliss* and then it's like *Just Seventeen*, *Nineteen* and it's *More!* And then *Woman's Own* and stuff like that, so you get the range.

The 'going up' that Sophie refers to can be related to the gendered experience of moving from girlhood to adolescence and into womanhood where particular magazines may be seen as cultural markers in the developmental process. McRobbie (1978; 1981; 1991) has commented on the ways in which *Jackie* magazine of the 1970s introduced girls to adolescence by mapping out the personal terrain, 'outlining its landmarks and characteristics in detail and stressing the problematic features as well as fun' (1991:83). McRobbie's analysis of *Jackie* argues that the different features of the magazine were involved in reproducing a culture of femininity that cohered around the concept of romance. From this perspective *Jackie* can be seen as preparatory literature for a feminine rather than a feminist career. The search for a 'fella', the privileging of true love and the emphasis upon repetitive beauty routines can be read and understood as an induction into the future world of marriage and domestic labour.

Barker's (1989) study of comics and magazines suggests other ways of looking at girls' magazines which challenges the feminist assumption that *Jackie* is 'bad for girls'. Barker's analysis suggests that a history of production can contribute to our understanding of the ways in which magazines can be seen as specific cultural products, produced within a context of technical constraints and compromises which change over time. Factors relating to the technology of magazine production such as machinery, financial resources, artistic input and marketing complicate notions of ideological 'reproduction', forming part of Johnson's elaborate 'circuit of culture' (1986:283) that exists between texts and readers. Thus seeing *Jackie* as an ideological purveyor of femininity overlooks many other factors which make the magazine what it is. Barker's reading of *Jackie* postulates that the magazine has an agenda that is based upon 'living out an unwritten contract with its readers' (Barker, 1989:165). The 'contract' is premised upon the active engagement of the reader with the magazine:

> The contract involves an agreement that a text will talk to us in ways we recognise. It will enter into a dialogue with us. And that dialogue, with its dependable elements and form, will relate to some aspects of our lives in our society. (1989:261)

Barker points out that the contractual understanding between magazine and implied reader is reliant upon social context. The act of reading can be seen as a process capable of creating feelings of mutual recognition and familiarity between the reader and the features of the magazine. Barker emphasizes the interactive engagement of the reader with the magazine, where both parties are involved in a conversation premised upon shared social experiences and expectations. The dialogic nature of magazines as social texts (Volosinov, 1973; Billig, 1987) facilitates conversational flows between text and reader and between groups of readers linked by their relationship to the text. Volosinov's (1973) analysis of language emphasizes the importance of the social in all forms of conversation. For Volosinov, all speech acts are addressed to another's word or to another listener; even in the absence of another person, a speaker will conjure up the presence of a listener. The concept of 'inner speech' defined as 'utterance still in the process of generation' (Volosinov, 1973:87) captures the social character of thought processes as emergent forms of dialogue one has with oneself and imaginary others. Volosinov describes writing as 'verbal performance in print' engaged in an 'ideological colloquy of large scale' (1973:95). The open structure of the teenage magazine format prompts the performance of multiple speech acts. Girls are addressed by the magazines, individual girls' dialogue with themselves as part of the act of reading and collectively girls' dialogue with each other as a response to reading magazines. The latter activity involving collective forms of identity and belonging has been conceptualized by Winship (1987) as 'communities of interpretation' – a term that captures the shared readership patterns and common understandings generated by a social text.

Our discussions with young women indicate that they too are implicated in a textual social dialogue:

> Anoop: What are the differences between the things you learn from magazines and television and the things you learn in the classroom?

Emma: There's more information in the magazines and things, more
　personal. . . .
Nicky: They have problem pages and people write in with their problems
　and you're given like a full explanation and they say, 'Well, if you want
　a book, write to this place and ask for so and so book'. They give you all
　the information and it's really good.
Emma: The teachers just tell you the basics.
Carla: They just wash over it.

Emma, Nicky and Carla value magazines as interactive texts that provide
them with detailed information on personal matters. For these young women a
commercially produced magazine *feels* more personal, addresses them directly
and provides a fuller explanation than that offered by teachers and school-based
learning. They are also sites of desire, discussion, information and opinion. The
rapport between magazine and reader may invoke real or imaginary scenarios
as it seeks out points of identification and communication:

Nicky: In the problem pages, kids write in and say, 'I think I'm gay', and
　like, 'I'm getting like feelings for some boy in my class and that', and
　the woman who writes back says, 'You're just going through this stage.
　Most teenagers do and it's like, just because you haven't discovered your
　sexuality yet. If you want more information then like get this book or
　phone this number'. It's really good actually.

Further discussions with young men and women indicate that the practices
with which young people read magazines play a key role in shaping the
gendered subject positions available to young people. Many young women
interviewed spoke of magazine reading as a regular *collective* practice among
friends that provided a springboard for discussions about parents, boyfriends
and friendships. Many of the discussions were concerned to establish a moral
consensus in which friendship groups 'drew the line' between acceptable and
unacceptable behaviours.

　By contrast the reading of magazines did not appear to occupy a similar social
space among male peer groups. In a group discussion with boys, the general
absence of magazines for adolescent males appeared to generate feelings of
emasculation and suspicion:

Mary Jane: Do you wish there was a boys' magazine?
Blake: Nah, you'd get called a sissy wouldn't you?
Christopher: Well there are some like *Loaded* and *Q* and *Maxim* as well with
　things like football, sex and clothes.
Blake: You're an expert you are! (*all laugh*).

Mary Jane: If there was a magazine like that for your age group – what about that?

Andrew: Yeah, I wouldn't mind buying a magazine like that sometimes but I wouldn't like the girls do, buy it every week, that's just too – I wouldn't like that. I'd only buy it when there was something in it like an article or something. You know, sometimes like when you get into a situation and you don't know what you're doing it would help then if there was a magazine to tell you what to do then.

The responses of the boys suggest that their reading of magazines is more of an individual than a collective activity. The boys indicate that reading magazines risks the charge of 'sissy', suggesting that such practices could be seen as less than manly. Christopher's awareness of magazines aimed at a male readership and his willingness to name and discuss them is viewed by Blake as a form of 'expertise' that generates laughter. As we discuss elsewhere (Kehily and Nayak, 1997), humour among boys in school serves a range of regulatory functions, positioning young men hierarchically in relation to each other while simultaneously consolidating patterns of inclusion and exclusion. In the context of school-based male peer groups, Christopher's 'knowledge' may be hazardous to the presentation of a socially recognized male identity. Andrew's comments specifically see magazines as a manual or reference book to be consulted as and when necessary in order to solve particular individual problems. His expressed distaste for regular readership 'like the girls do' implies a distancing from forms of dependency and attachment associated with the feminine and the overtly rational articulation of an emotional self-sufficiency based upon investments in an imagined masculine ideal.

Peter Jackson, Nick Stevenson and Kate Brooks have worked collaboratively on men's magazines. Reflecting upon joint work in this field, Jackson points to the 'new visual codings of masculinity' (2000:12) present in some of these texts. Thus Stevenson *et al.*'s (2000) study of men's lifestyle magazines implies that these texts are marked by ambivalence. Their audience-based study also found that men spoke of distancing themselves from the magazines, not taking them too seriously while simultaneously engaging with the advice and features. Their analysis suggests that men's lifestyle magazines reflect contemporary contradictions in masculinity. The magazines offer advice on relationships, health and body image, while also celebrating ladishness, hedonism and unfettered forms of leisure. Within this context male readers can be seen as subjects-in-transition, caught between the changing worlds of work and domesticity that has eroded the notion of male privilege in significant ways as discussed in Chapter 3. The ambivalence of men as readers reflects their experiences as subjects positioned by the contradictions and tensions inherent in changing times. The previous ethnographic vignette also suggests that men's magazines serve different purposes and different audiences. As Jackson reveals, 'While media commentaries have insisted on homogenizing the magazines as apart of a depressingly singular "lad culture", our own research insists on differentiating among the magazines and, especially, among the different ways in which they are read by their consumers' (2000:12).

A celebratory reading of the changes in teen magazines is delineated by McRobbie in her work on girl's magazines. McRobbie (1996) notes the ways in which contemporary magazines such as *More!* break with the ideology of romance found in *Jackie* magazine of the 1970s. McRobbie suggests that teenage magazines such as *More!* embrace and display an intensification of interest in sexuality. The sexual content is marked by features such as exaggeration, self-parody and irony which suggest new forms of sexual conduct for young women: 'this sexual material marks a new moment in the construction of female sexual identities. It proposes boldness (even brazenness) in behaviour . . . Magazine discourse brings into being new female subjects through these incitations' (McRobbie, 1996:177–178).

Our ethnographic evidence suggests that this 'new moment in the construction of female sexual identities' is actively resisted by the young women we spoke with. A closer look at the content of *More!* magazine may offer an insight into practices and behaviours which appear as points of concern for the young women. A regular feature of *More!* magazine is a two-page item called 'Sextalk'. This includes an assortment of information about sex such as answers to readers questions, sex definitions, sex 'factoids', short 'news' items and 'position of the fortnight' – a line drawing and explanatory text on positions for heterosexual penetrative sex such as 'backwards bonk' and 'side by side' (see appendix for an example of 'position of the fortnight'). The following are examples of a 'sex definition' and 'sex factoid' from two issues of *More!* A regular feature of *More!* magazine is a two-page item called 'Sextalk'. The combination of 'fact', definitions, drawings and advice found in 'Sextalk', expressed colloquially and with humour, points to a departure from the ideology of romance as expressed in teen magazines such as *Jackie* (McRobbie, 1981; Winship, 1985) and a move towards the *technology of sex* where consensual procedures organize and monitor human activity (Foucault, 1976). From a Foucaultian perspective the proliferation of sexual material in teen magazines demarcates a terrain for social regulation in which the exercise of power is productive rather than repressive. Sexual identity is privileged as a way of knowing our 'inner' selves and, of course, 'our man'. 'Sextalk' appropriates a discourse of sexual liberation resonant of the popular 1970s sex manual *The Joy of Sex* (Comfort, 1974). In both examples the language, style and diagrammatic mode of instruction suggests to readers that the route to sexual emancipation lies in the intimacy of male–female intercourse. Altman's (1984) study of 1970s sex manuals demonstrates the way in which anecdotes and clinical case studies are used in these texts and act as devices to inscribe ideology within the sex manual format. Altman argues that the combination of the familiar with the medical gives the texts an authoritative tone that conceals the fiction of ideological constructs. The 'Sextalk' feature can be viewed in a similar way as 'information' that utilizes 'medical' and 'personal' discourses to impart ideological messages. However, the responses of young people suggest that they are not beguiled by the approach.

So do young women identify with the mediated image of sexually assertive new femininities and the promise of girlpower? In an earlier study (Kehily, 2002) many young women regarded *More's* up-front, 'over the top' approach to sex as embarrassing, disgusting and 'too much' (Lara). The responses of many young women indicate that *More!* literally is 'too much'; its sexual excesses denote that it is not to be taken seriously and requires regulation at the level of the peer group. In the context of increased regulation in school life through testing, monitoring and individualized modes of assessment, young people's sexual cultures may become important to them as 'adult-free and education-free zones in which students can collectively negotiate what is acceptable, desirable and what is "too much"' (2002:207). The regular feature 'position of the fortnight' was spoken about in ways that fused embarrassment with a moral discourse of censorship and self-censorship:

> Catrina: Oh, I saw that, totally -
> Laura: Yeah.
> (*all laugh*)
> Sara: Yes, well.
> Catherine: I don't think we should say anymore about that!
> Mary Jane: Are we talking about position of the fortnight?
> (*all laugh*)
> All: Yeah
> Laura: My sister has one and it had like the best positions or something [unclear]
> All: Ughhh.
> (*muted laughter*)
> Mary Jane: What do you think of that then?
> Catherine: I think there should be age limits on that kind of thing.
> Laura: There should be a lock on the front!

The embarrassment of the young women can be seen in the half sentences, laughter and exclamations of disgust, demonstrating a reluctance to name and acknowledge the topic they are speaking about. Their responses suggest that *More!* transgresses the bounds of the speakable for these young women. Catherine and Laura's expression of censorship may indicate that appropriation of a moral, parental discourse, in this case, offers an unambiguous way of censoring 'position of the fortnight' illustrating their distaste of the feature.

Explicit details of sex or as they put it, 'that kind of thing' is clearly not *their* kind of thing. The young women discursively position themselves as potentially tainted by the sexual material of *More!* and resistant to the possibility of the new female sexual subjectivities referred to by McRobbie (1996), post-feminist girlpower advocates and other sexual libertines.

In keeping with Skeggs' (1997) study of white working-class young women, these young women were also concerned with issues of morality and reputation and were keen to create their own values of acceptability and respectability. The moralism of the young women and expressions of disgust in relation to issues of sexuality find points of resonance with Freudian analysis where middle childhood is seen as a period of (relative) sexual latency producing shame, disgust and claims of aesthetic and moral ideals which impede the course of the sexual instinct (Freud, 1905). In the transition from childhood to adulthood these negative associations can be expressed and reconciled in the consolidation of heterosexual relations. The girls' adverse reactions to the sexual content of *More!* may be seen to produce a moment of collective psychic and social positioning where young women take refuge in childhood approaches to sexuality rather than the older and potentially threatening domain offered by *More!* Of course this does not mean that young women do not enjoy talking about sex or engaging in sexual activity. Rather it suggests the power and agency of female friendship groups wherein, at certain moments, a collective approach to sexuality can be shared, regulated and expressed in opposition to media-based and commercially produced sexual cultures. In this example the subject positions made available through consumption such as the sexually active and desirous young woman are resisted in favour of locally generated meanings and practices.

The comments of young men and women in our study illustrate the point that Barker and Winship make – reading comics and magazines is an interactive activity producing collaborative acts of interpretation. Young people integrate what they read into the texture of daily life and make points of connection between the reading material and their own experiences (Hermes, 1995). This activity may involve overlooking experiences that do not fit so readily into the spaces between the lived, the text and the imagined. Second, living, reading and imagining have implications for gender identity. In Western societies gender becomes an important way of defining yourself in relation to others and in opposition to others. For young women, collective reading of magazines offers an opportunity for dialogue where femininities can be endlessly produced, defined and enhanced. The responses of young men, however, indicate that teen magazines take on a different gendered significance where boys express a reluctance to engage in regular readership or collective acts of readership and view such practices as emasculating. The relationship between reading practices and gender differences indicate that acts of readership provide a sphere for producing and conveying gender identities in youth culture. Here peer group relations play a part in the mediation and regulation of reading practices, where embracing magazines and repelling them can be viewed as a *gender display* intended to purvey a particular masculinity or femininity. Cultural products have the power to tap into social and psychic investments, producing gender-differentiated enactments, repetitions and practices. Here it is the meanings and associations ascribed to magazines by young women and men that provide public demonstrations of being and doing gender. The performative expression of masculinities and femininities suggest that gendered identities operate simultaneously as imagined ideal and everyday practice in the lives of young people.

Virtual Youth: New Technologies, Electronic Media and Cyber-Feminism

Contemporary research on girlhood suggests that the notion of femininity is also undergoing change. Many commentators describe this as a process of unfixing, to be supplanted by the emergence of *new femininities* – multiple ways of living and identifying as female. Aapola *et al.* (2005) suggest that the lives and experiences of young women in the contemporary period can be understood in relation to two competing discourses – 'girlpower' and 'Reviving Ophelia'. The 'girlpower' discourse has gained currency in popular culture through girl-bands and 'girlpower' attitude. Girlpower suggests to young women that they can get what they want and do what they want. In this respect the girlpower discourse exists as a seemingly new version of femininity that can be seen as a riposte to the constraints of the past, an assertive and individualized expression of power. Drawing upon a best-selling book of the same name (Pipher, 1994), the 'Reviving Ophelia' discourse articulates a set of moral and social concerns in relation to young women such as: loss of sense of self; pregnancy and sexually transmitted disease; drug use; involvement in crime and other forms of crisis. Within the context of these competing discourses, Aapola, Gonick and Harris suggest that young women are active in shaping their own identities in new, reformulated cultural spaces. The authors argue that the Internet has become an important site for girls to express themselves as individuals and, through dialogue with other girls, develop a collective identity and attitude. Since electronic communication allows for the reformulation of various sorts of cultural activity, it becomes clear that youth cultures do not necessarily need to be face-to-face or local. The proliferation of electronic magazines, written by and for girls, points to a level of energy and agency that is active in redefining feminine identities and provides a commentary on the 'virtual girl' of contemporary times. Here they describe the activities of middle class, mainly white girls in the US who call themselves 'Riot Grrrls':

> In addition to face to face meetings, gigs, workshops and conventions, the Riot Grrrls network through zines, which are self written and designed photocopied publications they hand out and mail to other girls. The writings take up a full range of themes and styles: angry, supportive, advice-giving, on issues like relationships, harassment, mental, physical and verbal abuse, and rape . . . Zines are often attempts to forge new communities beyond their locales. The capacity to build a global grrrl movement through these media is critical to many zine creators . . . Girls are also turning to cyberspace and the creation of e-zines as a alternative site for self-expression. In comparison to print zines, online zines have the advantage of limited production and distribution expense after the initial investment of a computer. (Aapola *et al.*, 2005: pp. 20–22)

The radical potential of virtual realities are further celebrated by 'cyberfeminists' such as Sadie Plant (1996:182) who suggests cyberspace provides 'a dispersed, distributed emergence composed of links between women, women and computers, computers and communication links, connections and connectionist nets'. For Plant (1998), the ones and zeros of machine code resist the phallic economy of patriarchal binaries and can be productively compared to the type of fused replication envisioned in Haraway's (1990) postmodern, hybrid and open-ended idea of a 'Cyborg Manifesto'. For Haraway the attraction of the cyborg is that it is thoroughly inauthentic, 'a kind of disassembled and reassembled, postmodern collective and personal self' (1990:205). And while Haraway makes little reference to cyborgs themselves, cyber-films such as *Bladerunner* or the *Terminator* series skilfully disclose the fluid intermeshing between bodies, machines and replicants that serve to make any ideas of the authentic impossible through the forging of what we may describe as 'mutant bodies'. Like trans-gendered, transsexual and inter-sex subjects, *Bladerunner* and the *Terminator* films repeatedly subvert and play around with our ideas of real bodies, simulations and machine assemblages. They offer a futuristic world in which non-human replicants can 'pass' as human, where the act of reproduction is as much technological as biological. However, despite the possibilities afforded by new assemblages and bio-technologies it is clear that the relations between gender, computers and bodies are more complex in late-modernity than hitherto may have been imagined. For example the Internet has emerged as the dominant sphere for pornography and the transformation of women's bodies into a high-tech spectacle that blurs the virtual with the real, but in rather different ways to those anticipated by the corpus of cyber-feminists. The capacity for computers to transcend the body should not be over-estimated either, as the Sociology students at Berkeley, University of California, found when working collaboratively under the tutelage of Burowoy in the writing of the book *Global Ethnography* (2000) discussed in Chapter 2. They recall how 'the fusing of body and machine into cyborg ethnographer met its physical limits in the increase in repetitive strain injuries (RSI) among members of the group'. This gives way to an innate contradiction: 'The compressed keyboard of the laptop computer injured our hands, wrists, and elbows even as it allowed us to be globally mobile and connected' (2000:xiv). In late-modernity, technology has also become a form of entrapment in which many modern workers may feel themselves to be 'slaves to computers' as personified in *Fight Club*, forever available by e-mail, blackberry or mobile communications as it penetrates the privacy of leisure and home-life. Similarly the image that many parents have of their children as 'glued' to the screen when watching television, engaging in e-messaging or playing computer games adds to this sense of cyber-alienation.

The more dystopian picture of gender, work and play cited above rewrites the radical potential of cyborg hybridity and transmutes it into a numbing techno-assimilation. It is akin to the practice of incorporation undertaken by the mutant, mechanized Borg in *Star Trek* who must submit, in automaton-fashion to a Collective, within which 'resistance is futile'. This bleaker tone contrasts with, and provides a context for, the more resplendent possibilities of the digital future imagined by cyber-feminists, global dreamers, Actor Network Theorists and other writers who attempt to quickly short-circuit the ever-evolving networks of power. In youth cultures, technology and cyberspace though liberating in some aspects are also found to have powerful regulatory devices. Electronic bullying by text messaging, the irate disparagement of individual reputations through 'flaming' on e-message boards and, most notably, the phenomena of 'happy slapping' (see Kehily, 2007), in which young people use mobile phones to film other youth being beaten up and post this onto the web are the darker side of these virtual assemblages.

Young people's bodies are frequently represented as sites for an emerging cybernetic fusion, encased in a soundscape of iPod tunes, connected to the World Wide Web and lovingly attached to mobile communications from which it would appear they would have to be surgically removed. In particular young women are increasingly positioned as the ideal neo-liberal subjects – flexible, technologically savvy, open to change and in control of their destiny. But how do young women themselves feel about new femininities? How do they position themselves in contemporary constructions of new femininities and what part does popular culture play in this process? Blackman (2004) suggests that late-modern accounts of subjectivity largely evade the ways in which the injunction to make sense of one's life is culturally translated in popular discourse. In an analysis of media forms considered feminine, Blackman notes the increased volume of advice and self-help literature in women's magazines. Women are presented with the need for transformation and self-improvement in order to be successful in personal relationships. In a series of contradictory messages encoded in media cultures, women are encouraged to develop emotional detachment and openness while waiting for a man. Autonomous selfhood is produced as a project of self-transformation and personal development. Blackman argues that the psychopathology of contemporary femininities is culturally produced in women's magazines by presenting women's experiences as dilemmas that can be resolved through personal development. The development of e-zines, message boards, virtual communities, text messaging, computer gaming and mobile communications now suggests new ways of performing gender and youth in an increasingly interconnected world.

Television, Fandom and Film

It is commonplace to draw a distinction between being a fan and participating in creative art forms. The former is seen to be an act of consumption whereas creating and performing are seen as acts of production. It is interesting to note therefore that many young people do not draw a distinction between the two when they speak about their relationship to popular culture. For many young people fandom and performance are both forms of self-expression that make them feel good while providing engagement in forms of identity work.

Being a fan is usually regarded as less important, less significant and secondary to participating in the cultural form at first hand. Jenkins (1992) characterizes fandom in the following way:

> To speak as a fan is to accept what has been labelled a subordinate position within the cultural hierarchy, to accept an identity constantly belittled or criticised by institutional authorities. Yet it is also to speak from a position of collective identity, to forge an alliance with a community of others in defence of tastes which, as a result, cannot be read as aberrant or idiosyncratic. Indeed, one of the most often heard comments from new fans is their surprise in discovering how many people share their fascination . . . their pleasure in discovering they are not 'alone'. (Jenkins, 1992)

Here Jenkins indicates that fandom cannot be viewed entirely in negative terms. Being a fan gives individuals a cultural reference point and a feeling of affiliation with others that produces recognition. For Jenkins, fans are not 'cultural dupes', but 'textual poachers', who gain enormous pleasure through fantasy.

Ehrenreich *et al.*'s (1992) study of the Beatlemania phenomenon in 1960s UK and US further explore these ideas by suggesting that fandom creates something new. Ehrenreich *et al.* suggest that Beatlemania was remarkable as the first mass outburst of the 1960s to feature women. The authors argue that the mob-like behaviour of Beatles fans was in itself a form of protest against the sexually repressive climate of the period and the stifling authoritarianism of the adult world. The authors point out that this rebellion may not be entirely conscious and draw upon Freudian theory to explain the unconscious motiv-ations of teenage fans who they consider to be releasing sexual energy and asserting their sexuality in their pursuit of the Beatles. The authors point out that the experience of being a Beatles fan stands in marked contrast to the exper-iences of young women in school and the domestic sphere where the emphasis is upon propriety and vigilance in order to maintain a 'good girl' reputation. Ehrenreich and her colleagues also consider the pleasures and enduring appeal of fandom for young women. They suggest that stars appeal to the fantasy lives of girls by providing them with romance without the hassle of a rela-tionship or the monotony of marriage. The authors suggest that being a fan is based on activity that is positive, affirming and overwhelmingly creative; in its heyday the screams of abandonment and adulation expressed by Beatles fans swamped the music to the point where the fans as much the band became the spectacle.

Young men and women we spoke with were invested in many different forms of fandom. Soap operas had a ubiquitous appeal for many young people. Story-lines and characters from the soaps provided a common talking point for a range of issues and events. As with teen magazines, the open structure of soaps invites multiple forms of dialogue and interactivity (Barker, 1998; Buckingham and Bragg, 2003). Young people were aware of the dramatic scope of soaps, associating popular prime time programmes such as *Home and Away* and *Neighbours* with themes aimed at a child audience, while *Coronation Street*, *Emmerdale*, *Brookside* and *Eastenders*, placed later in the schedule, risked sensitive and controversial adult themes:

Lucy: [*Brookside*] deals with it all really strictly.
Imogen: Like *Neighbours* and *Home and Away*, it's like, nothing happens like that -
Claire: Just fantasy.
Lucy: All the girls are like innocent little goody goodies and all the boys would never take advantage . . .
Claire: Yes, none of them smoke or drink. But in *Brookside* it's all realistic and that. It's like they've done things like drug abuse and everything.
Imogen: Yes, and then there's the lesbians.

The realism of the 'adult' soaps and their incorporation of issues such as drug use and sexuality forms part of the appeal for young people. For the young people we spoke with, soap operas provided a form of fandom where the performance is everyday life. Following the soaps involved an evaluative appraisal of their ability to capture the rhythms and texture of 'real life'. Soap operas, and identifications with the characters within them, have the potential to challenge young people's views and opinions. They also offer spaces in which new femininities can be performed through the relatively safe mediated genres of television fiction. In a discussion of lesbianism, Emma remarked 'Since watching Brookside – and now Eastenders have got them – I don't feel as bad as I used to now'. Soaps and shows aimed at a teenage audience such as the *OC* and *Buffy the Vampire Slayer* (the latter includes a 'phallic' young woman as the lead character and her friend who is a teenage lesbian) extend the repertoire of youthful sexual knowledge and incite a wider proliferation of young femininities.

Barker's (1998) study of British Asian girls' television viewing practices in the UK suggests that soap operas provide young women with resources to discuss issues that may not be sanctioned within some of the religious and cultural spaces they inhabit. Of particular significance to young women in his study is the development of moral identities and moral responsibility, which echoes Dwyer's (1999) conceptualization of 'appropriate femininities' (Chapter 2), once again suggesting that self-generated notions of respectability inform youthful femininities in significant ways (Skeggs, 1997; Kehily, 2002). Barker found that young women's 'soap talk' provided them with a set of tools to make moral and ethical judgements. Girls were concerned with morally disciplining characters in soaps for bad behaviour and simultaneously to 'make themselves' through such discourses. Barker suggests that girls' treatment of soaps as 'real life' drama rests upon gendered conceptions of realism. Boys, he suggests, are concerned with mimetic and naturalistic forms while girls are more concerned with emotional and mythic forms of realism. Significantly girls in his study appeared to reserve the full weight of their condemnation for female characters who acted like 'sluts'. In keeping with Skeggs (1997), girls rework moral values for themselves; however, their refashioning of gender values may draw upon many of the traditional and conservative features of dominant versions. Barker's (1998) media study of British Asian girls and soap operas and our own ethnographic discussions with young people about film, music, e-zines and magazines indicate that popular culture and the ways in which it is consumed forms a key site for the learning of gender identities.

While soaps offered many opportunities for active viewing we found that girls in our study also spoke of film in similar ways. For many young women romantic film more than other media provided a cinematic template for relationships:

Mary Jane: When you were a bit younger and you imagined relationships
    did you imagine them to be a certain sort of way?
Vicky: Yeah, off the telly, never argue, never fight.
[*all laugh*]
Catrina: Well I used to think that you used to walk down the street holding
    hands and he bought you all these gifts . . .
Mary Jane: What's the reality been like?

Vicky: Much more arguments and fights, get presents but not all the time. In the films you always get the idea it's all –

Catrina: Happily ever after . . .

Vicky: The man trying to please the girl who is nasty to him and I used to think that I had to be nasty too . . . I'm nicer now . . . We used to fight when I couldn't have my own way.

Catrina: You know what I got from films? You know when they have an argument and the woman starts to cry, I says whenever I have an argument with one of my boyfriends I wouldn't cry like they do on the telly.

In this discussion popular tropes of the romance genre are juxtaposed with their own experiences of intimate relationships. The romantic gestures of the form and the promise of future happiness are exposed as 'tricks' that do not retain their illusory power in real life. Themes of romance and trickery are further explored in Gill's (2006) study of 'chick lit' and post-feminism. Gill considers whether the burgeoning of this genre aimed at young women and spearheaded by the success of *Bridget Jones* can be seen as an endeavour to rewrite romance fiction for a new generation of women in new times. Echoing Blackman's (2004) concerns regarding media forms aimed at a female market, Gill notes the intensification of romance in late-modernity, evidenced in an increasingly lucrative wedding industry and the general revival of interest in romantic themes and symbolic markers of romance such as hen parties, overnight weekend breaks, dinner for two. She suggests that chick lit as text has much in common with its romantic predecessor, the Mills and Boon style novel. Chick lit heroines may be sexually experienced with a job and/or a child; however, they largely conform to the values of normative femininity in their search for romance, marriage and long-term happiness with a male partner. The formulaic development of the plot inevitably includes a 'rescue scene' in which the heroine is saved from the ravages of single life/workaholism/single parenthood/dead end job by a man who melts her heart with true love. But, like Vicky and Catrina's viewing of romantic films, do readers of romantic fiction consume the narrative in ways that textual analysis may indicate? As Radway (1984) and Walkerdine (1990) have demonstrated romantic fiction creates spaces for individuals that may be occupied in diverse and unanticipated ways. Significantly romantic fiction provides the opportunity for 'magical' thinking, offering women potential resolutions to the lived contradictions of femininity.

Versions of femininity in romantic films are rehearsed in personal encounters, tried on, adapted and repelled. Among young men and women we found that being a fan and following fashion did not necessarily entail dedication or adulation. Engagement with popular culture was inevitably mediated by the context in which these encounters took shape. In school-based settings being a fan may be a response to peers, teachers and the culture of the school. We found young men wearing football badges and other signifiers of support in school as a gesture of resistance to school rules banning all football insignia. Similarly, as discussed in Chapter 6, many young women maintained a high fashion, hyper-feminized appearance as a challenge to school authority rather than a straight forward embracing of femininity.

Consuming Locally and Globally

Globalization has had a much discussed impact upon youth and culture. A commonly held view suggests that globalization in the cultural sphere produces Western hegemonic structures at the expense of local cultures. Cultural globalization has been characterized as a series of flows from the Western 'core' to the 'periphery' of non-Western locations. A recurrent theme within this body of literature points to the emergence of social inequalities based upon the ability to consume and the ability to move. Skeggs (2004) suggests that globalization offers the possibility of cosmopolitan citizenship, marked by the participation in the global capitalist economy. Full citizenship and access to cosmopolitan spaces, she contends, appears to rest with some groups rather than others, the working-class and particularly working-class women forming the commonly excluded category. Empirical studies, however, suggest a more complex melange marked by reconfigurations of the local and the cosmopolitan in which individuals rework connections with family and community while undergoing personal change and social mobility (Thomson and Taylor, 2005; Henderson *et al.*, 2007).

Further empirical work points to moments of ambivalence and fragmentation that challenges the Western idea of 'global community' and cosmopolitan citizenship. Salo's (2003) study of gender and personhood in the new South Africa offers a closely observed and richly nuanced account of the ways in which cultural flows may be incorporated into local practices and given new meanings. The focus of her study is Manenberg township, Cape Town, a predominantly 'coloured' neighbourhood where motherhood was regarded as the epitome of femininity. Under apartheid, adult women exercised moral authority over young people's position in the community and their transition to adulthood. In the post-apartheid era the influence of adult women was in decline and young people were looking to other sources for a developing sense of personhood. Salo demonstrates that the media and public transportation offered young people access to a cosmopolitan style that had a transformative effect upon their lives. Watching television 'transformed these domestic locales into transgressive hybrid spaces from which new ideas and practices of divergent new feminine identities emerged' (2003:356). In a locality where male violence remained a routine feature of sexual relationships, television offered young women alternative images of gender relations based upon pleasure, desire and mutual respect. Through televisual portrayals, young women 'imagined gender relations beyond the narrow choices their mothers proscribed' (2003:358). Television programmes such as soaps placed emphasis upon individuality, connections with peer group and the dismantling of older, apartheid-styled signifiers of race.

Watching these programmes gave young women a glimpse of new forms of cultural capital, inspiring some to seek cosmopolitan experiences in other parts of the city – an agentic move that usually brought both new forms of freedom and constraint. Salo cites the example of Chantel, a 17-year-old respondent in her study who traded upon her good looks and fashionable style in order to gain access to cosmopolitan spaces and social experience beyond her local community. Her mobility was made possible through the exchange value of youthful femininity suggesting that, in her case, working-class femininity/sexuality can carry symbolic value and may not necessarily exist as a barrier to cosmopolitan citizenship.

Like young women, young men also sought alternative spaces for themselves in Manenberg. Youthful male activity in the neighbourhood centred round the hokke, a building that served as the gang headquarters, local shop, radio station and social club. Through the functions of the hokke, young men in the locality were more visible than their female counterparts, having a public presence that was broadcast through local media. Young men in Manenberg were heavily influenced by African-American rap culture, adopting the gangland style and practices of inner city US neighbourhoods. Their activities challenged the authority of senior women in the community while establishing the position of 'gangster' as an alternative means of achieving status in the local context. Ironically, while young women looked outside the neighbourhood to realize new forms of femininity and sociality, young men's attempts at new style masculinity further rooted them in their locality as their gangland status depended upon remaining local.

McGrellis (2005) reports a similar pattern in her study of young people in Northern Ireland. Young women appeared able and willing to access cosmopolitan culture in urban spaces beyond the local, while young men remained rooted in sectarian structures that harnessed them within local boundaries. Interestingly it is this aspect of Salo's study and McGrellis' work that runs counter to Skeggs' argument that working-class women remain among the most excluded and vilified of groups. Salo argues that local meanings of personhood were reformulated through young people's engagement with global youth culture. Consumer culture and new cosmopolitanism played an important part in deconstructing gender relations and racial divisions. Far from imposing Western hegemony, globalized youth culture offered young people in non-Western contexts alternative structures and practices for refashioning gender identities.

The importance of place, particularly the locale in which young people live and move, remains pivotal to reworkings of the local and the global.

Kjeldgaard's (2003) study of youth identities among 17–18 year olds in Denmark and Greenland illustrates differences between urban and rural locations and their impact upon youthful identities. Using an interesting range of methods such as consumption diaries and photographic life description, Kjeldgaard concludes that urban youth searched for uniqueness and authenticity from a range of choices and resources available to them. By contrast, youth in rural areas emphasized their lack of choice that defines what it means to live and grow up in that locality. In this context being unable to choose becomes, in itself, a site for identity. Significantly, in remote areas of Greenland young people articulated a more collective identity while Danish informants expressed more individualized identities redolent with discourses of the reflexive project of self found in late-modern social theory. The particular geographies of gender and youth are acutely marked in Kenway *et al.*'s (2006) recent study of young masculinities in Australia. By exploring 'out of the way' places such as rural fruit-growing areas, sparsely populated desert spaces and isolated coastal locations, the authors provide an evocative description of the different ways in which globalization is configured in these more remote spaces that give rise to the formation and discursive representation of what they term 'masculinities beyond the metropolis'. Such studies exemplify the way in which place is central to the production of gender identity and how it is lived and understood in the doing of global ethnographies.

A sense of place also transforms practices of consumption in significant ways. While a Western audience may be tempted to read *Ally McBeal* in similar ways to McRobbie's reading of Carrie Bradshaw, place-specific interpretations suggest alternative ways of looking. Ally McBeal may appear as the sad but funny woman in a perpetually regressed state of pre-pubescent girlhood; however in the Slovenian context this way of looking shifts considerably. Vidmar-Horvat's (2005) audience-based study of gender in post-socialist Slovenia indicates that the programme allows local audiences to re-imagine their own biographies. In the Slovenian context, *Ally McBeal* is read positively against the post-Soviet backdrop of attempts to pull women back into the home. Their mothers, the previous generation of women, lived under Soviet ideology in which liberation was achieved through participation in the workplace. Now this ideology was in reverse and the domestic was revered as the new site for women to excel. Watching Ally's rambling and comic attempts to reconcile feminist desires with feminine sensibilities, the programme facilitates space for young women to imagine their own world of work and home.

The empirical studies discussed above suggest that class, femininity, cosmopolitan citizenship and mobility may not be as fixed as Skeggs claims. It is possible to suggest that some cultural characteristics may be highly valued in the symbolic economy and may be successfully utilized by working-class subjects. It is also possible that high exchange value may be attached to 'hot' qualities and attributes that traverse class boundaries such as beauty, style, sporting ability, musicality and ICT wizardy. Here working-class and once-colonized subjects with the appropriate symbolic capital can entertain the possibility of 'passing' in terms of class or ethnicity, a move that is enabled by the prioritization of their high exchange value qualities. Studies also suggest that a sense of place and local context become important in the configuration of relationships between local and global. Through the local, processes of globalization have an impact on citizenship, cosmopolitanism and social mobility which, in turn, take on different meanings for young people, offering different and sometimes unanticipated points of connection and desire.

The diverse nature of local–global relations can be traced in the complex 'communities of interpretation' that emerge around global media. Ien Ang's (1985) cultural studies account of the popular 1980s American soap opera *Dallas* reveals how readers in the Netherlands may derive emotional pleasure by situating texts within their own lives. To research *Dallas*, Ang drew upon 42 letters she received (39 from women and girls), after advertising for responses in a magazine. It may seem strange how a soap essentially based upon the families of multimillionaire Texas oil barons could have global appeal. Amidst the wealth, Cadillac cars and swimming pool cocktail parties Ang discovered viewers were implicated in complex modes of identification. Ang found that for her mainly female Dutch audience *Dallas* offered 'emotional realism' as readers came to associate with what Ang depicts as a 'tragic structure of feeling' that connects with the ups and downs of their own everyday lives. This theme is reworked by Miller (1992) while conducting ethnographic research in Trinidad where he was struck by the way in which everyday life came to a standstill while the US soap *The Young and Restless* was broadcast for an hour. Rather than fostering an Americanized cultural imperialism the soap was rapidly resituated into the rhythms of island life. Miller found that viewers did not use the soap as a window on the West but felt it resonated with the theme of 'bacchanal', where hidden truths are exposed through scandal, in a similar way to the workings of Carnival. Here a seemingly homogenous global product is transformed into a highly distinctive Trinidadian commodity that is part and parcel of an enduring but ever-changing national culture.

Music, Dance and the Cosmopolitan

The global flows of music, images, style and other cultural commodities are said to give rise to new cosmopolitan forms of consumption. As we explored through an analysis of gender, ethnicity and Japanese *enka* music (Chapter 2), these 'circuits of culture' (Johnson, 1986) may entirely rework local–global relations beyond Western postcolonial frames. Here we saw how understandings of globalization, hybridity and the cosmopolitan need to be regarded as much more than just a Western enterprise when Korean and Japanese cultures inter-twine. The specificity of postcolonial relations is evident in Saldanha's (2007) vivid ethnography of the Goan trance scene, taking place in the Indian village of Anjuna. Amidst the tropical sands, sounds, sunlight, drugs and masala tea we may expect to find something approaching a 'global youth community'. What Saldanha discovers though is a deeply divided, racially demarcated terrain upon which rave tourists deploy the privileges of whiteness and cosmopolitan consumerism to make race a highly viscous sign that has yet to be superseded in late-modernity.

Gender and race signs are subject to geographical context. Through detailed observations of *di-si-ke* (i.e., Chinese disco) in Shanghai and beyond, Farrer (1999) provides a fascinating insight into the global spectacle of gender perform-ance amongst young people in China. According to Farrer *di-si-ke* is a fantasy space that allows young people to travel beyond the mundane world of neigh-bourhoods, work or family life to participate in a 'glamorous modernity in which one does not distinguish oneself by class or locality' (p. 149), in the immediate and intense spectacle of dance. The cosmopolitan spaces of *di-si-ke* become sites for new sexual and gendered imaginaries in which the global is not so much resisted but appropriated, localized and transfigured into new modes of being. Chinese disco culture is a colander-like sexual arena through which various foreigners, global videos, urban music and other commodities leak through. Chinese youth decipher, pilfer and make anew these mediated signs of Western sexual culture. By drawing upon the sexualized imagery of dance, dress and musical lyrics Farrer suggests that Chinese youth perform as sexual cosmopolitans. Here scantily dressed 'young women – whose modesty had been encouraged in Chinese society – simulate sexual excitement with lithe pelvic motions' (p. 159). This simulation of image and sound occurs by mimicking the media signs of Western video and the cacophony of musical and cultural forms that interplay and overlap across one another. This sexual inter-textuality reveals Shanghai *di-si-ke* to be a multilayered arena in which Chinese youth are adept 'textual poachers' of Western images, music and bodies, using these resources to reflexively enhance their own projects of self. This eclectic bricolage suggests that for indigenous youth communities a more progressive cosmopolitanism is available in the Shanghai metropolis than in the coastal Goan beach village. As Farrer reflects, 'Foreigners became the objects of sexual fantasy and occasional sexual adventures, but even more so were the mirrors for the construction of a cosmopolitan sexual self-image' (p. 157). Evidently foreigners and foreign sexual imagery can each be transformed into mutable props through which a new cosmopolitan sexuality can transpire. It would appear that in a world of signs, 'image is everything'. Here, 'The disco is a place for the visual consumption of others but even more for offering oneself up for visual consumption' (p. 162), a willing transformation of subjects into signs, economies into 'flows'.

The relationship between dance, music and the cosmopolitan are configured differently across time and space. As we saw in the case of Brazilian carnival (Chapter 4), postcolonial contexts are spaces where race, sexuality and religious discourses are struggled over. In her work in the Caribbean, Skelton's (1995) analysis of ragga music – the rougher, toasting version of reggae – found that the homophobic lyrics of artists such as Buju Banton and Shabha Ranks had particular appeal to young men in Jamaica. Skelton claims that while negative attitudes to homosexuality were evident in the islands of Antigua, Barbados and Grenada, it was Jamaica where these sentiments were most powerfully expressed, often through what we may deem to be a 'muscular Christianity'. The worldwide appeal of reggae/ragga, according to Skelton, came to be accompanied by a rise in homophobic abuse and violence by white but especially black youth in places like Brixton and south London. We would be extremely cautious about making any claims about the links between popular culture and violence (Barker, 1989). We would also wish to look more closely at any constructions of homophobia as a particularly racialized practice that holds particular appeal to young black men. However, what Skelton's study noticeably reveals is that global cities, and the cosmopolitan cultures that lie therein, can also become strategic sites of resistance. Skelton charts the way in which a number of gay alliances in London and New York made record companies accountable for the violent, anti-gay diatribes voiced by their artists. This was to lead to various ragga artists (under pressure of being sidelined by radio and television networks and being dropped by their corporate labels) to issue apologies and disclaimers about the violent homophobic intent in their lyrics. These geographies of power, binding Jamaica and the Caribbean with the production and consumption of youth scenes in the UK and US, inform us of the meaningfulness of place and how particular cultures can accommodate, celebrate or resist hegemonic ideas of gender and sexuality.

Ali's (2003) research with 'mixed-race' children in southern England further offers a glimpse into how collective readings of popular culture can enable flexible, cosmopolitan, post-race productions of identity to emerge. Ali's empirical work, undertaken in three schools, excels at deconstructing and making problematic the term 'mixed-race'. The children she converses with come to identify as 'mixed' (or not) on the basis of colour, culture, the step-parents they may have acquired and a whole host of other shifting configurations and alliances that go beyond genetic inscription. Thus 'mixed-raceness is often about desiring and holding *multiple* texts of belonging and mis/re/presentation' (p. 91). These multiple texts are vividly displayed through children's consumption of the renowned 'Girl band' the Spice Girls who became an iconic motif of the sassy, kung-fu kicking 'can-do' girl repertoire we discussed previously. Ali considers the Spice Girls as a thoroughly sexualized and racialized musical text that is given particular meaning through children's positive interpretations of these modes of being. Her analysis discovered that, ' "Race" was less salient in children's "readings" of attractiveness and desirability than their perceived ideas about *sexual* attractiveness' (p. 171). In short, children had the potential to occupy post-race subject positions in consumer culture where desire could negate the imposition of race boundaries. How race and gender are 'spoken' through the social act of consumption, and how it comes to bespeak these acts, is central to our understanding of their complicated interplay in young lives.

These porous openings are evident in a previous study (Nayak, 2003a) where 'Cross cultural fusion is found to be a refreshing tonic that can at once loosen local vernacular and enable a new multiculture to speak' (p. 10). However, the potential for post-race subject positions to emerge is always bound by the 'power-geometries' of youth culture as situated in the everyday context of consumption. The following ethnographic vignette is developed from a discussion with an Anglo-Norwegian 17-year-old school student who held a passion for black music and came to critically reflect upon the attitude adopted by some of her white Nordic friends:

Helena: One of my friends is like, 'I'd love to be black but . . . ', and they're okay about it. Some of them are racist, I'm talking to them and everything, saying, 'I really like you as a friend but don't like that opinion'.
Anoop: They're racist even though they're into black music?
Helena: Yeah, black music but not black anything else! They wear some Hip-Hop clothes. They go on about how the government spend the money on black people and everything, rather than on white. They don't say it in front of me cos I'll cut their head off in me words, with me arguments.

This extract discloses much about the relationship between cosmopolitan urban cultures and everyday life. Popular texts such as magazines, music, film and soap opera cannot be extrapolated from the stuff of everyday life, to be hygienically decoded outside of their daily contexts. These cultural texts rely upon recognition, identification and, as we shall go on to see in the following chapter, modes of dis-identification in order to become meaningful.

It is widely reputed that widespread international travel, global media and diasporic movements are widening youth horizons and encouraging cosmopolitan forms of citizenship for new generations. As our discussion of Goan trance and Shanghai *di-si-ke* reveal there are multiple possibilities for the creation and transformation of certain youth identities, but these subjectivities tend to rely upon mobile forms of whiteness. This 'flexible whiteness' does not always extend to indigenous communities, who remain highly imaginative in how they develop forms of cosmopolitan capital that are meaningful to their own cultural worlds. As we have seen the openness to new experiences may also engender particular forms of 'exoticism' and the elaboration of 'taste cultures' through an ever more refined palate, what Thornton (1995) calls 'subcultural capital' – the distinguishing marker of youth 'cool'. This appropriation can lead to 'an aesthetic cosmopolitanism dependent upon certain scopic regimes' (Urry, 1995:167) that may still be written through a more parochial and mundane etiquette of whiteness.

Conclusion

In this chapter we have discussed the many ways in which practices of consumption form an integral part of young people's cultural worlds. Earlier parts of the chapter explore the changing ways in which consumption has been viewed as a negative or positive force in young people's lives. We note the increasing significance of practices of consumption as a means of creating gendered meanings and shaping identities. Our analysis explores the multiple ways that acts of consumption create subject positions for young people. Using examples of young people's engagement with different cultural forms, the chapter demonstrates that popular culture provides a key site in which young people are implicated in the making of gender, race and class as both subject and objects of the processes of consumption. We also discuss the ways that young people may be ascribed to class and gender as commodities that can be 'read' in the cultural sphere, providing a shorthand for the location of class-cultural social hierarchies and their potential (or otherwise) for social mobility. The chapter discusses late-modern and postmodern readings of consumption as the triumph of the sign over the commodity and the celebration of superficiality and 'hyperreality' in cultures where new technologies offer both radical and regulatory potential. Interestingly we found that young women could resist mediated images of new femininities at the same time as they enact aspects of this trope but within local contexts that make sense to them. In this way the chapter points to the significance of place and social context in all engagements with popular culture and consumption. The latter part of the chapter particularly explores the relationship between local and global practices of consumption and the importance of place-specific encounters to the generation of new ways of looking and thinking. We conclude by looking at the production, consumption and circulation of gender and sexual signs within musical and dance cultures. Through cultural and semiotic analysis we suggest that for many young people the biographical project of the self is as much about fantasy, escapism and creative imaginaries. This is seen as the making of a new sexual cosmopolitanism, consumed through the technologies of image, dance and musical cultures.

8

Performing Gender

The deconstruction of identity is not the deconstruction of politics; rather, it establishes as political the very terms through which identity is articulated

(Judith Butler, *Gender Trouble*, 1990, p. 148).

Queering Identities

Arguably the most generative critique of gender relations in recent years has emerged in the dialogic, fraught exchanges that have occurred between feminist, gay and lesbian theorists and activists, from different generations and of different political persuasions. Where some scholars have displayed a desire to cling steadfastly onto categorical ascriptions of the subject, especially those identifications felt to be 'under siege' – for example 'women', 'gay' and 'lesbian' identities – a new group of thinkers have sought to disrupt the very idea of identity itself. In doing so queer theorists, as this cluster of firebrand writers are defining themselves, are offering a direct challenge to the foundational constitution of identity itself as a mode for theoretical and political mobilization. In the field of gender research this has created a split between those who continue to operate *through* Identity Politics and those who strive to work *against* it. For example, where many feminists have invoked the notion of 'woman' as a base for shared experience and collective support, those writing against identity point to the intrinsic fundamental impossibility of all sex categories as Butler's opening quote purveys.

Moreover if early lesbian and gay politics was policed by biting feminist debates on the violence of male sexual power, pornography and abuse, queer theory revels in the undeniable *pleasure* of sexual politics. This has included, for example, a commitment to the complicated relations of power entwined in the once seemingly outlawed practices of gay porn, sado-masochism or bondage – a timely response to the puritanical zeal of the AIDS era which crystallized most evidently on the bodies of gay men. The new politics of pleasure is discussed by Smith (1994) in her account of New Right discursive regimes which have sought to police race and sexuality in recent times. Smith makes

157

a distinction – evident in political debates in the House of Commons, the press and much colloquial discourse – between what she identifies as the 'good homosexual' (law abiding, sexually faithful, without disease, closeted) and the 'dangerous queer' (politically assertive, sexually promiscuous, potentially HIV+ and openly out and proud). Smith explains:

> The good subject is closeted in every sense of the term, hidden and contained within closed frontiers, while the subversive element comes out of the closet, shows itself in its own self-staged spectacle and refuses to be contained. The goodness of the 'good homosexual' consists precisely in her self-disciplining, self-limiting, fixed subject status, an otherness which knows her proper place. The dangerousness of subversive queerness lies in its unfixity and 'excessiveness', its insatiable drive towards expansion and self-reproduction, its contamination of the space of normalcy through its entry of the wrong orifices, and, above all, its pursuit of unlimited pleasure. (p. 205)

Young people we spoke with expressed contradictory sentiments regarding sexuality. Even those who saw homosexuality as a legitimate practice could engage in the type of split Smith identifies pertaining to the production of the 'good' and 'bad' gay subject.

> Emma: People make a big deal out of lesbians and gays. I mean I'm not [gay]. I don't like it myself, but it's up to them. It's up to them if that's the way they feel about somebody else.
>
> Nicky: I reckon they ought to keep it to themselves though. We went [*name of place*] for the day and like she looked over to these two lads and said, 'I think they're gay', and I went, 'Oh aah'. I was just about to order my food as well and like, I looked over and they were both standing there and like wiggling their bums and everything!

The liberal idea that gay subjects should 'keep it to themselves' rather than being 'out and proud' is seen as contradictory. There is recognition of individual rights, 'it's up to them' as well as a sense that they are ultimately implicated in unpalatable stomach-turning practices, 'I was just about to order my food as well!' The new queer emphasis on sexual fantasy, domination and submission brings sex out of the closet, not only for heterosexual cultures but also within gay and lesbian politics, rewriting the cornucopia of sexual practices through bodily pleasure and desire. Of course this binary may be one that operates between and within subjects themselves and is part of what Sedgwick (1990) depicts as the complex 'epistemology of the closet'. Indeed an aspect of queer theory and activism lies in the implosion of the homo/hetero divide through a revelation of the variety of sexual identifications, practices and beliefs that abound on either side of the binary.

Queer theorists such as Dollimore (1996[1991]), Eve Kosovsky Sedgwick (1990) and, most notably, Butler (1990; 1991; 1993; 1994; 2004) whose work we shall go on to interrogate in finer detail, have combined Foucault's writings on sexuality with deconstructionist tendencies found in poststructuralist and post-modernist theory and allied this to the insights on subjectivity derived from psychoanalytic theories. These techniques have been deployed to hollow out the subject from within by unhinging gender and sexuality from the founda-tional wall mountings of the subject. In doing so, queer theorists have imploded the ontological basis of identity as the founding principle upon which gender and sexuality is constituted, a key issue we will discuss in the following section. Thus where social constructionist and poststructuralist writers have focused upon the 'making of men' (Mac an Ghaill, 1994), or women, queer theorists contend that there is no 'man' or 'woman' to be made. This is a radical gesture that disturbs the taken-for-granted assumptions of sex made in much previous research on masculinities and femininities. In refusing to stabilize the subject, as Rasmussen (2006) has recently shown, it may be better to conceive of sex as the repertoire of tropes through which we engage in the impossible acts of 'becoming subjects'. Rasmussen's study investigates the politics of representation surrounding young LGBTI (lesbian, gay, bisexual, transgender and intersex subjects). In the following chapter we consider the instability of sex and gender through the chimera of performing 'drag kings', where we provide a critical appraisal of Halberstam's (1998) work on this topic.

It could be said that the very act of reclaiming the disparaged identity of 'queer' and giving it new signification through parody, pastiche and politics is an effective strategy through which queer politics can disturb identities. The disruption of identity is reflected in Nick's practices in Chapter 5, where he was able to 'trouble' and critically rework the meanings of masculinity through becoming a gay Skin. By engaging in same-sex practices, yet appearing 'straighter-than-straight', Nick throws into confusion what is understood by such categorical terms as 'gay', 'straight' and 'male'. For queer theorists these enactments involve a radical displacement of identity, through what Dollimore (1996[1991]) describes as 'transgressive reinscriptions'. This entails 'a mode of transgression which seeks not an escape from existing structures but rather a subversive reinscription within them, and in the process their dislocation or displacement' (p. 285). The gay Skins that Healy depicts, the illicit practices of carnival discussed by Parker and the reinvention of the term queer beyond the discourse of abuse are just some illustrations of this radical reinscription of language, action and identity. The activities of performance, pleasure and masquerade are strategies that can lead to a proliferation of gender in ways that blur the meaning and multiply the signification of what is understood by the terms 'male' or 'female', to the extent that these identities are rendered thoroughly inauthentic, plastic.

It is here that the writings of the North American feminist philosopher Judith Butler have become remarkably influential, challenging the very ontological status of identity itself and providing new routes for rethinking sex-gender categories. Butler's work is providing inspiring, if occasionally 'troubling', ways of rethinking gender. In galvanizing a new generation of queer theorists and gender scholars, Butler's provocative writing has also caused much consternation amongst older feminists and gay and lesbian activists. Most disturbing for this latter group has been Butler's insistence on the intrinsic impossibility of sexed identities and the recognition that 'gender norms are finally phantasmic, impossible to embody' (1990:141). In developing a paradigm of performativity Butler's work takes us beyond the territory of identity secured in much previous feminist poststructuralist debate. She does so in part by providing an ontological critique – a type of 'queering' if you will – of such seemingly knowable categories as 'man', 'woman', 'girl' or 'boy'. This radical interruption in identity theorizing argues that identity is a type of 'doing' only made manifest at the point of action. To explore the theoretical, empirical and political issues at stake we draw especially upon Butler's writings on identity and ally this to some of our own ethnographic research on gender performance and youth. Here we explore young people's compulsion to enact and display stylized forms of gender embodiment. Of particular interest is the way in which these performances can produce spectacular enactments of transgression that can elicit a practice of gender dissimulation. Our focus is upon the subversion, regulation and embodiment of gender identities and its implications for young people's relationships.

Subversion

In her path-breaking book *Gender Trouble: Feminism and the Subversion of Identity*, Butler (1990) provides a thorough ontological critique of subjecthood. As the subtitle suggests, Butler is driven by a radical impulse, not only to complicate and multiply identity formations by recognizing difference across time and space – a key feature of many feminist poststructuralist accounts – but, above all, to subvert and implode the very basis of identity itself. This involves much more than the deconstruction of gender into its socially constitutive parts as either masculine or feminine. It entails the stark recognition that the seemingly knowable sex categories of 'male' or 'female' are themselves fundamentally unstable discursive productions that in effect serve to make masculinity and femininity intelligible.

By uncoupling sex/gender categories Butler disrupts any notion of a subject that prefigures action. Consider, for example, the seemingly straightforward act of a girl putting on lipstick. Rather than attribute this action to a knowable female subject, in *Bodies that Matter* Butler describes such activities as a mode of 'girling' (1994:7) through which the 'subject' is only made intelligible through action. 'My argument', she recounts elsewhere, 'is that there need not be a "doer behind the deed", but that the "doer" is variably constructed in and through the deed' (1990:142). In contrast to the notion of a subject (the girl) producing action (putting on lipstick), Butler suggests that it is the action that produces the subject or at least the semblance of what the subject, the girl, 'is'. To this extent, 'There is no gender identity behind the expressions of gender; that identity is performatively constituted by the very "expressions" that are said to be its results' (p. 25). In this regard Butler's work provides a provocative and compelling *anti-foundationalist* critique of identity, a critique that has divided some feminist scholars while at the same time enabling new positions to emerge across the landscape of queer theory and gender politics.

But if there is something profoundly 'troubling' for feminism about the negation of a female subject, its antidote lies, perhaps, in the subversion and dramatic proliferation of identity possibilities. What happens, we may wonder, to our notions of gender if the lipstick the girl in our example puts on is black and used to exhibit an alternative Goth-girl identity; if she is what the media term a 'lipstick lesbian'; or if the 'girl' is really a boy? Here the incitement of normative gender behaviour and sexual codes of practice gives rise to an irrepressible proliferation of 'Other' sex/gender possibilities – the tomboy, the lesbian, the drag queen and so on. In these instances 'genders can be rendered thoroughly and radically *incredible*' (p. 141). These new discursive positions are not set apart from a rigidly circumscribed heterosexual femininity but are central to its constitution as they are produced, in effect, through the deployment of these norms. For as Connell (2002) has noted, when it comes to gender practices 'the reality keeps escaping from the orthodox categories' (p. 21), a theme we shall go on to illustrate in finer detail.

In Chapter 6 when exploring the production of gender we discovered that sexual jibes, mythic stories and name-calling were an intimate part of student cultures. We also saw how the discursive production of gender and sexuality operated as an *organizing principle* in young people's relations in school. These tropes of gendered imagining defined the 'appropriate' from the 'inappropriate', the 'normal' from the 'deviant', the 'moral' from the 'immoral'. In so doing, they produced complex and dynamic heterosexual hierarchies in which the lives of subordinate males, girls and young women were most open to sexual scrutiny especially from more dominant male students. Yet as the following school-based discussion with white, working-class girls, aged 14–15 years reveals, although sexual name-calling is commonplace, the iteration of sex/gender norms and the meanings they carry can, at least occasionally, be radically overturned.

Sam: We could be sitting together like now and the boys could say, 'Oh–yer lesbian' or summit, and you just take it in.

Carla: Laugh it off.

Sam: We just laugh it off.

Julie: Me and Carla do.

Carla: We'll just say, 'Oh yes!'.

Anoop: And they'll actually say that to you?

Samantha: Mmm. And we'll just carry it on and say, 'Oh, are you coming up in the bush?' or summit, and like carry it on as a joke or summit.

Julie: Me and Carla get called lesbians [by the boys] all the time but we just say, 'Oh yeah, we're proud of it!' and we just shrug it off.

Emma: Yeah. Because you know you're not.

Samantha: When you answer back, they can't say anything because like . . .

Carla: Exactly! We say, '*Yes, we are . . .* '

Nicky: . . . [Name of a male student] We turn round and say, 'Oh, do you want a threesome' or something, and he'll go, 'Oh, I don't know' and they just like be quiet.

This discussion alerts us to what Butler terms the 'performativity of gender' (1990:139) in all its vibrancy and subtle shadings. The sign 'lesbian' is initially deployed by young men as a vernacular form of abuse against Julie and Carla. In the context of our ethnography it became evident that the term is not used to signify that the girls are gay, but rather that they are 'frigid', boring and uninterested in boys. By affirming this sign lesbian ('we're proud of it!') and locating it through the more familiar signifying chain of same-sex relationships the girls are able to overturn the sign-value and enact a discursive repositioning of their sexual identities. While girl-on-girl action is a popular trope of hetero-porn, it is the excessive qualities of femininity that the girls rework to embarrass the boys. This 'semiotic guerrilla warfare' is then taken a step further when the identity, 'lesbian', is transformed into a sexually assertive style of femininity through the invocation of a 'threesome' and remarks about going over to the bushes; statements which dramatically reverse any prior association with frigidity, through 'inversion, perversion, and reinscription' (Dollimore, 1996[1991]:285). In doing so, the discursive enactment opens up the sign of gender to a multiplicity of subject positions that simultaneously bespeak a heterosexual femininity, lesbianism, bisexual identifications and sexual practices with multiple partners.

The multiplication of sex acts not only inverts the charge of frigidity but points to the insecurity of all sex-gender categories where each of these imaginary identifications is ambivalent, split and inscribed within the other. Because there is no authentic subject to speak of, the proliferation of sex-gender categories renders the sign excessive by prising open the closed signifier 'girl', giving rise to what Butler describes as 'hyperbole, dissonance, internal confusion and proliferation' (p. 31). For the French feminist Irigaray (1985), such discursive strategies are exemplary of the infinite possibilities of femininity, enabling 'the sex that is not one' – subordinate, but also infinite, impossible and beyond categorization – to become a site of 'disruptive excess' (p. 78). Here the initially derogatory remark 'lesbian' is subjected to a frisson which transforms its signification through discursive interplay, parody and subversion. That is to say, the production of these 'logical impossibilities' leads to the incitement of what Butler (1990:17) refers to as the 'subversive matrices of gender[disorder]'.

There is much that is disturbing about the adoption and adaptation of sex/gender categories. For what does it say about gender identity if heterosexuals can 'pass' as lesbian, if the sexually passive suggest threesomes or if hyper-heterosexual boys are silenced by the daunting reality of sex beyond the discursive regimes they seek to impose? It could be argued that recourse to any type of gender ontology is in itself an epistemological impossibility as Butler expands:

> If the inner truth of gender is a fabrication and if a true gender is a fantasy instituted and inscribed on the surface of bodies, then it seems that genders can be neither true nor false, but are only produced as the truth effect of a discourse of primary and stable identity. (p. 136)

In this way, the 'girls' – for the compulsion to interpellate the subject is barely avoidable in language – are able to resist and transgress the culture of heterosexual masculine schooling by disturbing the sacred ground upon which an authentic gender identity can be cultivated. Butler's anti-foundationalist approach reveals how the naming or 'interpellation' (Althusser, 1971) of subjectivities as gay, straight or something in-between is a process of 'hailing' that summons these configurations to life. But of more interest is the actions themselves, the 'doings' and how the different performative tropes can come to unsettle the social constructionist idea of gender as a real category, a true foundation of 'being'. The lesbian masquerade by seemingly straight girls not only discloses lesbianism as a performance, but reveals all sexual identifications as performative, rewriting the rubric that inscribes heterosexuality as natural. This 'oblique' version of lesbianism, straight-but-not-straight, has the capacity to resignify the heterosexual constructs through which it is partially and inevitably spoken, thus rendering problematic the very category of girlhood. The girls are temporary and tenuous occupants of a 'zone of uninhabitability' (Butler, 1993:3) who 'twist' meanings of sex and gender. They enact lesbianism ('We're proud of it!') at the same time as they refute it ('because you know you're not'), holding in tension presence and absence. 'These "ever-new" possibilities of resignification' (p. 224) occur because the subject is constructed on contingent foundations and, in the words of Dollimore (1996[1991]), may engage in acts of 'sexual dissidence' in which the ontology of the subject itself is queried and thereby 'queered'. For this latter scholar, 'the perverse is', ultimately, 'the worm at the centre of the normal' (p. 146), which is of course what makes the counter-response by the girls so deliciously challenging.

Such stylized enactments parody gender from the 'inside-out' and can be considered transgressive forms of mimicry that transfigure identity and give rise to gender dissimulation. The postcolonial literary critic Homi Bhabha (1994), writing about the fraught colonial encounters between nation-states, has also remarked upon the role of 'irony, mimicry and repetition' (p. 85). He has argued that 'in order to be effective mimicry must continually produce its slippage, its excess, its difference' (p. 86). In the rather different, but no less power-ridden terrain of gender relations we also find that mimicry means there can be no original female subject and no gender authority upon which lesbianism, straightness, nymphomania or frigidity can rightly be accorded. As Bhabha explains, 'Mimicry conceals no presence or identity behind its mask' (1994:88), rather it operates as 'the metonymy of presence' (p. 89), the part that stands in for the whole. Here we find that the sexed body is a highly dubious zone upon which to anchor difference and a treacherously slippery surface on which to sustain gender meaning. In this way Dollimore views such forms of mimicry as an enticing, 'scandalous inversion' (1996[1991]:287).

And if we consider mimicry as Bhabha does, as 'a discourse uttered between the lines and as such both against the rules and within them' (p. 89), the appropriation of lesbianism by young women is, then, a thoroughly ambiguous subversion of gender relations. A neat illustration of the unsettling aspect of mimicry is evident in Fanon's (1978) exemplary account of postcolonial race relations, *Black Skin/White Masks* which, as the title suggests, opens up the possibility – through a type of 'splitting' – for black skinned subjects to subconsciously masquerade and identify, however precariously, as 'white'. A contemporary example of mimicry is found in Puar's (1995) research with young second-generation Sikh women in northern England who skilfully utilize their hybrid subject positions to parody whiteness and Asianness from the 'inside out'. Through a strategic deployment of heavy-accented migrant spoken English – of the type deployed in the BBC comedy sketch series *Goodness Gracious Me* – the young women were found to produce a shared discourse that at once subverted whiteness and their culturally assigned category of being Asian women. Puar explains how this shared language game 'seems to be an act of solidarity and exclusion; dominant white gazes are unable to participate in the parody. Reclaiming this "language" renders the objectifiers impotent. We were sharing in the solidarity of the double gaze...' (p. 41).

Nevertheless these strategic transfigurations are not without their costs. Sara Ahmed (1997) has written about her middle-class upbringing, being raised by her Pakistani father and English mother, and the possibility it occasionally afforded for her to 'pass' as white if she chose to erase associations with her father. Moments of passing and the fear of being discovered can make for highly fraught experiences which may not necessarily involve a direct politics of subversion. As Skeggs (1997) reveals, when discussing the enactments of young working-class women to pass as bourgeois, 'their attempts to pass are not a form of insubordination; rather they are dissimulations, performances of a desire not to be shamed but a desire to be legitimated' (p. 87). Passing is always a rule-bound and power-coded affair. For example the act of minstrelsy or blackface, like the stereotypical 'rugger lads' who dress in women's gear on a boys' night out, is hardly a moment of radical disturbance.

Passing, mimicry and masquerade are then situated acts that offer only the potential to transgress within particular frames of reference. In terms of the subversion of identity queer theorists would argue that because signs are ultimately arbitrary constructions, wherein 'The sign represents the present in its absence' (Derrida, 1991:62), there is no semantic reason why the working classes cannot try on the emperor's clothes, why blacks cannot 'be' white or girls cannot 'be' boys: a disturbing challenge that some feminist and gay and lesbian scholars have yet to fully reckon with.

If gender reinscription has the potential to subvert and displace established categories it continues to have burning consequence for those undertaking these acts. For example Kieran, a 15-year-old British Asian young woman, wore short closely cut hair, trousers, no make make-up or jewellery and chose to hang around in male-dominated groups in school. In her appearance she resembled the archetypal 'tomboy' and eventually fulfilled her dream of becoming a car mechanic having successfully completed a work-based apprenticeship. However, as a consequence of her 'tomboy' appearance, attitude and mechanical interests she was consistently de-sexualized by boys as someone who 'didn't count as a girl', yet could never quite become 'one of the lads'. Gender reinscription for gay and lesbian young people is also a difficult undertaking in what are still quintessentially heterosexual youth cultures where homophobia presides. An illustration of the limits of inversion, mimicry and gender reinscription can be seen when Tina spots a teenage couple in the park, one with long hair and the other with hair cut short.

> Tina: I took my dog out for a walk the other day, in the park up by our house and I would have argued black and blue [. . .] *that* was a boy. And I was arguing and arguing with these lads and these girls, 'That is a boy'. And this girl grabbed what I thought was a boy and I said, 'See – would they be doing that [i.e. kissing] if it was a girl?' And they all looked at me and I goes, 'No, that's a boy and a girl', and she did look like a boy and they was sitting on the swing kissing right. And these three lads come over and goes, 'The lemons am off again'. They were only lesbians! And after a while the wench took her coat off and you could tell [she was a girl].

And this girl come along and she says, 'Hi Jen, hi Mandy', and she goes at the top of her voice, 'them are lemons you know!', and I was sitting there like this [*demonstrates shocked open mouthed expression*]. And all the lads were having a go at them, but I'd have sworn it was a boy and it shocked me – not being a lesbian, but all the lads. Cos the girl who she's going out with Mandy, she's really pretty and all the lads keep on saying to Mandy, 'What you going out with that ugly bat for?', and everything. And you can guarantee whenever you go [to the park] there's all this writing about them.

Mary Jane: So they get teased quite a lot?

Tina: It doesn't seem to bother Mandy, cos Mandy really loves Jen. But Jen doesn't like it cos Jen was saying to Catrina the other day, 'The people always having a go at Mandy, she thinks that Mandy's going to dump her and go out with a lad instead', but Mandy says she wouldn't. They've been going out with each other for ages.

Being able to 'pass' as a member of the opposite sex can enable spaces for gender subversion, but it is evident that these spaces are highly constrained by a grid of power relations, homophobia and the unending desire to know the truth of sex categories. In the passage this ensues in name-calling ('lemons'), sexual graffiti and various attempts to 'straighten out' Mandy, who at least conforms to the visual aesthetic of what a 'girl' should be, a dynamic that ultimately causes anxiety and insecurity in her relationship. Similarly for young people from minority ethnic backgrounds who are seen to pass as white or choose to dissimulate from their allotted racialized subjectivities, they may in turn be rigidly categorized as 'coconuts' or 'bounty bars' – brown on the outside, but white on the inside.

It appears, then, that gender reinscription does not necessarily displace the prevailing relations of power. Certainly Nick's account of being a gay Skin could suggest otherwise. Queering the value of Skin did not stop Nick from beating up 'queens' or enacting aggressive forms of masculinity in social interactions across the local landscape. More recently in gay youth culture, several gay men's magazines have attempted to resituate the lower working-class Chav subculture, famed for wearing Burberry baseball caps, tracksuits, Rockport boots, brassy jewellery and tattoos. Transforming the male Chav into an object of desire has resulted in some gay youth mimicking Chavs through a performance that has seen the excesses of heterosexual masculinity attempt to be reclaimed. Where previous gay generations have fetishized the 'butch' denim look of manual labourers, the moustachioed black leather pose of biker boys or the tough crew-cut of Skinheads, the contemporary queer fascination with Chavs is part of a longstanding legacy of gender subversion and parody by sexual minorities. The radical gesture does not rest in producing a copy of authentic masculinity, but in revealing

that this is a copy of a copy, that all gendered styles are ultimately fabricated. These performances may serve to unsettle masculine identity at the
same time as it is enacted. But what does it mean to continually transfigure
working-class culture into gay masculine fetish? What if the embodiment
of gay skinheadism, for example, is underwritten by the threat and enactment of racist violence as Murray Healey disclosed? And could the celebration of masculine excess also not invoke the repudiation of femininity,
through intense homosocial rituals that are tinged with an unspoken mark of
misogyny?

There is little doubt that the stylistic approximation of taken-for-granted identities can engender a radical deployment of gender and sexuality. However,
as Lynne Segal demonstrates, this 'can succeed only if it can be seen as a
collective struggle over representation: context, reception and, above all, articulation within wider political struggle makes the difference' (1994:196). Similarly
in the field of race and ethnic relations the globalization of particular aspects of
black culture – music, language, gestures and style – though widely imitated
by countless white teenagers worldwide has yet to usher in a new moment
in which race no longer matters. As bell hooks has proclaimed, these global
styles of consumption are also ways of 'eating the Other', offering an exotic
taste of spice to enrich the blander palate of whiteness without ever removing
white identity from its position as dominant, hegemonic and normative. A
tantalizing illustration of eating the Other can be seen in a semiotic analysis
of whiteness in Haagen-Dazs advertising which employed highly sexualized
black bodies to convey particular flavours of ice-cream (e.g. equating blackness
with chocolate, cappuccino with mixed race identities and Latino bodies with
Cuban rum and raison flavourings) (see Nayak, 1997). The selling of 'difference'
and the marketing of hybridity are in effect emblematic of the contradictions
of capitalism: contradictions which enable rather than suppress its expansion.
As McEwan enquires, in a lucid discussion of global culture, 'Why is it that on
the one hand difference is celebrated through a consumer market that offers
a seemingly endless choice of identities, sub-cultures and styles, yet on the
other hand hybridity continues to shock?' (2001:176) (for further discussion see
Werbner, 1997). Hybrid transgression may indeed engender a cultural reinscription of sexuality, gender, race and class. But as we have seen the act of
imitation, simulation and performance while unquestionably compelling, is not
necessarily a twisting gesture of defiance that inevitably turns itself against
authoritative powers.

Such complexity takes us back to Parker's account of Brazilian carnival in
which festivals offer a potentially radical site wherein performance, parody
and gender subversion proliferate. This radical potential, though, is always
reliant upon the 'power-geometries' of postcolonial histories, existing gender
relations and the different meanings these events have for the various actors
who perform within or come to regulate carnival. The popularity of Mardi

Gras in Sydney, Australia, carnival in Rio de Janeiro, Brazil, and festivals worldwide indicate that gender blurring is neither new nor in and of itself subversive. The transformation of carnival into commodified spectacles for global appeal – like the mainstreaming of much black, gay and working-class culture discussed previously – would suggest that power can indeed be recuperated in different forms and at different scales. As Fuss (1991:6) remarks, 'Homosexuality, read as a transgression against heterosexuality, succeeds not in undermining the authoritative position of heterosexuality so much as reconfirming heterosexuality's centrality as that which must be resisted'. Moreover the persistence of gender categories in late-modernity would suggest that 'hegemonic heterosexualities' are not so easily obliterated, rather they function in and through contradiction, a recuperation issue we shall now turn to.

Regulation

If the enactment of lesbian masquerade in the previous extract enables the subversion of identity to occur, it also throws into relief the extraordinary compulsion to 'act straight'. In our discussions with young men we found that heterosexual masculinity was an impossible ideal that was struggled over, negotiated and reconstructed anew in the effort to make it appear 'just-so'. Evidently heterosexual masculinity was not something that could lie still, but continually had to be asserted, regulated and performed. The following extract, generated from school-based discussion with young people, provides an example of these regulatory processes. The context for our 'sex talk' developed from ethnographic investigation into the teaching and understanding of sex education and sexual practices in schools. One of the teachers we had spoken with mentioned using an HIV/AIDS video to promote safe sex to the class as part of the Personal and Social Education (PSE) curriculum. The teacher explained to us that the video she deployed included black and white actors and focused upon two male protagonists: one gay, the other straight. In an attempt to subvert stereotypical associations that conflate homosexuality with AIDS, the film goes on to reveal that it is the straight man that is HIV+. However, the gap between teaching and learning became apparent when we enquired how young people understood the film.

　　Jason: We had that film once.
　　Clive: Which one?
　　Savage: It was about homosexuals weren't it?
　　Clive: That was in Science.
　　Samantha: The only video we had in PSE was about crime and vandalism.

Jason: Was it in Science? That one about, how do . . . I can't say it.

Clive: Homosexuality.

Jason: That's the one.

Mary Jane: What was that then?

Shane: And you sat there and watched it?!!

Jason: We had to! We had to sit and watch it! We had no choice, we had to stay there and watch it!

Anoop: What lesson was this?

Jason: Science, arh, we don't wanna know, we had to sit there and watch it.

Samantha: What was it about?

Jason: It was about these chaps, they told you they were gay.

Clive: Oh that. That was boring.

Where the teacher had referred to this method of teaching sex education as a model of 'good practice', the responses of students and in particular the young men we spoke with would suggest otherwise. Their resistance to pedagogy lies in part with the powerful identifications they are making with masculine heterosexuality. The careful regulation of this identity is seen when Jason is unable to speak about homosexuality, when Shane challenges the others for watching the film, when Jason responds that he was forced into the viewing practice and when Clive dismisses the event as 'boring'. We may read Shane's charge, 'And you sat there and watched it?!!' as a powerful performative act in peer-group cultures. For Butler 'Performative acts are forms of authoritative speech: most performatives, for instance are statements that, in the uttering, also perform a certain action and exercise a binding power' (1993:225). This 'binding power' involves the 'regulation of identificatory practices' (p. 3) and is seen when other students attempt to legitimate their viewing activities and blame the teacher for imposing the video upon them. Indeed Jason's response to the challenge erupts into excitable speech and iterations that contravene conventional understandings of heterosexual masculinity as secure, stable and rooted in certainty. For as Segal wryly remarks, in her critical engagement with masculinity, 'the more it asserts itself, the more it calls itself into question' (1990:123).

This compulsion to perform straight masculinity is collectively imposed, yet taken up with relish by the young men we spoke with. In Foucaultian terms, it would appear that the individual is both an effect of power and the element of its articulation. However, being a 'proper boy' – whatever that means – remains an imaginary ideal, the impossibility of which makes it no less a desirable subject position to inhabit. In this sense we could describe identification as the never-touching encounter that exists between the desiring subject and the desired object. For Butler, our sex is not something that lies beyond the discursive realm but is always produced as a reiteration of hegemonic norms. Being a 'proper boy' or 'proper girl' is, then, a fantasy that is both hankered after and embodied through an approximation of its norms. In writing 'against proper objects' Butler (1994:1) has remarked upon the everyday violence committed through the imposition of such normative phantasms. To this extent identity is also always an act of exclusion, a point of closure, the feverish demarcation of a boundary that elides the mercurial qualities of subjectivity itself. Moreover this struggle for sex-gender signs (what it means to be a 'lesbian', 'Chav', gay Skin, 'proper boy' and so on) is not an activity that is happening outside of our doing. Rather it is an inter-subjective process wherein we both act and are acted upon: we are concurrently the subjects and objects of the sign-making world.

What is also evident from these ethnographic encounters is the realization that gender signs are constituted through *difference*. Words such as masculine and feminine are then social constructs, inscribed in a wider signifying chain of meaning within which one term refers to another, or more likely others, through a systematic play of differences. It is because signs are arbitrary and differential that the relationships between them, how they are constituted in systems of meaning, are significant. The distinction between gender identity and gender identification is similar in many senses to the dissonance which exists in semiotics between objects and signs. Gender identity, like the signified, is the ideal meaning, the point at which the sign and the signifier come together; gender identification, on the other hand, can be likened to the sign, the free-floating signal that can only communicate meaning within a given encoded system of representation. This dissonance we describe between identity and identification, what Derrida (1991) calls 'spacing', means that the two never quite occupy the same spatial and temporal zone, but engage in a complex shadow play where image, imago and the imaginary intersect. Identification as an act of desiring is always subject to its 'lack', an issue we can productively further develop.

Because discourses are fused with power particular signs may come to take on a differing social status within the symbolic regime of language. Derrida deploys the term logocentricism to describe the Western pattern by which meaning is produced through a binary of presence and absence. The binary, designed around opposition and exclusion, seeks to avoid intermixture through the polarization of categories, for example man/woman, white/black, straight/gay, able-bodied/disabled. In these examples the former component of the dichotomous equation subsumes and dominates the latter, performing its roles as a 'master signifier' whereupon the absented sign is impelled to take on a subordinate position as the 'not said', absence or 'lack'. It is through this lacuna that gender subjectivities are styled, not only in the choices we make but implicitly through those we do not, the uncomfortable 'not-like-me' of identity we choose to repress, expel or mark ourselves against. We can consider this as a powerful act of *disidentification* in which the sign is dependent on this absence – its Other – in order to 'be'.

In our discussions with young women concerning gender, practices of identification and dis-identification were consistently deployed to negotiate femininities. Tina who was of mixed heritage developed a strong identification with the singer Whitney Houston embodied through consumption, 'I had all her records, I even had a leather jacket the same as hers'. She goes on to add, 'I think she's ever so pretty and she's got a good singing voice'. However, for Tina and her best friend Samantha, the singer Madonna represented a more problematic and at best partial identification, due to her ambiguous sexuality and what they perceived as a sexually assertive, excessive femininity that needs to be held in check.

Tina: I used to like Madonna, but I think Madonna is a ****.

Samantha: I used to like Madonna, but I don't like the image she's got now [this is prior to Madonna's more recent demure look].

Anoop: And you don't like her anymore, what it is about her you don't like?

Tina: Her's showing herself up now. Her's using... like this was in a magazine I had the other day, she just uses her body to get attention.

Samantha: She's using her stardom to get attention, her used to make good songs an' that.

Tina: In my magazine I got the other day it had got pictures of her how she is. Remember when she used to sing 'Holiday', she didn't look nice but she looked better compared to them silly pictures where she's just changed. You want to see how she's changed.

Samantha: I got all her records.

Mary Jane: Her body's changed a lot hasn't it?

Tina: Dyed hair, no end of colours.

Anoop: What image of Madonna did you like best?

Tina: When she did 'Vogue'. I thought she looked really nice when she did 'Vogue'.

Samantha: Yeah, she did. I got a video of her when she did the 'Like a Virgin' tour when her was young and I got her Italian tour.

Tina: I tell you which one she looks weird on, her new one 'Erotica'. When she's got her hair all slicked down like that, her looks like a . . . like a man. And it was on the telly the other day, and she went to a fashion show and she was a celebrity and she walked on. She'd got a dress and had cut out the holes round there [indicates to breasts] and nobody realized until she took off her jacket. And she was standing round like that with her hands on her hip.

Mary Jane: Do you think she might've been deliberately trying to shock?

Tina and Samantha: Yeah!

Samantha: I think its cos not many people liked her again, cos her started
    looking like a whore and her wanted to make a comeback.
Tina: I still like her records but I don't like her act at all.
Samantha: I don't like her act – I don't like 'Erotica'.

It is interesting to consider this extract in the light of Madonna's more recent
biography and the manner in which she is technically proficient in the marketable reinvention of self. In the 1980s Madonna went from sexy pin-up girl
to no-nonsense 'Material Girl' in the blink of an eye, offering something for
everyone. In the 1990s Madonna self-consciously flirted with the borders of the
allegedly 'perverse' including S/M imagery, lesbianism, black sexuality and a
gambit of illicit sexual signifiers that construed her as the 'dirty-sexy-bad-girl'
Tina and Samantha are so repelled by. The manner in which past images of
Madonna have been marketed through a fetishization of black sexuality and
lesbian iconography is a further testimony to the ways in which 'difference'
is incorporated, transfigured and sold back to us as titillating. However, if we
look at Madonna today her lived sexual biography is much more mundane
and far less 'out there' than may be imagined. She has opted for a traditional
marriage, lives with a multi-millionaire, has entered middle age, given birth,
written children's books, attends English elocution lessons and professes to
aspects of religious spiritualism. Despite these practices, Madonna remains
adept at 'working the sign', seamlessly producing her 'self' as the desirable
soft-focus, cinematic sex symbol for popular music video.

As the illustration reveals, it is apparent that Tina and Samantha are
in part performing their femininities through active identification and dis-
identification with Madonna and other celebrities. These gender productions
take place across the body of Madonna which, it is alleged, she uses to get
attention through her hairstyles 'dyed . . . no end of colours', dress and sexually provocative 'hands on her hip' posture. The process of dis-identification
is discursively enacted when Madonna's image is revealed in 'silly pictures' in
which 'she looks weird', 'like a man' and behaves in sexually explicit fashion,
'like a whore'. In the end Samantha and Tina negotiate their femininities
through these contradictory cultural representations, partially resolved through
making distinctions between Madonna's old image where 'she looked really
nice' and her Erotica performances. The careful regulation of gender is seen
where a balance must be struck between lacking femininity (looking 'like a
man') and the enactment of an excessive, hyper-sexualized femininity (looking
'like a whore'). These comparisons enable Tina and Samantha to demarcate
between liking Madonna's music while hating her act, a split that enables
them to perform a particular femininity fashioned through and against these
complex contradictions.

In recent work Butler has gone on to regard this strategic displacement as a
form of gender *melancholia*. The refusal to take up particular subject positions

results in a permanent state of mourning for the abject identifications that are disavowed. Aspects of this gender melancholia can be traced in the above passage, when Samantha brings to utterance the need to relinquish identific-ations with Madonna. The mournful pang is felt when she reflects, 'her used to make good songs an' that'. The melancholic attitude is seen in the desire to capture these yearnings in records, musical videos and other memorabilia as a passing life. Gender melancholia is an act of grieving for past and impossible identifications, a wound that can never fully heal.

These acts of repudiation, expulsion and disavowal remain double-edged and reverberate with the costs of submitting oneself to becoming, say, a 'proper girl'. As Butler explains:

> This 'being a man' and this 'being a woman' are internally unstable affairs. They are always beset by ambivalence precisely because there is a cost in every identification, the loss of some other set of identifications, the forcible approximation of a norm one never chooses, a norm that chooses us, but which we occupy, reverse, resignify to the extent that the norm fails to determine us completely. (1993:126–127)

Rather than achieve a seamless replication of sex/gender norms Butler declares, 'identification is the phantasmatic staging of the event' (1993:105), as seen in the early discussion of HIV/AIDS. What is it, we may ask, that enables some identifications such as heterosexuality to be repeatedly 'staged', in music, film, literature, advertisements and art while others remain, as the ethnographic vignettes reveal, barely speakable? For if we accept that 'identity is a signifying practice' (Butler, 1990:145), then the act of identification remains a strategy through which other signifiers are negated, repudiated or erased. The examples we have discussed are similarly marked by a series of 'signifying absences' (Butler, 1990:136) that reveal a dis-identification surrounding gay men, lesbians, being HIV+, looking like a man or appearing as a slut. Using the psycho-analytic insights deployed by Butler, these identities can be cast in abject, mournful and grief-stricken ways. The trope of gender melancholia features in Halberstam's (1998) biographical account discussed in Chapter 9 where she mournfully reflects upon aspects of masculinity that were denied to her in the move from childhood to adolescence. As we shall go on to see, Halberstam's project involves a return to the wound and an attempt to heal that which can never be fully recovered.

What is evident from our discussions of Madonna and the AIDS/HIV video is that identities are internal constructions that are constituted in relation to one another. As queer theorists such as Sedgwick and Dollimore elaborate the obsessive denouncement of homosexuality by straight culture only serves to reveal how integral it is to the ever-fragile constitution of heterosexuality. We can make similar comparisons in the field of race relations with regard to whiteness, for example in Parker's account of Brazilian culture discussed in

Chapter 5 which remarks upon how the indigenous community inherited the melancholic attributes of the colonizer, only to be reinvigorated by the ecstatic *jouissance* of carnival. The over-sexed depiction of blackness as an expression of bodily excess – virility, athleticism, rhythm and musicality – when compared with disembodied constructions of whiteness, often as 'death' (Dyer, 1997) – demonstrates how the other is fundamental to this mutual affirmation. Identity is, then, simultaneously, not just an assertion of the Self but a constructed act of closure in that it defines what is excessive, outré or abject.

However, we would be mistaken in assuming that dis-identification fully obliterates those 'Other' possible identifications or renders them obsolete. Rather identification is a partial, split and ambivalent process which, in the moment it announces itself as 'identity' (in common statements such as, 'As black man . . . .', or 'Speaking as a woman . . . '), conceals its incurable multiplicity and precarious contingency. At the same time, the momentary claim to be 'representative' of a particular group or community is made impossible. In this respect the act of identification is always an approximation as Hall explains:

> Identification is, then, a process of articulation, a suturing, an over-determination not a subsumption. There is always 'too much' or 'too little' – an over-determination or a lack, but never a proper fit, a totality. Like all signifying practices, it is subject to the 'play' of difference. It obeys the logic of more-than-one. (2000:17)

Because identities are constructed within, rather than outside discourse, they remain subject to the complex discursive interplay, strategic repositioning and repetitive regulation we have seen. But identities are also internally fabricated through imaginings, identifications, projections and silent disavowals. The presence of the abject Other within hollows out the meaning of identity and makes it unfamiliar to itself. Gender simulation is in keeping with Bhabha's description of racial mimicry which 'rearticulates presence in the terms of its "otherness", that which it disavows' (1994:91). It is precisely because identity is incomplete, a signifying act open to excess, that gender norms 'are continually haunted by their own inefficacy; hence, the anxiously repeated effort to install and augment their jurisdiction' (Butler, 2000:114).

Embodiment

Having outlined the anti-foundational approach to gender identity adopted by Butler and the accompanying regulatory and subversive tendencies that arise, a series of questions transpire. If gender identity is a fantasy, projected through the eye of imaginary sex difference, why is it such a compelling fiction to behold? If gender remains an impossible assignment to accomplish, why do so many of us continue to submit to its exigencies? And if the subversion of gender is barely avoidable, a consequence of our inability to fully approximate its regulatory ideal, then how has it maintained its position as a hegemonic norm in the social world?

Poststructuralist theory has done a good job of recognizing how gender relations are inscribed with power but it frequently underplays the gestures, emotions and performance of the body. Butler has suggested that in order to better understand how social processes are made to appear 'as real' we need also to comprehend how the discursive and the material are embodied in everyday life. She develops Foucault's insight that even the human body– that fleshy and seemingly most 'natural' of beings – is constituted in the discursive capillaries of medical, educational, judicial, military and religious technologies. Foucault has argued that the body is subject to an historical and discursive genealogy, being part of what Butler (1990:141) describes as a 'social temporality'. The body is, in Foucaultian terminology, the product of a unique 'bio-power' (1978:143). While Foucault (1978), at least in his early work, has been criticized for neglecting the materiality of the body through a type of 'discursive determinism' which depicts the corporeal as 'the inscribed surface of events, traced by language and dissolved by ideas', Butler (1993) emphatically contends: bodies matter. Her concern, then, has not been to discount bodily experience as a few critics of *Gender Trouble* had suggested, but rather in 'initiating new possibilities, new ways of bodies to matter' (1993:30). Nevertheless and much to the chagrin of her critics, there is little discussion in Butler's work of the anatomical constraints engendered by such bodily regimes as puberty, menstruation, childbirth, lactating, dieting, aging, disease or disability, to say nothing of such racialized markers as colour. Instead, in deploying the notion of embodiment, Butler has sought to reconcile the historically conceived signing of the body with an active notion of the performative. The way we style our bodies is neither a matter of sex (nature) nor simply an adjunct of the prevailing gender order (culture), rather it is one of the techniques through which we perform, enact and 'do' gender. In this respect Butler regards sex and gender as 'illusions of substance – that bodies are compelled to approximate, but never can' (1990:146). In this reading gender identity is an embodied action that does not exist outside of its 'doings', rather its performance is also a reiteration of previous 'doings' that become intelligible as gender norms.

Throughout our ethnographic research on the meanings of gender and sexuality in young people's cultural worlds we discovered that ideas about gender were habitually embodied. We would further suggest that for youth the performance of gender and its imaginary attachments to 'masculinity' and 'femininity' are different to those of adults or the aged. As our examples of Kaguru people in Tanzania indicate, gender ideals differ across time and space, registering uniquely in particular places, and are embodied anew according to their cultural happenstance.

The sign-wearing body appears the final repository of truth for who the subject 'is', a performance belied through bodily deportment. Connell (2002) has remarked how 'Much of young people's learning about gender is learning *gender competence*' (p. 81), an issue that was strikingly evident in the corporeal enactments and discursive ascriptions that featured in our investigations:

> Susan: Like if a boy crosses his legs or makes a comment and everybody – like rumours just spread.
> Anoop: Why would it be certain people that would be called gay and not others, even if they don't know like, in class?
> Libby: I don't know, they've just got this picture of a gay person in their heads . . .
> Susan: They pick on Gavin because he hasn't got a masculine voice and he's not very well built like everyone else in our year.
> Amy: And if they walk funny, they're gay.

The styling of the body through gestures, actions and utterances is a primary technique through which gender is performed. A failure to comply with the severe bodily regime of valorized masculinity could soon lead to homophobic comments and the creation of a disparaged or failed masculinity. As the illustration reveals, embodiment is pivotal where 'crossing your legs', not having a deep 'masculine voice' or being 'not very well built' can rapidly lead to the assertion of effeminacy, an accusation against young men which soon translates into being 'queer'. The idea of 'true' masculinity as an embodied art was critically reflected upon in conversations with young women who dissected the masculine desire to link bodily practices to gender and sexuality.

> Amy: They think they can point out like gay people just by the way they walk or the way they act.
> Susan: It's really pathetic!
> Lucy: Like if he's got a squeaky voice, 'Oh he's gay!'
> Sally: Just like a normal man. He could be walking down the street and you could think, 'Oh, I bet he's got a really nice girlfriend', but for all you know, he could be gay or he could be homosexual.
> Susan: People still think they can tell.
> Libby: People do shout it out and start calling them gay. Well, the boys do.

These illustrations of young people's life-worlds demonstrate that although gender may indeed be performative, we are not so freely able to perform gender as we wish. Rather gender relations are powerfully constrained and tightly corseted around acceptable forms of femininity and masculinity. To capture this notion of structure and agency Connell prefers to speak of 'gender projects' rather than performativity, as it 'makes it possible to acknowledge both the agency of the learner and the intractability of gender structures' (p. 82). While we would also emphasize the need for theories of performance, dance, emotions and the body to be located in relations of power and social structures we are also keen not to overlook the radical impulse behind new queer theorizations of identity. For this reason we describe the enactment of gender by young people as a mode of *choreography*, a set of culturally patterned activities which bring the subject into being but at best can only ever approximate the sexed identity that is desired. Moreover as we have already seen there are occasions where the choreography of gender is resisted, transgressed and reconfigured in new routines. The development of new choreographies of gender may occur where an appropriated style forms part of a collective enactment, as with the subculture of gay Skins. Alternatively these choreographies may in turn be recuperated in new discursive formations such as the recent deployment of 'ladettes'. In Britain the term 'ladette' has been attributed by the media and popular press to young women who display a hedonistic desire to 'binge drink', go clubbing, have casual sex and behave, at least in many ways, like 'lads' (see Jackson, 2006). On the other side of the globe, Australian women have been styled 'ockerettes', identified through the shared characteristics of drinking, swearing and sexual availability. These activities, in large part a product of the changing economic situation of women described in Chapter 4, were not so long ago a source of tabloid fascination imbued with a moral repugnance for 'ladies' who acted as 'lads'. However, it is also apparent that women drinkers are an increasingly acceptable part of much of the modern night-time economy where sex, money and a large consumption of alcohol are the necessary ingredients of this urban cocktail (Chatterton and Hollands, 2003). It is possible then, that over time, gender tropes become stretched and exceed their initial moral restraints. This does not mean that the traces of negative ascriptions cannot return in words, images and other discursive representations, in fact they frequently do. Rather it shows how a collective choreography of gender practices can make what was once unacceptable culturally palatable within new generations.

In our discussions with young people the choreographic power of masculinity is seen where young men would admonish one another through homophobic insults for sitting too closely together, speaking in high-pitched 'squeaky voices', crossing their legs, walking in a supposedly 'mincing' fashion, being slightly built or displaying an earnest, academic prowess. As a consequence of exhibiting a conformist, academically minded persona Miles had previously been branded as 'queer'. This homophobic abuse dissipated when he became a Sixth Former and those who taunted him had left. He recalled, 'It's a sort of stigma, ain't it? A quiet person in a class would be called "gay" or summat. I was for a time cos I was fairly quiet in the classroom and for a while everyone was callin' me a gay'. Bodies are then implicated in what Connell (2002:51) describes as 'the bringing-into-being of social reality'. Here a whole disciplinary regime is deployed to bolster and purport 'the regulatory fiction of heterosexual coherence' (Butler, 1990:137) through embodied activity. These daily actions demonstrate how gender is regulated, performed and embodied in youth cultures. Butler outlines the significance of the body as an agent and medium through which the discursive signs of gender are given corporeal significance. We discover 'words, acts, gestures and desire produce the effect of an internal core or substance, but produce this on the surface of the body, through the play of signifying absences that suggest, but never reveal, the organising principle of identity as a cause' (p. 136).

Alongside the mundane choreography of gender we encountered we also witnessed some spectacular displays of heterosexual embodiment among young people. An example of this was evident through a type of crucifix performance, described here by young women when asked whether they felt boys or girls tended to be more homophobic in school.

> Lucy: I think that boys are.
> Susan: Yes, definitely.
> Lucy: Because they go, 'STAY AWAY!' [demonstrates crucifix sign with fingers]
> All: Yes!
> Susan: Like as if he's contagious.
> Amy: If they're all sitting together like that (i.e. huddled up) one of them will move away.

We can consider the crucifix performance as an embodied display of hyperbolic heterosexuality. It entails the regulation of self and others and forms part of the self-convincing rituals of masculinity. Where the 'borderwork' Thorne described in Chapter 6 was frequently undertaken by boys against girls at Elementary School, our findings would suggest that by Secondary School this strategy is further being deployed by boys against other boys who are deemed gay in what comprises a new source of contagion. It is worth reflecting here upon Kaguru young men who undergo circumcision to be separated from a polluting foreskin, 'Because the foreskin keeps the glans moist, like a woman's genitals are thought always to be, it is said to have feminine attributes' (Beidelman, 1997:127). Circumcision is a ritual epitomizing the 'purity and danger' described by the anthropologist Douglas (1966). Where circumcision is a very literal form of splitting and removal, at a psychoanalytic level homophobia can also be seen as means through which young men expel femininity and purvey a competent heterosexual masculinity. The abject nature of homosexuality is seen when Miles adds, 'In the First Year if you got a girlfriend you're the laughing stock: now if you haven't got a girlfriend you're the laughing stock!'

For Butler the crucifix enactment and heterosexual coupling can be seen as a performed identification, an act of 'repudiation without which the subject cannot emerge' (1993:3). The construction of masculine heterosexuality is then dependent upon the iteration of the abject, the unliveable, the uninhabitable: what Butler calls 'that site of dreaded identification' (p. 3). Failure to comply with expected bodily modes of behaviour could result in a young man being labelled 'gay', symbolically crucified and subjected to bullying and harassment. Within the horror genre the invocation of Christian regalia (holy water, biblical scripture, crucifixes) is used to ward off vampires, spirits and dark forces. The construction of the homosexual as predatory vampire forms a double threat. Gay men and vampires are abject figures, leaky bodies with the potential to pollute your blood through HIV and blood-sucking respectively, the consequences of which can lead to becoming part of the living dead. But underlying this outward fear is a deeper, internal anxiety that in being 'taken' by a vampire/gay man, you too are transformed into that repudiated object through the return of the abject.

In *The Powers of Horror* Kristeva (1982) configures Douglas's (1966) anthropological accounts of pollution and taboo through Lacanian psychoanalytic frames. These insights are valuable for considering misogyny, homophobia and Kaguru male initiation. Drawing upon Kristeva's concept of abjection as derived through these readings, Butler explains the relationship between the body and defilement:

The 'abject' designates that which has been expelled from the body, discharged as excrement, literally rendered 'Other'. This appears as an expulsion of alien elements, but the alien is effectively established through this expulsion. The construction of the 'not-me' as the abject establishes the boundaries of the body which are also the first contours of the subject. (1990:133)

The production of HIV+ and gay identities as 'monstrous Others' is an embodied act deployed to provide heterosexual masculinity with the illusion of substance, whilst unintentionally summoning the abject to life. In the perpetual effort to convey its authenticity gender identity can only concede its inadequate fallibility. The need to perform, embody and anxiously repeat at once undermines and makes implausible gender accomplishment. Because gender is a rule that can only ever be approximated these stylized enactments fall short of the ideal they seek to inhabit. Although this makes gender subjectivity no less desirable to occupy, it does point to the impossibility of identity acquisition:

The parodic repetition of gender exposes as well the illusion of gender identity as an intractable depth and inner substance. As the effects of a subtle and politically enforced performativity, gender is an 'act', as it were, that is open to splittings, self-parody, self-criticism, and those hyperbolic exhibitions of the 'natural' that in their very exaggeration, reveal its fundamentally phantasmatic status. (1990:146–147)

What is evident through the embodied performance of heterosexuality is the recognition that gender signs forever carry with them the abject signifier they seek to repress. Indeed the abject Other must continually be expelled, disparaged and spliced from the fictive being of the subject. For Butler this is a mutually constitutive relationship where, 'the subject is constituted through the force of exclusion and abjection, one which produces a constitutive outside to the subject, the abject outside, which is, after all, "inside" the subject as its own founding repudiation' (1993:3). The act of enforcing imaginary queer Others to 'stay away' is, then, a performative and deeply psychic gesture that aims to evacuate the sign of gayness from without and within.

But as Derrida has shown signs are not so readily displaced, rather their meanings are deferred, carried forward in traces as encapsulated by his preferred term *différence*, which is used to convey difference and deferral. The impossibility of subjectivity, which is marked by presence and absence, has led Derrida to rewrite the term 'woman' through a deleted inscription, a crossing-out that demonstrates how identity is always under erasure. When it comes to the suturing of identities in this way we find, 'The line which cancels them, paradoxically, permits them to go on being read' (Hall, 2000:16). For these reasons, gender continues to be constituted through numerous 'styles of the flesh' (Butler, 1990:139) and forever bound to the circle of repetition as it struggles to come to terms with the disturbing, troubling impossibility of what it means to 'do' identity. Ultimately it is an act that can be done differently, undone or done away with altogether.

Conclusion

In this section we have focused upon the new challenges offered by queer theorists to gender, sex and subjectivity. We show how the category of sex can no longer be seen as a stable point of departure for our analyses of gender. The chapter has been structured around the subversion, regulation and embodiment of gender. Through a detailed consideration of the work of Butler we have shown how queer theory can engender new ways for rethinking the subject in late-modernity. Inspired by writing in this field we have tried to connect some of these radical ideas to the everyday lives of young people and the numerous ways in which they 'do' gender. We have suggested that some of the philosophical ideas concerned with gender melancholia, performativity and abjection can productively be used to examine everyday gender practices and the choices and identification we make. We appreciate that queer theory and politics is a troubling terrain for many feminist and youth scholars to traverse, but it may be a rewarding one (see Rasmussen, 2006). In this way we have drawn upon psychoanalytic and queer perspectives to unsettle gender and sex categories. To further disturb the taken-for-granted assumptions of sex categories we will now turn to the possibilities and prospects for ending gender. The focus in this final chapter is upon the manipulation of bodies and the biographical making – and faking – of sex.

9
Ending Gender?

Our starting point for this book considered the ways in which gender relations, particularly among young people, are being shaped by late-modernity. The late-modern era signals a break with the industrial past and the familial arrangements associated with Western industrial societies. De-traditionalization – a key feature of late-modernity – is commonly presented as a point of fissure with the industrial past marked by economic restructuring, social mobility and the loosening of family and regional ties. These processes are also characterized by increasingly individualized biographies and new ways of thinking reflexively about the self. Within the context of new times it appears self-evident that gender relations are being reconfigured in the face of emergent new forms of masculinities and femininities, highlighting change and discontinuity with the past. Familiar themes of the new gender order, as discussed in Chapters 3 and 4, suggest that young men are in crisis while young women appear as the victorious beneficiaries of new ways of working, living and being. While young men may be positioned as the recently dispossessed, haunting a defunct, de-industrial landscape, young women are cast as the ideal neo-liberal subjects – adaptable and forward looking, the perfect bareback riders to suit the flexible economies of contemporary times. Our concern throughout the book has been with the ways in which gender relations in late-modernity are culturally represented and lived. In focusing upon these representations we have sought to place young masculinities and femininities within their cultural context in order to explore the possibilities and discursive limits of these constructions. Central to our approach is recognizing the importance of the body as a conveyor of signals and a dense economy of signs.

The 'crisis' of masculinities is commonly represented as an identity crisis in which the settled certainties of a patriarchal past have been disrupted, throwing men off course in displaced and sometimes self-destructive ways. The ritualistic pugilism of *Fight Club*, the defensive recriminations of D-FENS, protagonist of *Falling Down* and the identifications working-class males make with *Rocky* can be seen as deeply symbolic portrayals of loss and longing, a riposte to the indignity of losing status and power and simultaneously an attempt to recuperate this. Central to an understanding of these accounts is an appreciation of social change as an affective process in which social and psychic processes are experienced as 'structures of feeling' (Williams, 1973). We are also concerned to explore the limits and contradictions of 'crisis' as a way of understanding youthful masculinities. Viewing masculinity as a sign with no tangible essence undermines the idea of masculinity as an object or *thing* that can be in crisis. This point also applies to femininity as a sign that struggles to embody neo-liberal personhood. We also point to the imprecise nature of a contemporary 'crisis', a representation that implodes in the face of historical accounts and a consideration of young men over time and place. In all of the chapters we draw upon empirical accounts to illustrate the ways in which masculinities and femininities are culturally imagined by young people and played out across a range of sites.

Unshackled from the patriarchal past and the confines of domesticity, new femininities are empowered to take centre stage in the newly reconfigured spheres of work and leisure through the cultivation of an active and agentic personhood. That life has changed for many young women appears as an undeniable truth of the present. Work, leisure and consumption provide spheres for the emergence of new feminine subject positions. In popular representations these new femininities appear everywhere from girls sporting *Playboy* logos on tight-fitting crop-top tee-shirts, high-flying middle-class school achievers, binge-drinking ladettes in the night-time economy, to needy and vulnerable career women in professional and corporate institutions. In its own way, each of these portrayals tell us something about the new girl order: femininity is no longer invisible, but *excessive*. And how do we know it is excessive? Because in schools, workplaces, drinking cultures and personal relationships girls – or so we are told – are now 'outdoing' the 'lads'. This is of course a highly selective representation that falls back upon a familiar binary of sexual difference. We agree that young women's lives are markedly different than in previous generations, but we contend, first, that these opportunities do not apply to all women and, second, that they are much more contradictory than they may at first appear. The new girl order as a Western neo-liberal construct is designed around individual opportunity, personal makeovers and the reflexive production of self. It is a club that carefully excludes peripheral femininities from 'pramface' teenage mums on unemployed estates, to plastic sandal-wearing peasants toiling in the Andean foothills.

However, the apparent freeing up of at least some Western young women in late-modernity has not necessarily met with the approval of older generations of feminists whose search for new ways of being female was politicized and trouble-torn. In the struggle to embrace the political project of feminism, second wave feminists commonly repressed many features of the feminine and particularly the self-consciously girly. The feminine was commonly presented as unnecessarily decorative: superfluous, trivial and unworthy, a forlorn fantasy of what men wanted women to be. The 'oh-my-god-I-might-break-a-nail' sensibility was disavowed in favour of the demonstration of ability and competence in the public domain and a sharing of responsibilities in the domestic sphere. To the dismay of many feminists, young women appear to want the fun and froth of femininity. Immersed in hyper-sexualized styles of adornment, their unself-conscious enjoyment of femininity and its accoutrements speak some previously unspeakable truths back to feminism. It appears the ideal of sisterhood is not a treasured inheritance for many young women; female subjectivity is marked by diversity and fragmentation rather than unity; women can emotionally betray other women; choice and opportunity may invoke more individualist modes of being. The renunciation of the foundational category 'women' as a basis for identity and political mobilization, in favour of the pleasures of the feminine, signals a break with the activism of the past and the possibility of a move towards other modes of collectivism. Among young women the popularity of Internet grrl-zines, mobile telecommunications and the widely celebrated girls' nights in or out suggest other ways of forming and reforming female friendships. However, girl-talk continues to be peppered with a liberal sprinkling of hetero-romance and perhaps a stronger sense of entitlement to sexual pleasure and satisfaction than ever before.

So can the refusal of a traditional feminist identity politics be regarded as a progressive move in itself? Young women's dalliance with the feminine bears all the hallmarks of a passionate new love affair – intense, all-consuming and powerful. Hyper-femininity is everywhere – to be lived and worn, produced and consumed. The visibility of young women and the reconfigured presence of the feminine as loud and 'out there' can be read as an attempt to bring the invisible labour of gender into public view. The work of 'doing' girl is no longer hidden in the margins of the domestic or the confines of the bedroom. The burgeoning of the beauty industry evidenced in the proliferation of businesses such as nail parlours, salons and treatment rooms, cosmetic surgery and clinical procedures testifies to the work ethic of appearing gendered as a committed endeavour involving serious amounts of time and money. However, this 'work' can also be seen in late-modern terms as integral to modes of *individualization* and the shaping of a reflexive project of self. Here young women are positioned as self-regulating subjects, compliantly bringing their bodies and themselves into line with normative modes of femininity that can be marketed and exchanged in the flexible global economies of new times. Their bodies are their biographies, the curriculum vitae upon which the glowing success of getting the 'right job' or the 'right fella' may yet depend. These 'bodyographies', as we can call them, involve the intermeshing of self with commodity and service. Bodyographies are perhaps most evident in the service sector where the quality of service is integral to the delivery and value of the product as conveyed through the management of emotion. In many cases this 'added value' or personal touch is what makes the product, as seen in the personal attention and lingering smile of the airhostess, sales representative, waitress, tour guide or sex-worker.

One of the advantages of looking at gender on a global scale is that it enables us to gain an insight into alternative modernities and world systems. It also allows us to address the limits of Western theories and concepts as well as short-circuit some of the wider generalizations made about social change. In doing so we can gain an insight into how the 'flows' of globalization are negotiated and reformed in peripheral places and the different social, political, cultural and economic transformations that may occur within these areas. In seeking to understand gender relations in contemporary times we have been mindful of the dominance of Western perspectives and the impact of globalization. We have deliberately sought out non-Western accounts to illustrate the value of looking cross-culturally. Looking at gender relations in a global context throws Western empirical studies into sharp relief, demonstrating above all else the mutable and diverse ways of doing gender across time and place. The critical readings considered in Chapter 5 illustrate young masculinities and femininities in process, revealing gender as a fragile and complex practice that is forever in the making. The successful 'doing' of gender in social relations becomes a highly accomplished enactment, constantly reworked through modes of production, consumption, regulation and performance. The ethnographic readings drawn from Brazil, UK, Russia and Tanzania consider the ways in which the performance of gender works at and struggles for meaning within its cultural context. Collectively they reveal that attempts to fix gender remain a quixotic project caught in the quicksand of time and place. The sexual exploits of Nick, the gay skin, the postcolonial spectacle of *carnaval*, the ritualistic circumcision practised by the Kaguru and the consciously crafted cultural affiliations of the 'normals' and 'progressives' exist as richly diverse examples of gender in process, brought into being by the interrelationship of socio-cultural arrangements and biographical trajectories. In keeping with our own approach, the studies attribute high value to the epistemological status of the subject as skilled and insightful interpreters of their social worlds. Collectively the readings prioritize lived relations, observing people over time, paying attention to what they say and do as central to meaning making and modes of analysis.

Female Masculinity

An interesting approach to gender relations considers what happens when women engage with masculinity as part of themselves rather than a male Other. Halberstam's (1998) US-based study of female masculinity has been instrumental in demonstrating that gender can be unhinged from the gender-appropriate body and that such disruptions offer us a glimpse into the ways in which masculinity is constructed. Halberstam argues that masculinity cannot be reduced to the male body; rather women can take on the semblance of masculinity in ways that reveal the workings of masculinity itself. She contends, 'the shapes and forms of modern masculinity are best showcased within female masculinity' (1998:3). Using what she terms 'queer methodologies', Halberstam draws upon interdisciplinary approaches to film, literary text, primary documents, performance art and photographic visual media in order to explore the contours of female masculinity.

Halberstam's starting point lies in a concern that ambiguously gendered bodies receive little recognition in Western societies. Despite the presence of female masculinity across many decades dating back to the nineteenth century and beyond, there remains a collective 'disbelief' in its presence and a general lack of acceptance of masculine women and boyish girls. As an illustration of this, Halberstam conceptualizes the category of tomboy as a childhood expression of female masculinity. She suggests that in many cases tomboyism is viewed benignly as a girl's agentic desire to enjoy the freedoms associated with boyhood. Tolerance evaporates, however, as girls enter puberty and the regulatory power of female adolescence kicks in to ensure that young women subscribe to the boundaries of normative femininity.

Refusing to let female masculinity die with adolescence, Halberstam, following Sedgwick (1990) argues for the production of new taxonomies of desire, physicality and subjectivity that claim to be premised upon a non-engagement or refusal of conventional masculinities and masculine power in order 'to explore a queer subject position that can successfully challenge hegemonic models of gender conformity' (1998:9). The details of these new taxonomies provide a richly diverse document, visual and textual, of female masculinities. Under the performance umbrella of 'drag king', we find nuanced versions of female masculinity such as butch realness, femme pretender, male mimicry, fag drag and denaturalized masculinity, carefully codified in relation to their simulation of masculine styles. The limitations of such taxonomic categories are acknowledged by Halberstam as a difficulty that has emerged as a consequence of being left to sexologists. She expresses some regret that the production of more 'accurate' and elaborate taxonomies has not continued, presumably led by academics and sexual activists rather than sexologists. In an interview with Annamarie Jagose (1999), Halberstam elaborates upon these themes, saying that she embraces categorization 'as a way of creating acts, identities and modes of being which otherwise remain unnameable' (1999:4), providing a counterpoint to humanist claims that categories inhibit subjects. Halberstam further suggests that her interest is in the categories produced and sustained by sexual subcultures, a theme pursued in a subsequent paper on queer subcultures, their use of time and space and the role of the academic in documenting and celebrating this fluid and creative set of activities (Halberstam, 2003). There is little evidence of subcultural voice in *Female Masculinity*, however, as all the categories are produced by Halberstam's reading of the drag king scene rather than by attempts to understand participant's views and experiences of it. It may be worth questioning the formulation of new taxonomies as a desirable project in itself regardless of who takes responsibility for devising the classificatory system. A Foucaultian argument could suggest that the production of taxonomies brings the sexual subject into being, giving them an identity that remains a powerful discursive production, forever premised upon a particular sexual behaviour, thereby producing visible subjects that can be known and regulated. Queer sensibilities commonly embrace the demise of the subject and the breakdown of the hetero–homo divide. The production of new taxonomies within a queer framework can be seen in contradictory ways as a curiously conservative project, attempting to give substance to the insubstantial. Furthermore Halberstam attaches special significance to performances of female masculinity staged by lesbians rather than heterosexuals, claiming that lesbians have a capacity to 'expose the artificiality of all genders and all sexual orientations and therefore to answer the charge of authenticity that is usually made only about lesbian identity' (1998:240). While these comments address some of the frequently replayed issues relating to identifying as lesbian and particularly butch, they also bespeak some residual investment in forms of identity politics that desire lesbian identity to *be real*, to provide a basis for particular identity claims. There remains an on-going tension throughout the text between recognizing masculinity as a fragile and ultimately hollow construction while simultaneously holding the notion of masculinity in place as a thing-in-itself that can be approximated, copied and performed.

Halberstam makes some big claims for female masculinity:

> I am arguing that the very existence of masculine women urges us to reconsider our most basic assumptions about the functions, forms and representations of masculinity . . . The first claim is that women have made their own unique contribution to what we call modern masculinity and that these contributions tend to go completely unnoticed in gender scholarship. The second claim is that what we recognise as female masculinity is actually a multiplicity of masculinities. (1998:45–46)

Additionally Halberstam expresses a commitment to 'make masculinity safe for girls' (1998:268), thus implying that there is something inherently 'dangerous' about masculinity that must be tamed if women are to assert this identification. These claims, however, do not emerge from engagement with drag kings themselves. Respondents interviewed by Halberstam in clubs, participating in drag king contests and on the scene had little to say about the transgressive or subversive potential of their performance. Women who performed as men reported dressing up in drag, ' "Just for fun", "It seemed like a crazy thing to do" or "I didn't really think about it" ' (1998:244). Such nonchalant responses suggest that their performances were not fuelled by a radical gender agenda. Rather as researchers such responses should act as signals to encourage us to pay more attention to what respondents say and do in order to understand the social world from their perspective. It is, of course, entirely possible that performing as authentically male may mean *nothing* to many drag kings and this 'meaninglessness' may be important to understand in its own terms. Subcultural activity has often been a temporary and part-time affair for participants, providing differing levels of significance for those involved. For some drag king performers the Saturday night spectacle of dressing up as a man may be a brief moment of little consequence for the rest of their week. But for others it may be that precious moment in their lives where they feel, 'This is me, this is who I am!' However, this is not the response of Halberstam's drag participants. The fallacy of meaningfulness can be a kind of intellectual indulgence for investigators that we entertain at the expense of ethnographically generated insights into the social lives of people whose epistemological status in this context is inevitably greater than that of researchers.

In the final chapter of the book, Halberstam draws upon her personal experience to consolidate her argument for female masculinity. She recalls her girlhood self wanting a pair of boxing gloves and a punch-bag for her thirteenth birthday. This recollection is presented as her desire to keep adult womanhood in abeyance while being able to beat up boys of her own age. Growing up in 1970s England, her desires were met with regulatory reminders, prohibitions and the offer of 'alternative' activities befitting of normative femininity of the period. Halberstam presents a moving account of adolescence as:

> the shrinking of my world . . . no explanation needed to be given for the narrowing of a girl's life once she hit puberty; indeed, adolescence produced a logic all its own and all challenges to that logic were simply more evidence of one's irrational attachment to inappropriate behaviour. (1998:267–268)

She goes on to argue that girls should avoid femininity in girlhood as it is all too readily associated with pathologies that may endanger their well-being. Rather Halberstam appears to suggest that girls and young women embrace their masculinity through sport and play as an agentic alternative to normative femininity. While sympathetic to these expressed ideals of childrearing, we admit to being puzzled by the framing of such practices. Why promote female masculinity when one could as easily take a bolder stride towards 'the end of masculinity' (MacInnes, 1998), use performance to 'trouble' all gender identities (Butler, 1990) and perhaps begin the difficult project of undoing gender as at least some young people signalled in Chapter 8.

In the final pages of the book Halberstam pays homage to boxing as an ultimate expression of female masculinity. Appealing especially to women who identify as butch, boxing represents a ritualized and highly physical expression of power; within the ring underdogs can punch above their status to emerge as champions against all the odds. Halberstam suggests the absence of powerful images of masculine women encoded in representations of butch produces a need to cross-identify with male heroes. Resonant with themes found in our earlier discussions of the *Rocky* movies and *Fight Club*, Halberstam's discussion of *Raging Bull* presents pugilism as a magical solution to the contradictions of white masculinity, with the added twist, however, that Raging Bull can emerge as Raging Bull Dyke in an animated moment of cross-identification:

> The male boxer from Rocky Bilboa to Jake La Motta, represents for me the spectacle of a battered white masculinity that always finds a way to win. By replacing the pugilist with the butch raging bull, I offer masculinity a new champion, a legitimate contender, ready to fight all comers and determined to go the distance. (1998:43)

Such fighting talk presents quite a challenge to the gender order. At the risk of appearing unfit for the fight we would like to suggest that boxing only offers a subversion of gender if we hold in place masculinity and its symbolic associations. Halberstam's study gives a great deal of power to female masculinity as a style that is capable of subversion, transgression and transformation. In doing so the emphasis upon physicality and *looking like a man* risks reifying the category of masculinity as a stylization valorized in endless emulations in search of the authentic embodied form. Related to this, there is a concern that female masculinity remains rooted in the pursuit of activities associated with boys and men and the accompanying signifiers of looking like a boy/man. Can hyper-feminine girls do female masculinity or does their very girliness preclude them? The tension inherent in the text weaves a faint and sometimes invisible line between viewing masculinity as a construction while engaging with it as real. In this respect Halberstam's taxonomy of female masculinity comes dangerously close to assuming 'copies of an original' rather than 'copies of a copy'. Baudrillard's (1983) use of the term simulacrum is useful here in implying a copy without an original, which we feel offers a more appropriate way of rethinking sex/gender categories. Healy's (1996) study of *Gay Skins*, discussed in Chapter 5, points out that simulation and mimicry is not necessarily transgressive outside of relations of power. His study closely observes the texture of gay skinheads' lives and experiences as they work to reveal the masquerade of *all* masculinity; here gay Skinhead style is not the queering of an original, but copy to copy. The studies diverge in one crucial respect – the contrast between the portrait of gay skins and the classification of female masculinity illustrates the ensuing differences that emerge in treating masculinity as an empty sign and imbuing it with meaning.

Finally it is worth considering Halberstams's approach to femininity. There is a striking lack of engagement with femininities in any form throughout the text. Where femininity does appear in childhood and adolescence it is treated as uniformly *bad*, a repressive regulatory force that inhibits and confines girls. However, as popular representations and late-modern accounts of femininity show, it can simultaneously be experienced as pleasurable, occasionally powerful but inevitably contradictory. It is these popular representations of femininity that many young (and not so young) women are embracing. Related to this, there is a further assumption throughout Halberstam's account that female masculinity is orientated to the world of masculinities. As a mirror opposite of masculinity, femininity appears a pale reflection of 'being'. In this respect femininity is conceived as the shadow of masculinity, its two-dimensional, not-yet-there Other – it is absence or 'lack' rather than substantiated presence.

As we have tried to show, masculinity and femininity are better understood as mutually constitutive relations, once arbitrary signs that have now become endowed with specialist meaning in late-modernity. As the various international examples we draw upon illustrate, gender is accorded different value and meaning in different societies. Above all these signs are given meaning through historical relations of power that have enabled masculinity to appear as the 'master' signifier of a Western logocentrism. Halberstam's depiction of female masculinity offers some resistance to these modalities but inevitably lapses into the construction of femininity as a lacuna awaiting the penetration of masculinity, that affirmative presence that can render it to life. There is a further assumption that the performance of drag king involves the negation or refusal of the feminine. Drag king performers are presumed to be in dialogue with masculinity, providing a comment upon and a re-presentation of masculine styles. It is worth considering, however, the possibility that the phenomenon of drag king may have valuable things to say about femininity and particularly the assertive new femininities of late-modernity. Could it be that identification with the representation of raging bull dyke conceals a thinly veiled desire to express the guilty pleasures of phallic womanhood that, potentially, have as much to say about constructions of femininity as masculinity?

Ultimately *Female Masculinity* is a book about bending – not ending – gender. As Sennett notes, 'Despite a detailed examination of the complexities and paradoxes of performing masculinity, Halberstam's reliance on a stable, definable body "underneath" the drag king performance remains essential to her definition of drag' (2002:40). While Halberstam is willing to queer the category of gender then, through the notion of female masculinity, she is unable to fully transcend the ontological bedrock of sex. The woman that is masculine is still, somehow, always a woman. In Derrida's terms, she is not exposed as a category under erasure, but instituted as a 'proper object'. The sexed body of the woman is then much more than the canvas upon which gender subversion is enacted through drag, female boxing or other gender-bending activities. As Cream queries:

> We don't simply add 'sex' to the body and we definitely don't add 'the body' to something called 'sex'. What, then is this thing we call the sexed body? The sexed body is a construction that requires explanation. It does not simply exist, it is not a starting point. (1995:31)

It is these, more 'troubling' questions about gender, sex and the body that we feel offer a rather different theoretical and political trajectory than the body-bound notion of female masculinity. For Cream 'gender *and* sex are historically and geographically variable categories' which in turn means a radical questioning of terms such as 'girl', 'boy', 'male' or 'female'. In disrupting the taken-for-granted nature of the body, Cream's discussion focuses upon the abject bodies of transsexuals, intersex subjects and women athletes who have been 'exposed' as having XXY chromosomes as opposed to the XX chromosomes associated with 'woman' or the XY chromosomes ascribed to 'man'. In this latter example Cream remarks that it is 'highly contentious to assert that a woman with XXY chromosomes is not a woman' (p. 35). Indeed there are at least 15 different forms of intersexuality, including subjects with multiple and partially formed sex organs as well as those with chromosomes that do not fit the bi-polar definitions of 'male' and 'female' (Stanley, 2002). In troubling sex in this way it appears that it can no longer be invoked with any definitive clarity. A rather different, if equally compelling account of the manipulation of sexed bodies can be found in the fascinating narratives of Krystal Bennett, Renee Richards and Vincent (2006), the latter whose story is worthy of a detailed critical discussion below.

Making and Faking Sex

The uncertainty surrounding sex and the body are illustrated in the life-stories of lesbian, gay, bisexual, transgender and intersex (LGBTI) subjects as our account of sex and subculture in Chapter 5 disclosed. Rasmussen's media analysis of Krystal Bennett, described in the US media as 'a big, butch, out dyke who brought her girlfriend to the prom' (2006:175), vividly depicts the reworking of sex and gender categories. In Ferndale High School, Washington, Krystal Bennett was nominated Prom King by her senior class, an incident that was later to throw the national media, school and heterosexual institution of the Prom into apoplectic frenzy. As Rasmussen reports,

Bennett's story has such currency because it challenges not only discursive dividing practices relating to sexual identities but also divisions relating to gender identities. Effectively, Bennett's election momentarily reconfigures the sacred space of the prom and exposes its contingent foundations. (p. 178)

The contingent nature of sex, gender and the body are evident in the personal testimonies of the former tennis player Renee Richards who won one singles title in her career. Renee Richards was born a 'man' and had previously played in men's tournaments as Richard Rashkind. At a much later point, having become a 'woman', she returned to compete in women's tennis tournaments. 'The argument against me playing was that I would be physically stronger than the other girls, but I thought it was a fair fight', she contests. 'I was 43 at the time, 20 years older than most of the girls on the tour. It was an equal playing field, and that's the most important thing' (*The Guardian*, Sport, September 2, 2006, p. 2). Renee Richards records how she made numerous friends on court, including Billie Jean King and Martina Navaratilova whose lesbianism and fierce competitive spirit led each of them to be deemed 'mannish' in some quarters. However, Richards also received a notably cool reception from some women players about her sex-change and the perceived advantages it was felt to afford her on the women's circuit. 'At times the notoriety was almost overwhelming', she sighs. Retiring from the game, she went on to coach Navaratilova for 3 years before returning to medicine where she currently practices as an ophthalmologist in New York, under the working title of Dr Renee Richards. This snap-shot sporting biography illuminates the ways in which gender, sex and the body can be seen as *manipulations* of certain types of being, rather than a timeless essential set of qualities.

In contrast to Halberstam's study of female masculinity, Norah Vincent used herself as a way of directly experiencing the world of masculinity. Her project as a self-generated social experiment in experiential learning appears not dissimilar to George Orwell's (1986) attempt to understand the poverty of 1930s Britain in *The Road to Wigan Pier* where he seeks to shed light upon bourgeois privilege by living as working class and John Howard Griffin's (1960) personal documentation of racism and discrimination in 1960s USA who, as a white American, uses medication, ultra-violet and staining to 'become' black. The manipulation of identity is also deployed by undercover investigators as well as certain anthropologists and ethnographers who make ethical decisions about their research. Vincent, with friends on the New York drag king scene, dressed up as man and went out for a night on the town. She enjoyed passing as a man, her measure of success involved scanning faces to see if anyone gave her a second or third look. Being female and not being noticed when in drag was a new and exciting experience for her. She decided to live as a man for 18 months.

Vincent documents her detailed, painstaking and highly personal efforts to embody masculinity. Her first step is to call herself Ned, conjuring into being a male identity through the act of naming. Vincent describes 'doctoring' her head and face, cutting her hair to emphasize the jaw line, 'creating' stubble, strapping her breasts in and wearing baggy clothes, glasses and a baseball cap. Having simulated the appearance of masculinity she sets about embodying it: lifting weights to bulk up her arms and shoulders, eating more, gaining weight, learning the behaviours of male company, ways of talking, walking and interacting. The final item in the assimilated repertoire of masculinity was a prosthetic penis which she nicknamed 'Sloppy Joe'. She does not comment upon the significance of the naming process but perhaps it seems only fitting for her new member to be given an identity too. Bought from a sex shop in Manhattan, she held it in place with a jockstrap and felt it gave her, rather than anyone else, 'a more realistic experience of "manhood" '. Vincent started spending time with a group of men who played bowls regularly and, though Ned was much ridiculed for being seriously inept at the game, he was accepted into the group as a guy who they could hang with and share a joke.

Norah Vincent's insights into masculinity and the world of men were most marked in encounters with women. After a number of dates with women met through Internet dating sites, she reports feeling waves of misogyny, impatience and rage at the sexual power of women and the ways they exercised it. Most women did little to conceal their disdain for men, leaving Ned feeling judged and defensive. In a passage that indicates the powerful emotional investment Vincent made in Ned, she describes her experience of dating women:

> Many of my dates – even the more passive ones – did most of the talking. I listened to them talk literally for hours about the most minute, mind numbing details of their personal lives . . . [L]istening to them was like undergoing a slow frontal lobotomy. Weren't people supposed to be on their best behaviour on first dates? Weren't they supposed to at least pretend an interest in the other person, out of politeness if nothing else?

Women's capacity to condemn men, judge them and bore them at the same time feels like an intensely personal expression of misogyny that gains momentum over time as Ned gets close to women while simultaneously being repelled by them. Ned begins to feel sorry for heterosexual men caught in the double bind of trying to be guys and trying to please women. Vincent provocatively describes masculinity as a clanking and ill-fitting suit of armour in which men attempt to hide but can never completely conceal the vulnerability and insecurity at the heart of living and performing as male. Vincent concludes:

> I passed in a man's world not because my mask was so real, but because the world of men was a masked ball. Eventually I realised that my disguise was the one thing I had in common with every other guy in the room. It was hard being a guy.

Vincent's experiences point to the importance of the affective domain as a site where the work of gender can be played out. What it feels like to identify as masculine or feminine, to accomplish the enactment of gender with seeming ease becomes a highly charged and emotionally intense affair. The performance of gender requires constant work on the body and the process of embodying gender or 'passing' appears to carry affective affiliations and consequences that are powerfully felt.

But we can also take something more from Norah/Ned's experience as s/he meanders between the supposedly opposite poles of masculinity and femininity. There is a type of gender 'double consciousness' at work here that not only offers critical insight into the construction of masculinity in the way that Halberstam does, but more than this there is also to be found some intelligent criticism regarding the contemporary constitution of femininity in Western societies. Thus the clanking armour of masculinity is an interesting metaphor that we can extend into a sharp critique of young men's ironclad inflexibility to adapt to the challenge of feminism and the new conditions in late-modernity. But the gender arrangements through which new femininities are produced can also be called into question. Many modern modes of femininity are premised upon individualization and this can be traced in the self-absorbed characteristics of Ned's dating companions who are each immersed in their own endless project of the self. As Skeggs (1997:163) explains, 'The project of the self is a Western bourgeois project wherein "Individuals" are the product of privilege, who can occupy the economic and cultural conditions which enable them to do the work on the self'. These dynamics resonate in popular culture where the contours of individualization are seen in Ally McBeal, Carrie Bradshaw, Bridget Jones and many other fictional characters that have come to symbolize the ditzy but nevertheless self-obsessed performance of contemporary femininities. What these accounts disclose is the myth of the neo-liberal 'can-do girl' as a fiction premised upon beauty, whiteness and the never ceasing appeal of bourgeois possibility.

Closing Remarks

This book has explored the everyday activity of gender in the lives of young people. In particular theories of gender performance are highly useful for considering the role of bodies, action and 'doing'. New work in this area also alerts us to the way in which affect and emotion can yield important insights into the psychic realm of identification, dissimulation and disavowal. Moreover performance theories demonstrate the compulsion of routine and how the repetition of regulatory activities can impact upon individual subjects and the seemingly enduring structures they give meaning to. Our approach has been to bring together new theoretical insights on gender with the lived experience of young people. This has led us to a detailed consideration of neighbourhoods, schools, workplaces, bedrooms, shopping and night-life spaces as arenas within which gender is continually made and remade. This approach has shown how gender is institutionally orchestrated and materially conceived. In this respect, while it may be philosophically convenient to speak of gender performativity in theoretical abstraction, we suggest gender performance always occurs in a particular time and place and is subject to the lived context of those spaces.

In the previous chapter, we saw how institutions such as schools assume the presence of sex categories as known and knowable, the immutable basis of gendered subjectivity. Gender identity within this space remains realizable in different forms as young people rehearse, repeat and resist the fashionable tide of gender norms and meanings inherent in masculine cultures and hetero-sexual hierarchies. The effort expended in giving substance to the insubstantial suggests that the idea of gender occupies a kind of comfort zone for teachers and students, a settled certainty of the educative experience. While a notion of the curriculum and what counts as knowledge may mutate in response to changing educational policies or political realignments, notions of gender identity appear as an unassailable presence, a constant educational experience amidst the turmoil of reform and new initiatives. What is evident in such institutions is that adults and young people are performative beings that each contribute to and sustain the fiction of gender identity as real and significant in foundational terms. Similar gender assumptions can be found in work-based institutions such as factories, the banking sector or law societies (Willis, 1977; McDowell, 1997; Collier, 1998).

Work on the performance of gender should also invite a reconsideration of objects. According to Lash and Urry (1999:15), in the postmodern era 'What is increasingly being produced are not material objects, but signs'. These writers point to the way in which objects are 'emptied out' of symbolic and even material content but may take on an aesthetic value within circuits of production and consumption. 'This is occurring', they declare, 'not just in the proliferation of non-material objects which comprise a substantial aesthetic component (such as pop music, cinema, magazines, video etc.), but also in the increasing component of sign value or image in *material* objects' (1999:15). Youth cultures are saturated with objects such as lipstick, magazines, stationary and collectables of various kinds. In some studies these items appear as part of the underground economy of the student world, having use-value and symbolic significance to young people as members of total institutions (Thorne, 1993). In other studies these items constitute the paraphernalia of gender in young lives, the ephemeral stuff of boyhood and girlhood that exist in leisure time spaces – in the playground, in bedrooms, in activities with peers. We suggest that these objects are culturally significant and play a vital role in communic-ating the idea of gender. Indeed youth cultures are niche markets *par excellence*. The aesthetization of objects such as branded running shoes is not so much a statement of 'who one is' but 'who one wishes to be'. It is part of the gendered composition of 'self'.

Moreover the gendering of bodies and commodities (such as the adornment of a bunny girl logo, previously discussed) through production may take on new meaning at the level of consumption. For young girls the logo could appeal for its 'cutesie' rabbit motif, while for young women it can be used to 'hype-up' their own sex-value and 'knowingness' within particular peer groups. Even so, these are highly contradictory relations that cannot be separated out from market forces and gender regimes. We have argued, then, that the performance of gender is subject to material relations – including objects, social structures and institutions – as well as the discursive interplay of cultural signs. The endless simulacra Baudrillard (1983) identifies and the 'economies of signs and space' Lash and Urry (1999) speak of suggest that in a world of appearances it is the value of the sign that is significant, however artificial it may be. Regarding sex and gender as empty signs, but ones that have come to carry special meaning in late-modernity, enables us to see how gender processes are set in motion. Locating performance in time and space is then an important means of understanding how gender is signed through material, discursive and embodied practices.

If they are to retain any significance, queer theories need to engage more fully with everyday life. Butler's reading of gender, as brought into being by enactment, places a new accent on the action over the subject. This leads us to take seriously the material properties of objects as tools or technologies of doing that produce the subject. Such enactments point to the many ways in which gender identity is troubled and recuperated in everyday encounters. For example Halberstam's warrior challenge to deploy images of female boxing to disturb hegemonic masculinity may have to be revised where these signs are rapidly incorporated and 'emptied out' of their intended meaning in market encounters at the nexus of capital. As recent Hollywood films (e.g. *Million Dollar Babe*) and recurrent advertisements using women boxers show, even powerful signs can be 'flattened out' and sold back to women in endless commercials for tampons, leg-waxing and deodorant. Here it is not the use-value of the material product that is of such significance, but the sign-value attached to what a woman boxer might represent if the context is adjusted through modes of individualization that make capital out of feminist notions of 'power', 'independence' and 'taking control'. These affective qualities and the gender identifications they may elicit inevitably come at a price and are far in excess of what the commodity itself can achieve. These images also work at an inter-textual level, through symbolic references to the popular computer-generated image (and now film icon) Lara Croft or the high-kicking can-do girl that is *Buffy the Vampire Slayer*. It would seem that when we assume that sex is real and invoke strong gender images to overturn established gender types, in a sign-making world we quickly find that 'all that is solid soon melts into air'.

On the world stage, gender relations continue to remain an organizing principle in the arrangement of most human societies. Economic restructuring and
cultural globalization are certainly producing new masculinities and femininities through mobile signs that are taken on, embodied and brought to life
when inhabited by human actors. Film and popular culture abound with these
new, yet not-so-new gender styles. As we have seen, a familiar refrain in
late-modernity is that young men are 'in crisis', and young women are the
flexible beneficiaries of neo-liberal forms of thinking and being. However, this
representation seems less coherent when placed alongside the lived experience of young people. These experiences indicate that 'crisis' and 'opportunity'
are exceptionally wide-ranging subject positions – shaped by a variety of
forces – and that most youth biographies actually fall somewhere between
these extremes. Empirical studies, firsthand observations and interactions with
young people rather suggest that they utilize multiple gender strategies that
may be complicit, resistant or ironic of the prevailing gender order. What
close-up ethnographic portraits reveal is a much more subtle and varied
repertoire of experience in which gender relations are marked by a prosaic
patchwork that encompasses continuity and change, collective action and individualization, cosmopolitan mobility and place-bound forms of affective social
identification.

That social theory has yet to fully grasp the changing complexity of young
lives suggests a need to return to the emerging experiences of young men and
women themselves and locate this within and across particular sites and spaces.
By locating our accounts through recent debates on global ethnography, we
hope to have gone some way to showing the tenuous constitution of gender
across time and place and illustrated the contradictions of living gender in
late-modernity.

If our analysis of the production, consumption, regulation and performance
of gender is anything to go by, gender relations have come a long way and
there are certainly a variety of new practices in occurrence. Interestingly there
appears a greater range of new femininities in the circuits of representation
than of masculinity but even here age, ethnicity, sexuality and class give rise
to multiple masculinities. A main aspect of our work has been to look at
how global change and economic restructuring are impinging upon these sites
and changing gender relations within them. As we have seen, gender transformations in these spaces are highly uneven and contradictory. In these sites
we have also drawn attention to the importance of everyday culture and the
ways in which music, film, magazines, new technologies and television soaps
provide a flexible repertoire through which a host of gender identifications
and dis-identifications take place. Here we have seen how young men and
women are discerning subjects who negotiate and creatively rework the meanings of gender and give it embodied form in daily life. In doing so, we have
suggested that the crisis in masculinity and the opportunistic new girl order

are both 'out-of-scale' images that cannot capture the complexity and diversity of individual lives. Moreover this thoroughly modernist way of looking places Western youth centre stage relegating all others to the roles of minor supporting cast members.

The highly selective and emotive way of approaching the youth question through gendered notions of 'crisis' and 'opportunism' relies upon a preconception of what masculinity and femininity 'is'. It invokes these signs as 'real objects' that are tied to sexed bodies and practices assumed to be inherent in young men and women. The ontological security ascribed to sex and gender allows them to operate as seemingly stable points of reference in an increasingly insecure world. Yet despite the tenuous, pluralized and increasingly fragmented constructions of gender in late-modernity it appears as an incontrovertible truth, an immutable corporeal reality tethered to the weighty anchor that is sex. This implies that the process of ending gender will require a critical rethinking of sex and a detailed interrogation of what it means to be a young man or woman in late-modernity. For the time being, we are at least witnessing the rewriting of some gender signs and the erasure of others.

References

Aapola, S., Gonick, M. and Harris, A. (2005) *Young Femininity, Girlhood, Power and Social Change*, Basingstoke: Palgrave.

Adkins, L. (2002) *Revisions: Gender and Sexuality in Late Modernity*, Buckingham: Open University Press.

Ahmed, S. (1997) ' "It's a sun-tan isn't it?" Autobiography as identificatory process', in H.S. Mirza (ed.) *Black British Feminism: A Reader*, London: Routledge.

Alexander, C. (2000) *The Asian Gang*, Oxford: Berg.

Ali, S. (2003) *Mixed Race, Post Race?* Oxford: Berg.

Althusser, L. (1971) *Ideology and Ideological State Apparatuses, Lenin and Philosophy and Other Essays*, London: New Left Books.

Altman, M. (1984) 'Everything they always wanted you to know: The ideology of popular sex', in C. Vance (ed.), *Pleasure and Danger: Exploring Female Sexuality*, London: Pandora.

Ang, I. (1985) *Watching Dallas: Soap Opera and the Melodramatic Imagination*, London: Methuen.

Appadurai, A. (1990) 'Disjuncture and difference in the global economy', *Theory, Culture and Society*, 7, pp. 295–310.

Archer, L. (2003) *Race, Masculinity and Schooling: Muslim Boys and Education*, Maidenhead: Open University Press.

Arthurs, J. (2004) *Television and Sexuality, Regulation and the Politics of Taste*, Maidenhead: Open University Press.

Back, L. (1996) *New Ethnicities and Urban Culture: Racism and Multiculture in Young Lives*, London: UCL Press.

Back, L. and Nayak, A. (1999) 'Signs of the times? Violence, graffiti and racism in the English suburbs', in T. Allen and J. Eade (eds), *Divided Europenas: Understanding Ethnicities in Conflict*, The Hague/London/Boston: Kluwer Law International.

Barker, C. (1998) ' "Cindy is a please leave slut": Moral identities and moral responsibility in the "soap please leave talk" of British Asian girls', *Sociology*, 32 (1), pp. 65–81.

Barker, M. (1989) *Comics, Ideology, Power and the Critics*, Manchester: Manchester University Press.

Baudrillard, J. (1983) *Simulation*, Columbia University New York: Semiotext(e).

Bauman, Z. (1988) *Freedom*, Milton Keynes: Open University Press.

Beck, U. (1992) *Risk Society: Towards a New Modernity*, London: Sage.

Beidelman, T.O. (1997) *The Cool Knife: Imagery of Gender, Sexuality and Moral Education in Kaguru Initiation Ritual*, Washington: Smithsonian Institution Press.

Bennett, A. (1999) 'Subcultures or neo-tribes? Rethinking the relationship between youth, style and musical taste', *Sociology*, 33 (3), pp. 599–617.

Beynon, J. (2002) *Masculinities and Culture*, Milton Keynes: Open University Press.

Bhabha, H. (1994) *The Location of Culture*, London: Routledge.

Billig, M. (1987) *Arguing and Thinking, A Rhetorical Approach to Social Psychology*, Cambridge: Cambridge University Press.

Bjerrum Nielsen, H. and Rudberg, M. (1994) *Psychological Gender and Modernity*, Oslo: Scandinavian University Press.

Blackman, L. (2004) 'Self help, media cultures and the production of female psychopathology', *European Journal of Cultural Studies*, 7 (2), pp. 219–236.

Blackman, S. (1995) *Youth: Positions and Oppositions – Style, Sexuality and Schooling*, Aldershot: Avebury.

Blackman, S. (2005) 'Youth subcultural theory: A critical engagement with the concept, its origins and politics from the Chicago School to postmodernism', *Journal of Youth Studies*, 8 (1), pp. 1–20.

Bloustein, G. (1998) 'It's different to a mirror "cos it talks to you": Teenage girls, video cameras and identity', in S. Howard (ed.), *Wired Up: Young People and the Electronic Media*, London: UCL Press.

Bohnsack, R. and Nohl, A.M. (2003). 'Youth culture and practical innovation: Turkish German youth. "time out" and the actionisms of break-dance', *European Journal of Youth Studies*, 6 (3), pp. 366–385.

Bourdieu, P. (1984) *Distinction: A Social Critique of the Judgement of Taste*, Cambridge, MA: Harvard University Press.

Brewer, J.D. (2002[2000]) *Ethnography*, Buckingham: Open University.

Brunsdon, C. (1997) *Screen Tastes, Soap Opera to Satellite Dishes*, London: Routledge.

Buckingham, D. and Bragg, S. (2003) *Young People, Sex and the Media: The Facts of Life?* Basingstoke: Palgrave.

Burawoy, M., Blum, J.A., George, S., Gille, Z., Gowan, T., Haney, L., Klawiter, M., Lopez, S.H., Riain, S.O. and Thayer, M. (2000) *Global Ethnography: Forces, Connections, and Imaginations in a Postmodern World*, Berkeley Los Angeles and London, England: University of California Press.

Butler, J. (1990) *Gender Trouble, Feminism and the Subversion of Gender*, London: Routledge.

Butler, J. (1991) 'Imitation and Gender Insubordination', in D. Fuss (ed.), *Inside/Out: Lesbian Theories, Gay Theories*, London/New York: Routledge, pp. 13–31.

Butler, J. (1993) *Bodies that Matter, On the Discursive Limits of Sex*, London: Routledge.

Butler, J. (1994) 'Against Proper Objects', *Differences: A Journal of Feminist Cultural Studies*, 6 (2+3), pp. 1–26.

Butler, J. (2000) 'Critically queer', in P. Du Gay, J. Evans and P. Redman (eds), *Identity: A Reader*, London: Sage/Open University Press.

Butler, J. (2004) *Undoing Gender*, Boca Raton, FL: Routledge Taylor and Francis.

Byrne, B. (2006) *White Lives, the Interplay of 'Race', Class and Gender in Everyday Lives*, London: Routledge.

Caminha, P. Vaz de. (1943) 'A carta de pero Vaz de Caminha', in J. Cortesao (ed.), *A Carta de Pero Vaz de Caminha*, Rio de Janeiro: Livros de Portugal.

Campbell, B. (1993) *Goliath: Britain's Dangerous Places*, London: Methuen.

Canaan, J. (1991) 'Is "doing nothing" just boys' play? Integrating feminist and cultural studies perspectives on working-class masculinities', in S. Franklin, C. Lury and J. Stacey (eds), *Off Centre: Feminism and Cultural Studies*, London: Routledge.

Castells, M. (1997) *The Power of Identity*, London: Blackwell.

Charlesworth, S.J. (2000) *A Phenomenology of Working Class Experience*, Cambridge: Cambridge University Press.

Chatterton, P. and Hollands, R. (2002) 'Theorising urban playscapes: Producing, regulating and consuming youthful mightlife city spaces', *Urban Studies*, 39 (1), pp. 95–116.

Chatterton, P. and Hollands, R. (2003) *Making Urban Nightscapes: Youth Cultures, Pleasure Spaces and Corporate Power*, London: Routledge.

Clarke, J. (1977) 'Skinheads and the magical recovery of community', in S. Hall and T. Jefferson (eds), *Resistance through Rituals*, London: Hutchinson.

Cohen, P. (1997) *Rethinking the Youth Question*, Basingstoke: Macmillan.

Cohen, P. and Ainley, P. (2000) 'In the country of the blind? Youth studies and cultural studies in Britain', *Journal of Youth Studies*, 3 (1), pp. 79–95.

Cohen, S. (1972) *Folk Devils and Moral Panics*, London: Paladin.

Coffield, F. (1986) *Growing up at the Margins, Young Adults in the North East*, Milton Keynes: Open University Press.

Collier, R. (1998) *Masculinity, Crime and Criminology: Men, Heterosexuality and the Criminal(ised) Other*, London: Sage.

Comfort, A. (ed.) (1974) *The Joy of Sex, A Gourmet Guide to Lovemaking*, London: Quartet.

Connell, R.W. (1987) *Gender and Power*, London: Routledge.

Connell, R.W. (1989) 'Cool guys, swots and wimps: The interplay of masculinity and education', *Oxford Review of Education*, 15 (3), pp. 291–303.

Connell, R.W. (2002) *Gender*, Oxford: Blackwell.

Connolly, P. (1995) 'Boys will be boys? Racism, sexuality and the construction of masculine identities among infant boys', in J. Holland, M. Mlair and S. Sheldon (eds), *Debates and Issues in Feminist Research and Pedagogy*, Clevedon: Multilingueal Matters/The Open University.

Corrigan, P. (1979) *Schooling the Smash Street Kids*, London: Macmillan.

Couldry, N. (2000) *Inside Culture: Re-imagining the Method of Cultural Studies*, London: Sage.

Coward, R. (1984) *Female Desire*, London: Paladin.

Cream, J. (1995) 'Re-solving riddles: The sexed body', in D. Bell and G. Valentine (eds), *Mapping Desire*, London: Routledge.

Daniel, S. and McGuire, P. (eds) (1972) *The Paint House: Words from An East End Gang*, Harmondsworth: Penguin.

Davies, J. (1995) 'I'm the bad guy? Falling down and white masculinity in 1990s Hollywood', *Journal of Gender Studies*, 4 (2), pp. 145–152.

Dawson, G. (1994) *Soldier Heroes, British Adventure, Empire and the Imagining of Masculinity*, London: Routledge.

De Beauvoir, S. (1972[1949]) *The Second Sex*, London: Cape.

Delamont, S. (2001) *Changing Women, Unchanged Men? Sociological Perspectives on Gender in a Post-industrial Society*, Buckingham: Open University Press.

Derrida, J. (1991) 'A Derrida Reader: Between the Blinds', in P. Kamuf (ed.), New York: Columbia University Press.

Dollimore, J. (1996[1991]) *Sexual Dissonance: Augustine to Wilde, Freud to Foucault*, Oxford: Clarendon Press.

Douglas, M. (1966) *Purity and Danger*, London: Routledge.

Dubberley, W.S. (1993) 'Humour as resistance', in P. Woods and M. Hammersley (eds), *Gender and Ethnicity in Schools: Ethnographic Accounts*, London: Routledge.

Dwyer, C. (1999) 'Negotiations of femininity and identity for young British Muslim women', in N. Laurie, C. Dwyer, S. Holloway and F. Smith (eds), *Geographies of New Femininities*, Essex: Pearson, pp. 135–152.

Dyer, R. (1997) *White*, London: Routledge.

Dyson, A.H. (1997) *Writing Superheroes, Contemporary Childhood, Popular Culture and Classroom Literact*, New York: Teachers College Press.

Ehrenreich, B., Hesss, E. and Jacobs, G. (1992) 'Beatlemania: A sexually deviant subculture', in K. Gelder and S. Thornton (eds), *The Subcultures Reader*, London: Routledge.

Epstein, D. and Johnson, R. (1998) *Schooling Sexualities*, Buckingham: Open University Press.

Fanon, F. (1978) *Black Skin, White Masks*, New York: Grove Press.

Farrer, J. (1999) 'Disco "super-please leave culture": Consuming foreign sex in the Chinese disco', *Sexualities*, 2 (2), pp. 147–166.

Featherstone, M. (1998[1991]) *Consumer Culture and Postmodernism*, London: Sage.

Foster, V., Kimmel, M. and Skelton, C. (2001) ' "What about the boys"? An overview of the debates', in W. Martino and B. Meyenn (eds), *What About the Boys? Issues of Masculinity in Schools*, pp. 1–23, Buckingham: Open University Press.

Foucault, M. (1976) *The History of Sexuality*, vol. 1, treans R. Hurley, Harmondsworth: Penguin.

Foucault, M. (1978) *The History of Sexuality Volume 1: An Introduction*, Translated by R. Hurley, Harmondsworth: Penguin.

Foucault, M. (1988) 'Technologies of the Self', in L. Martin, H. Gutman and P.H. Hutton (eds), *Technologies of the Self, A Seminar with Michel Foucault*, London: Tavistock.

Frankenberg, R. (1993) *White Women, Race Matters: The Social Construction of Whiteness*, London: Routledge.

Freud, S. (1905[Edition 1977]) 'Three Essays on the Theory of Sexuality', Translated by J. Strachey, *Pelican Freud*, volume 7, Harmondsworth: Penguin.

Freyre, G. (1983) *Casa-frande e Senzala: Formacao Brasileira Sob o Regime da Economica Patriarchal*, Rio de Janeiro: Livrarria Jose Olympio Editora.

Frosh, S., Phoenix, A. and Pattman, R. (2002) *Young Masculinities*, Basingstoke: Palgrave.

Fuss, D. (1991) 'Inside/Out', in D. Fuss (ed.), *Inside/Out: Lesbian Theories, Gay Theories*, London: Routledge.

Giddens, A. (1986[1982]) *Sociology: A Brief but Critical Introduction*, Basingstoke: MacMillan.

Giddens, A. (1991) *Modernity and Self Identity, Self and Society in the Late Modern Age*, Cambridge: Polity Press.

Giddens, A. (1992) *The Transfomation of Intimacy: Sexuality, Love and Eroticism in Modern Societies*, Cambridge: Polity Press.

Giddens, A. (1993) *The Transformation of Intimacy: Sexuality, Love and Eroticism in Modern Societies*, Cambridge: Polity Press.

Gill, R. (2006) *Re-writing the Romance? Chick Lit and Post Feminism*, paper presented at ESRC New Femininities seminar, Milton Keynes: The Open University, 7 April.

Gittins, D. (1998) *The Child in Question*, Basingstoke: Macmillan.

Gordon, T., Holland, J. and Lahelma, E. (2000) *Making Spaces; Citizenship and Difference in Schools*, Basingstoke: Macmillan.

Griffin, C. (1985) *Typical Girls? Young Women from School to the Job Market*, London: Routledge.

Griffin, J.H. (1960) *Black Like Me*, London: Paladin.

Halberstam, J. (1998) *Female Masculinity*, Durham, NC: Duke University Press.

Halberstam, J. (1999) 'Masculinity without men', Annamarie Jagose interviews Judith Halberstam, *Genders*, 29, http://www.genders.org/g29/g29_halberstam.html.

Halberstam, J. (2003) 'What's that smell? Queer temporalities and subcultural lives', *The Scholar and Feminist Online*, 2 (1), http://www.barnard.columbia.edu/sfonline.

Halford, S. and Savage, M. (1997) *Gender, Careers and Organisations: Current Developments in Banking, Nursing and Local Government*, Basingstoke: Macmillan.

Hall, S. (1980) 'Encoding/decoding', in S. Hall, A. Lowe and P. Willis (eds), *Culture, Media, Language*, London: Hutchinson, pp. 15–47.

Hall, S. (1992) 'What is this "black" in Black Popular Culture?' in G. Dent (ed.), *Black Popular Culture*, Seattle, WA: Bay Press.

Hall, S. (1993) 'New ethnicities', in J. Donald and A. Rattansi (ed.), *Race, Culture and Difference*, London: Sage/The Open University.

Hall, S. (1996) 'When was the "postcolonial"? Thinking at the limit', in I. Chambers and L. Curtis (eds), *The Postcolonial Question: Common Skies Divided Horizons*, London: Routledge.

Hall, S. (1997) 'Introduction', in S. Hall (ed.), *Representation: Cultural Representations and Signifying Practices*, London: Sage/The Open University.

Hall, S. (2000) 'Who needs "identity"?' in P. du Gay, J. Evans and P. Redman (eds), *Identity: A Reader*, London: Sage/Open University Press.

Hall, S. and Jefferson, T. (eds) (1976) *Resistance through Rituals, Youth Subcultures in Postwar Britain*, London: Hutchinson.

Hall, S. and Jacques, M. (1989) *New Times: The Changing Face of Politics in the 1990s*, London: Lawrence and Wishart.

Haraway, D. (1990) 'A manifesto for cyborgs: Science, technology, and socialist feminism in the 1980s', in L.J. Nicholson (ed.), *Feminism/Postmodernism*, London: Routledge, pp. 190–233.

Harris, A. (2004) *Future Girl: Young Women in the Twenty-first Century*, New York: Routledge.

Healy, M. (1996) *Gay Skins: Class Masculinity and Queer Appropriation*, London/New York: Cassell.

Hebdige, D. (1979) *Subculture: The Meaning of Style*, London: Methuen.

Henderson, S., Holland, J., McGrellis, S., Sharpe, S. and Thomson, R. (2007) *Inventing Adulthoods, A Biographical Approach to Youth Transitions*, London: Sage/The Open University.

Henderson, S., Taylor, R. and Thomson, S. (2002) 'In touch: Young people, communication and technologies', *Information, Communication and Society*, 5 (4), pp. 494–512.

Henderson, S., Taylor, R. and Thomson, R. (2003) 'In touch: Young people and the mobile phone', in M.J. Kehily (ed.), *Children's Cultural Worlds*, Chichester: Wiley.

Hermes, J. (1995) *Reading Women's Magazines*, Cambridge: Polity Press.

Hermes, J. (2006) '*Ally McBeal*, "Sex and the City" and the tragic success of feminism', in J. Hollows and R. Moseley (eds), *Feminism in Popular Culture*, Oxford: Berg.

Hesmondhalgh, D. (2005) 'Subcultures, scenes or neo-tribes? None of the above', *Journal of Youth Studies*, 8 (1), pp. 21–40.

Hey, V. (1997) *The Company She Keeps: An Ethnography of Girls' Friendship*, Buckingham: Open University Press.

Hewitt, R. (1986) *White Talk, Black Talk, Interracial Friendship and Communication amongst Adolescents*, Cambridge: Cambridge University Press.

Hochschild, A. (2002) 'Emotional labour', in S. Jackson and S. Scott (eds), *Gender: A Sociological Reader*, London: Routledge, pp. 192–196.

Hoggart, R. (1957) *Uses of Literacy*, Harmondsworth: Penguin.

Hollands, R. (1995) *Friday Night, Saturday Night: Youth Cultural Identification in the Post Industrial City*, Newcastle upon Tyne: University of Newcastle upon Tyne.

Hollands, R. (1997) 'From shipyards to nightclubs: restructuring young adults' employment, household and consumption identities in the North-East of England', *Berkeley Journal of Sociology*, 41, pp. 41–66.

Hollands, R. (2002) 'Divisions in the dark: Youth cultures, transitions and the segmented consumption spaces in the night-time economy', *Journal of Youth Studies*, 5 (2), pp. 153–171.

Hollows, J. and Moseley, R. (2006) 'Popularity contests: The meaning of popular feminism', in J. Hollows and R. Moseley (eds), *Feminism in Popular Culture*, Oxford: Berg.

Hollway, W. (1989) *Subjectivity and Method in Psychology, Gender, Meaning and Science*, London: Sage.

Irigaray, L. (1985) *The Sex that is Not One*, Ithaca: Cornwall University Press.

Jackson, C. (2006) 'Wild girls? An exploration of "ladette" cultures in secondary schools', *Gender and Education*, 18 (4), pp. 339–360.

Jackson, D. (1990) *Unmasking Masculinity*, London: Unwin Hyman.

Jackson, P. (2000) 'Rematerializing social and cultural geography', *Social and Cultural Geography*, 1 (1), pp. 9–14.

James, A. and Prout, A. (eds) (1997) *Constructing and Reconstructing Childhood: Contemporary Issues in the Sociological Study of Childhood*, 2nd edn, London: Falmer.

Jefferson, T. (1996) 'From little "fairy boy" to the "compleat destroyer": Subjectivity and transformation in the biography of Mike Tyson', in M. Mac an Ghaill (ed.), *Understanding Masculinities: Social Relations and Cultural Areans*, Buckingham: Open University Press.

Jenkins, H. (1992) *Textual poachers*, in K. Gelder and S. Thornton (eds), *The Subcultures Reader*, London: Routledge.

Johnson, R.J. (1986) 'The story so far', in D. Punter (ed.), *Introduction to Contemporary Cultural Studies*, Harlow: Longman.

Kearney, M.C. (2005) 'Birds on the wire: Troping teenage girlhood through telephony in mid twentieth century media culture', *Cultural Studies*, 19 (5), pp. 568–601.

Kenway, J., Kraack, A. and Hickey-Moody, A. (2006) *Masculinities Beyond the Metropolis*, Basingstoke: Palgrave.

Kehily, M.J. (2002) *Sexuality, Gender and Schooling, Shifting Agendas in Sexual Learning*, London: Routledge.

Kehily, M.J. (2003) 'Youth cultures', in M.J. Kehily and J. Swann (eds), *Children's Cultural Worlds*, Chichester: John Wiley.

Kehily, M.J. (ed.) (2004) *An Introduction to Childhood Studies*, Maidenhead: Open Univeristy Press/McGraw Hill.

Kehily, M.J. (2007) 'Playing', in M.J. Kehily (ed.), *Understanding Youth: Perspectives, Identities and Practices*, London: Sage/The Open University.

Kehily, M.J. and Nayak, A. (1997) 'Lads and laughter: Humour and the production of heterosexual hierarchies', *Gender and Education*, 9 (1), pp. 69–87.

Kehily, M.J. and Montgomery, H. (2003) 'Innocence and experience', in M. Woodhead and H. Montgomery (eds), *Understanding Childhood, an Interdisciplinary Approach*, Chicheter: John Wiley/The Open University.

Kjeldgaard, D. (2003) 'Youth identities in the global economy', *European Journal of Cultural Studies*, 6 (3), pp. 285–304.

Kristeva, J. (1982) *The Powers of Horror*, Translated by L. Roudiez, New York: Columbia University Press.

Kuhn, A. (1995) *Family Secrets, Acts of Memory and Imagination*, London: Verso.

Lash, S. and Urry, J. (1999[1994]) *Economies of Signs and Space*, London: Sage.

Lees, S. (1986) *Losing Out: Sexuality and Adolescent Girls*, London: Hutchinson.

Lincoln, S. (2001) *Teenage Girls' Bedroom Cultures: Codes versus Zones, Unpublished Paper*, Manchester: Manchester Metropolitan University.

Lyman, P. (1987) 'The fraternal bond as a joking relationship: A case study of the role of sexist jokes in male group bonding', in M. Kimmell (ed.), *Changing Men*, London: Sage.

Mac an Ghaill, M. (1994) *The Making of Men*, Buckingham: Open University Press.

MacDonald, R. (1999) 'The road to nowhere: Youth insecurity and marginal transitions', in J. Vail, J. Wheelock and M. Hill (eds), *Insecure Times: Living with Insecurity in Contemporary Society*, London: Routledge.

MacDonald, R., Mason, P., Shildrick, T., Webster, C., Johnston, L. and Ridley, L. (2001) 'Snakes and ladders: In defence of studies of youth transition', *Sociological Research Online*, 5 (4), http://www.socresonline.org.uk/5/4/macdonald.html.

MacDonald, R. and Marsh, J. (2001) 'Disconnected youth?' *Journal of Youth Studies*, 4 (4), pp. 373–391.

MacDonald, R. and Marsh, J. (2005) *Disconnected Youth? Growing Up in Poor Neighbourhoods*, Houndsmill: Palgrave.

MacDonald, R. and Marsh, J. (2006) *Disconnected Youth? Growing up in Britain's Poor Neighbourhoods*, Basingstoke: Palgrave.

MacInnes, J. (1998) *End of Masculinity, the Confusion of Sexual Genesis and Sexual Difference in Modern Society*, Buckingham: Open University Press.

Maffesoli, M. (1995) *The Time of the Tribes, the Decline of Individualism in Mass Society*, London: Sage.

Massey, D. (1994[1991]) *A Global Sense of Place, in Space, Place and Gender*, Oxford: Polity Press.

Massey, D. (1999[1993]) 'Geography, gender and high technology', in J. Bryson, N. Henry, D. Keeble and R. Martin (eds), *The Economic Geography Reader*, Chichester: John Wiley & Sons.

Massey, D. (1998) 'The spatial construction of youth cultures', in T. Skelton and G. Valentine (eds), *Cool Places: Geographies of Youth Cultures*, London: Routledge, pp. 121–129.

Maynard, R. (2006) 'Sydney beach riots "fuelled by racial prejudice" ', *Guardian*, October 21, p. 21.

McDowell, L. (1997) *Capital Culture*, Oxford: Blackwell.

McDowell, L. (2002) 'Transitions to work: Masculine identities, youth inequality and labour market', *Gender, Place and Culture*, 9, pp. 39–59.

McDowell, L. (2003) *Redundant Masculinities? Employment, Change and White Working Class Youth*, Oxford: Blackwell.

McEwan, C. (2001) 'Geography, culture and global change', in P. Daniels, M. Bradshaw, D. Shaw and J. Sidaway (eds), *Human Geography: Issues for the 21st Century*, Harlow: Prentice Hall.

McLeod, J. and Yates, L. (2006) *Making Modern Lives, Subjectivity, Schooling and Social Change*, Albany, New York: SUNY.

McGrellis, S. (2005) 'Pure and bitter spaces: Gender, identity and territory in Northern Irish youth transitions', *Gender and Education*, 17 (5), pp. 499–514.

McNair, B. (2002) *Striptease Culture: Sex, Media and the Democratisation of Desire*, London: Routledge.

McRobbie, A. (1978) 'Working class girls and the culture of femininity', *Centre for Contemporary Cultural Studies, Women Take Issue*, London: Hutchinson.

McRobbie, A. (1981) 'Just like a Jackie story', in A. McRobbie and T. McCabe (eds), *Feminism for Girls: An Adventure Story*, London: Routledge & Kegan Paul.

McRobbie, A. (1991) 'Jackie Magazine: Romantic individualism and the teenage girl', *Feminism and Youth Culture: From Jackie to Just Seventeen*, London: Macmillan.

McRobbie, A. (1994) *Postmodernism and Popular Culture*, London: Routledge.

McRobbie, A. (1996) 'More! New sexualities in girls and women's magazines', in J. Curran, D. Morley and V. Walkerdine (eds), *Cultural Studies and Communications*, London: Arnold.

McRobbie, A. (2002) 'Notes on "What not to Wear" and post-feminist symbolic violence', *Sociological Review*, 52 (2), pp. 97–109.

McRobbie, A. (2004) '*Reflections on Young Women and Consumer Culture*', paper presented at HM Treasury, London, as part of the AHRC Cultures of Consumption Programme.

McRobbie, A. (2006) *Top Girls: Young Women and the Post Feminist Sexual Contract*, paper presented at ESRC Identities and Social Action public lecture, January, Milton Keynes: The Open University.

McRobbie, A. and Garber, J. (1975) 'Girls and subcultures', in S. Hall and T. Jefferson (eds), *Resistance through Rituals: Youth Subcultures in Postwar Britain*, London: Hutchinson.

McRobbie, A. and Garber, G. (1982) 'Girls and subculture', in S. Hall and T. Jefferson (eds), *Reisitance through Rituals, Youth Subcultures in Postwar Britain*, London: Hutchinson.

McRobbie, A. and Nava, M. (eds) (1984) *Gender and Generation*, London: Macmillan.

Mercer, K. (1990) 'Welcome to the jungle: Identify and diversity in postmodern politics', in J. Rutherford (ed.), *Identity: Community, Culture and Difference*, London: Routledge.

Miles, S. (2000) *Youth Lifestyles in a Changing World*, Buckingham: Open University Press.

Miller, D. (1992) 'The young and the restless in Trinidad. A case study of the local and the global in mass consumption', in R. Silverstone and E. Hirsch (eds), *Consuming Technologies*, London: Routledge.

Miller, D. (1997) 'Consumption and its consequences', in H. MacKay (ed.), *Consumption and Everyday Life*, London: Sage/The Open University.

Montgomery, H. and Woodhead, M. (2003) 'Introduction', in M. Woodhead and H. Montgomery (eds), *Understanding Childhood, an Interdisciplinary Approach*. Chichester: John Wiley/The Open University.

Muggleton, D. and Weinzierl, R. (2003) *The Post-Subcultures Reader*, Oxford: Berg.

Nakayama, T.K. and Krizek, R.L. (1995). 'Whiteness: a strategic rhetoric', *Quarterly Journal of Speech*, 81, pp. 291–309.

Nayak, A. (1997) 'Frozen bodies: Disclosing whiteness in Haagen-Dazs advertising', *Body and Society*, 3 (3), pp. 51–71.

Nayak, A. (1999) 'Pale warriors: Skinhead culture and the embodiment of white masculinities', in A. Brah, M.J. Hickman and M. Mac an Ghaill (eds), *Thinking Identities: Ethnicity, Racism and Culture*, Basingstoke: MacMillan.

Nayak, A. (2003a) *Race, Place and Globalisation, Youth Cultures in a Changing World*, Oxford: Berg.

Nayak, A. (2003b) 'Through children's eyes': Childhood, place and the fear of crime', *Geoforum*, 34, pp. 303–315.

Nayak, A. (2003c) 'White masculinities and the subcultural response to deindustrialisation', *Environment and Planning D: Society and Space*, 21, pp. 7–25.

Nayak, A. (2006) 'Displaced masculinities: Chavs, youth and class in the post-industrial city', *Sociology*, 40 (5), pp. 813–831.

Nayak, A. and Kehily, M.J. (1996) 'Playing it straight: Masculinities, homophobias and schooling', *Journal of Gender Studies*, 5 (2), pp. 211–230.

Nilan, P. (1992) 'Kazzies, DBTs and tryhards: Categorisations of style in adolescent girls' talk', *British Journal of Sociology of Education*, 13 (2), pp. 201–214.

Orwell, G. (1986) *The Road to Wigan Pier*, London: Secker and Warburg.

O'Sullivan, T., Hartley, G., Saunders, D., Montgomery, M. and Fiske, J. (1994) *Key Concepts in Communications and Cultural Studies*, London: Routledge.

Packard, V. (1957[1970]) *The Hidden Persuaders*, Harmondsworth: Penguin.

Parker, R.G. (1991) *Bodies, Pleasures and Passions, Sexual Culture in Contemporary Brazil*, Boston: Beacon Press.

Pearson, G. (1983) *Hooligan, A History of Respectable Fears*, Basingstoke: Macmillan.

Pilkington, H. and Johnson, R. (2003) 'Peripheral youth: Relations of identity and power in local/global context', *European Journal of Cultural Studies*, 6 (3), pp. 259–283.

Pilkington, H., Omel'chenko, E., Flynn, M., Bliudina, U. and Starkova, E. (2002) *Looking West? Cultural Globalisation and Russian Youth Cultures*, University Park, PA: Pennsylvania State University Press.

Pipher, M. (1994) *Reviving Ophelia: Saving the Selves of Adolescent Girls*, New York: Grosset/Putnam.

Plant, S. (1996) *On the matrix: Cyberfeminist Simulations*, in R. Shields (ed.), *Cultures of the Internet: Virtual Space, Real Histories, Living Bodies*, London: Sage, pp. 170–183.

Plant, S. (1998) *Zeros and Ones: Digital Women and the New Technoculture*, London: Fourth Estate.

Polhemus, T. (1997) 'In the supermarket of style', in S. Redhead, D. Wynne and J. O'Connor (eds), *The Clubcultures Reader*, Oxford: Blackwell.

Prado, P. (1931) *Retrato do Brasil: Ensaio sobre a tristeza Brasileira*, 3rd edn, Rio de Janeiro: F. Briguiet and Cia.

Puar, J.K. (1995) Resituating discourses of "whiteness" and "Asianness" in Northern England: Second generation Sikh women and constructions of identity, *Socialist Review*, 24 (1/2), pp. 21–53.

Radway, J. (1984) *Reading the Romance: Women, Patriarchy and Popular Literature*, Chapel Hill, NC: University of North Carolina Press.

Rasmussen, M.L. (2006) *Becoming Subjects: Sexualities and Secondary Schooling*, New York: Routledge.

Reay, D. (2005) 'Beyond consciousness? The psychic landscape of social class', *Sociology*, 39 (5), pp. 911–928.

Redhead, S. (1995) *Unpopular Cultures: The Birth of Law and Popular Culture*, Manchester: Manchester University Press.

Redhead, S. (1997) *Subcultures to Clubcultures*, Oxford: Blackwell.

Roediger, D. (1992) *The Wages of Whiteness: Race and the Making of the American Working Class*, London: Verso.

Rousseau, J.J. (1979[1762]) *Emile or On Education*, Translated by A. Bloom, New York: Basic Books.

Rutherford, J. (1997) *Forever England: Reflections on Masculinity and Empire*, London: Lawrence and Wishart.

Rutherford, J. (ed.) (1990) *Identity: Community, Culture, Difference*, London: Lawrence and Wishart.

Said, E. (1995[1978]) *Orientalism: Western Conceptions of the Orient*, Harmondsworth: Penguin.

Saldanha, A. (2007) *Psychedelic White: Goa Trance and the Viscosity of Race*, Minnesota: Minnesota Press.

Salo, E. (2003) 'Negotiating gender and personhood in the new South Africa', *European Journal of Cultural Studies*, 6 (3), pp. 345–365.

Savage, M., Bagnall, G. and Longhurst, B. (2005) 'Local habitus and working-class culture', in F. Devine, M. Savage, J. Scott and R. Crompton (eds), *Rethinking Class: Culture, Identities & Lifestyle*, Basingstoke: Palgrave.

Sedgwick, E.K. (1990) *Epistemology of the Closet*, Berkeley: University of California Press.

Segal, L. (1987) *Is the Future Female? Troubled Thoughts on Contemporary Feminism*, London: Virago Press.

Segal, L. (1990) *Slow Motion, Changing Masculinities, Changing Men*, London: Virago.

Segal, L. (1994) *Straight Sex: The Politics of Pleasure*, London: Virago.

Sennett, J. (2002) ' "I am the man!" Performing gender and other incongruities', *Journal of Homosexuality*, 43 (3/4), pp. 39–47.

Shahidian, H. (1999) 'Gender and sexuality among immigrant Iranians in Canada', *Sexualities*, 2 (2), pp. 189–222.

Simpson, K. (2004) 'Doing development: The gap year, volunteer-tourists and a popular practice of development', *Journal of International Development*, 16, pp. 681–692.

Skeggs, B. (1991) 'Challenging masculinity and using sexuality', *British Journal of Sociology of Education*, 12, pp. 127–137.

Skeggs, B. (1997) *Formations of Class & Gender: Becoming Respectable*, London: Sage.

Skeggs, B. (2004) *Class, Self, Culture*, London: Routledge.

Skeggs, B. (2005) 'The re-branding of class: Propertising culture', in F. Devine, M. Savage and R. Crompton (eds), *Rethinking Class: Culture, Identities & Lifestyle*, Basingstoke, Palgrave MacMillan, pp. 46–48.

Skelton, T. (1995) ' "Boom, bye, bye": Jamaican ragga and gay resistance', in D. Bell and G. Valentine (eds), *Mapping Desire*, London: Routledge, pp. 264–283.

Skelton, T. and Valentine, G. (1997) *Cool Places, Geographies of Youth Cultures*, London: Routledge.

Smith, A.M. (1994) *New Right Discourses on Race and Sexuality: Britain 1968–1990*, Oxford: Blackwell.

Sonnet, E. (1999) ' "Erotic fiction by women for women": The pleasures of post-feminist heterosexuality', *Sexualities*, 2 (2), pp. 167–187.

Stanley, L. (2002) 'Should "sex" really be "gender" – or "gender" really be "sex" ', in S. Jackson and S. Scott (eds), *Gender: A Sociology Reader*, London: Routledge, pp. 27–41.

Stainton Rogers, R. and Stainton Rogers, W. (1992) *Stories of Childhood, Shifting Agendas of Child Concern*, Hemel Hempstead: Harvester Wheatsheaf.

Steedman, C. (1986) *Landscape for a Good Woman*, London: Virago.

Steedman, C. (1995) *Strange Dislocations: Childhood and the Idea of Human Interiority 1780–1930*, London: Time Warner Books.

Stevenson, N., Jackson, P. and Brooks, K. (2000) 'Ambivalence in men's lifestyle magazines', in P. Jackson, H. Lowe, D. Miller and F. Mort (eds), *Commercial Cultures, Economies, Practices, Spaces*, Oxford: Berg.

Storey, J. (1997[1993]) *An Introduction to Cultural Theory and Popular Culture*, 2nd edn, Essex: Prentice Hall.

Taylor, I., Evans, K. and Fraser, P. (1996) *A Tale of Two Cities: Global Change, Local Feeling and Everyday Life in the North of England, a Study of Manchester and Sheffield*, London: Routledge.

Taylor, I. and Jamieson, R. (1997) 'Proper little mesters': Nostalgia and protest masculinity in de-industrial Sheffield', in S. Westwood and S. Williams (eds), *Imaging Cities: Scripts, Signs, Memories*, London: Routlege.

Thomson, R. and Taylor, R. (2005) 'Between cosmopolitanism and the locals, mobility as a resources in the transition to adulthood', *Young*, 13 (4), pp. 327–342.

Thorne, B. (1993) *Gender Play: Girls and Boys at School*, New Brunswick, NJ: Rutgers University Press.

Thornton, S. (1995) *Club Cultures: Music, Media and Subcultural Capital*, Cambridge: Polity Press.

Tinkler, P. (1995) *Constructing Girlhood, Popular Magazines for Girls Growing up in England 1920–1950*, London: Taylor and Francis.

Tolson, A. (1977) *The Limits of Masculinity*, Suffolk: Tavistock Publications.

Troyna, B. and Hatcher, R. (1992) *Racism in Children's Lives: A Study of Mainly-white Primary Schools*, London: Routledge in association with the National Children's Bureau.

Twine, F.W. (1996) 'Brown skinned white girls: Class, culture and the construction of white identity in suburban communities', *Gender, Place and Culture*, 3 (2), pp. 205–244.

UNICEF (2007) 'Child poverty in perspective: An overview of child well-being in rich countries', *Inocenti Report Card 7*, Florence: UNICEF Innocenti Research Centre.

Urry, J. (1995) *Consuming Places*, London: Routledge.

Urry, J. (2000) 'Mobile sociology', *British Journal of Sociology*, 51 (1), pp. 185–203.

Vail, J., Wheelock, J. and Hill, M. (eds), (1999) *Insecure Times: Living with Insecurity in Contemporary Society*, London: Routledge.

Valentine, G. (2004) *Public Space and the Culture of Childhood*, London: Ashgate.

Veblen, T. (1899, 1970) *The Theory of the Leisure Class: An Economic Study of Institutions*, London: Allen and Unwin.

Vidmar-Horvat, K. (2005) 'The globalisation of gender, Ally McBeal in post-socialist Slovenia', *European Journal of Cultural Studies*, 8 (2), pp. 239–255.

Vincent, N. (2006) *Self-made Man: My Year Disguised as a Man*, Atlantic Books, Extracted in The Guardian, 18.3.06.

Volosinov, V. (1973) *Marxism and the Philosophy of Language*, London: Seminar Press.

Walker, R. and Goodson, I. (1977) 'Humour in the classroom', in P. Woods and M. Hammersley (eds), *School Experience*, London: Croom Helm.

Walkerdine, V. (1990) *Schoolgirl Fictions*, London: Verso.

Walkerdine, V. (1991) '*Sex, Power and Pedagogy*', in *Schoolgirls Fictions*, London: Verso.

Walkerdine, V., Lucey, H. and Melody, J. (2001) *Growing up Girl, Psychosocial Explorations of Gender and Class*, Basingstoke: Palgrave.

Walsh, D. (2006) 'Taboo tolerated as gay men party in Pakistan', *The Guardian*, March 14, 2006, p. 22.

Ware, V. (1992) *Beyond the Pale*, London: Verso.

Warner, M. (1994) *Managing Monsters: Six Myths of Our Time*, London: Vintage.

Watney, S. (1991) 'Schools Out', in D. Fuss (ed.), *Inside/Out: Lesbian Theories, Gay Theories*, London/New York: Routledge.

Weeks, J. (1981) *Sex, Politics and Society: The Regulation of Sexuality since 1980*, Harlow: Longman.

Weeks, J. (1985) *Sexuality and its Discontents*, London: Routledge.

Weeks, J. (1986) *Sexuality*, London: Tavistock.

Weis, L. (2004) *Class Reunion: The Remaking of the American White Working Class*, New York: Routledge.

Werbner, P. (1997) 'Introduction: The dialectics of cultural hybridity', in P. Werbner and T. Modood (eds), *Debating Cultural Hybridity*, London: Zed Books.

Winship, J. (1985) 'A girl needs to get streetwise: Magazines for the 1980s', *Feminist Review*, 21, pp. 25–46.

Winship, J. (1987) *Inside Women's Magazines*, New York: Pandora.

Williams, R. (1973) *The Country and the City*, London: Chatto and Windus.

Williams, R. (1976) *Keywords*, London: Fontana.

Williamson, H. (2004) *The Milltown Boys Revisited*, Oxford: Berg.

Willis, P. (1977) *Learning to Labour: How Working Class Kids get Working Class Jobs*, Farnsborough: Saxon House.

Willis, P. (1990) *Common Culture: Symbolic Work at Play in the Everyday Cultures of the Young*, Milton Keynes: Open University Press.

Woods, P. (1976) 'Having a laugh: An antidote to schooling', in M. Hammersley and P. Woods (eds), *The Process of Schooling*, London: Routledge.

Woods, P. (1990) *The Happiest Days: How Pupils Cope with School*, Lewes: Falmer Press.

Wulff, H. (1995) 'Inter-racial friendship: Community youth styles, ethnicity and teenage femininity in South London', in V. Amit-Talai and H. Wulff (eds) *Youth Cultures: A Cross-Cultural Perspective*, London: Routledge.

Wyn, J. and Woodman, D. (2006) 'Generation, youth and social change in Australia', *Journal of Youth Studies*, 9 (5), pp. 495–514.

Yano, C. (2004) 'Raising the ante of desire: Foreign female singers in a Japanese pop music world', in A. Chun, N. Rossiter and B. Shoesmith (eds), *Refashioning Pop Music in Asia: Cosmopolitan Flows, Political Tempos and Aesthetic Industries*, London/New York: Routledge Curzon, pp. 159–172.

Zeigler, S. (2004) 'Sex and the citizen in Sex and the City's New York', in K. Akass and J. McCabe (eds) *Reading Sex and the City*, London: I.B. Tauris.

Zukin, S. (1991) *Landscapes of Power: From Detroit to Disney World*, California: University of California Press.

Films

Billy Elliot (UK), dir. Stephen Daldrey, 2000.
Bladerunner (USA), dir. Ridley Scott, 1982.
Brassed off, (UK), dir. Mark Herman, 1996.
Falling Down (USA), dir. J. Schumacher, 1993.
Fight Club (USA), dir. David Fincher, 20th Century Fox, 1999.
Kinky Boots (UK), dir. Gulion Garrold, 2005.
Million Dollar Babe (US), dir. Clint Eastwood, 2005.
Rocky II (USA), dir S. Stallone, 1979.
Terminator (US), dir. James Cameron, 1984.
The Full monty (UK), dir. Peter Cattaneo, 1997.
Total attraction (USA), dir. Adrian Lyne, 1987.

Index

Index